RIVERS OF LONDON
DETECTIVE STORIES

KU-263-207

Titan
COMICS

RIVERS OF LONDON: DETECTIVE STORIES
ISBN: 9781785861710
FP HC ISBN: 9781785865978

TITAN COMICS

EDITOR STEVE WHITE
ASSISTANT EDITOR LAUREN BOWES
SENIOR DESIGNER ANDREW LEUNG

Managing & Launch Editor Andrew James
Production Assistant Natalie Bolger
Production Controller Peter James
Production Supervisor Maria Pearson
Senior Production Controller Jackie Flook
Art Director Oz Browne
Senior Sales Manager Steve Tothill
Press Officer Will O'Mullane
Brand Manager Lucy Ripper
Direct Sales and Marketing Manager Ricky Claydon
Commercial Manager Michelle Fairlamb
Head of Rights Jenny Boyce
Publishing Manager Darryl Tothill
Publishing Director Chris Teather
Operations Director Leigh Baulch
Executive Director Vivian Cheung
Publisher Nick Landau

Published by Titan Comics
A division of Titan Publishing Group Ltd.
144 Southwark St.
London
SE1 0UP

Rivers of London is trademark™ and copyright © 2017 Ben Aaronvitch. All rights reserved.

Rivers of London logo designed by Patrick Knowles

No part of this publication may be reproduced, stored in a retrieval system, or transmitted, in any
form or by any means, without the prior written permission of the publisher. Names, characters,
places and incidents featured in this publication are either the product of the author's imagination
or used fictitiously. Any resemblance to actual persons, living or dead (except for satirical
purposes), is entirely coincidental.

A CIP catalogue record for this title is available from the British Library.

First edition: December 2017
10 9 8 7 6 5 4 3 2 1

Printed in Spain.
Titan Comics.

For rights information contact jenny.boyce@titanemail.com

WWW.TITAN-COMICS.COM

Become a fan on Facebook.com/comicstitan

Follow us on Twitter @ComicsTitan

RIVERS OF LONDON

DETECTIVE STORIES

WRITTEN BY

ANDREW CARTMEL & BEN AARONOVITCH

ART BY

LEE SULLIVAN

WITH HUMOUR STRIPS BY

CHRIS JONES (p77) & J B BASTOS (p78)

COLORS BY

LUIS GUERRERO

LETTERING BY

ROB STEEN

TITAN
COMICS

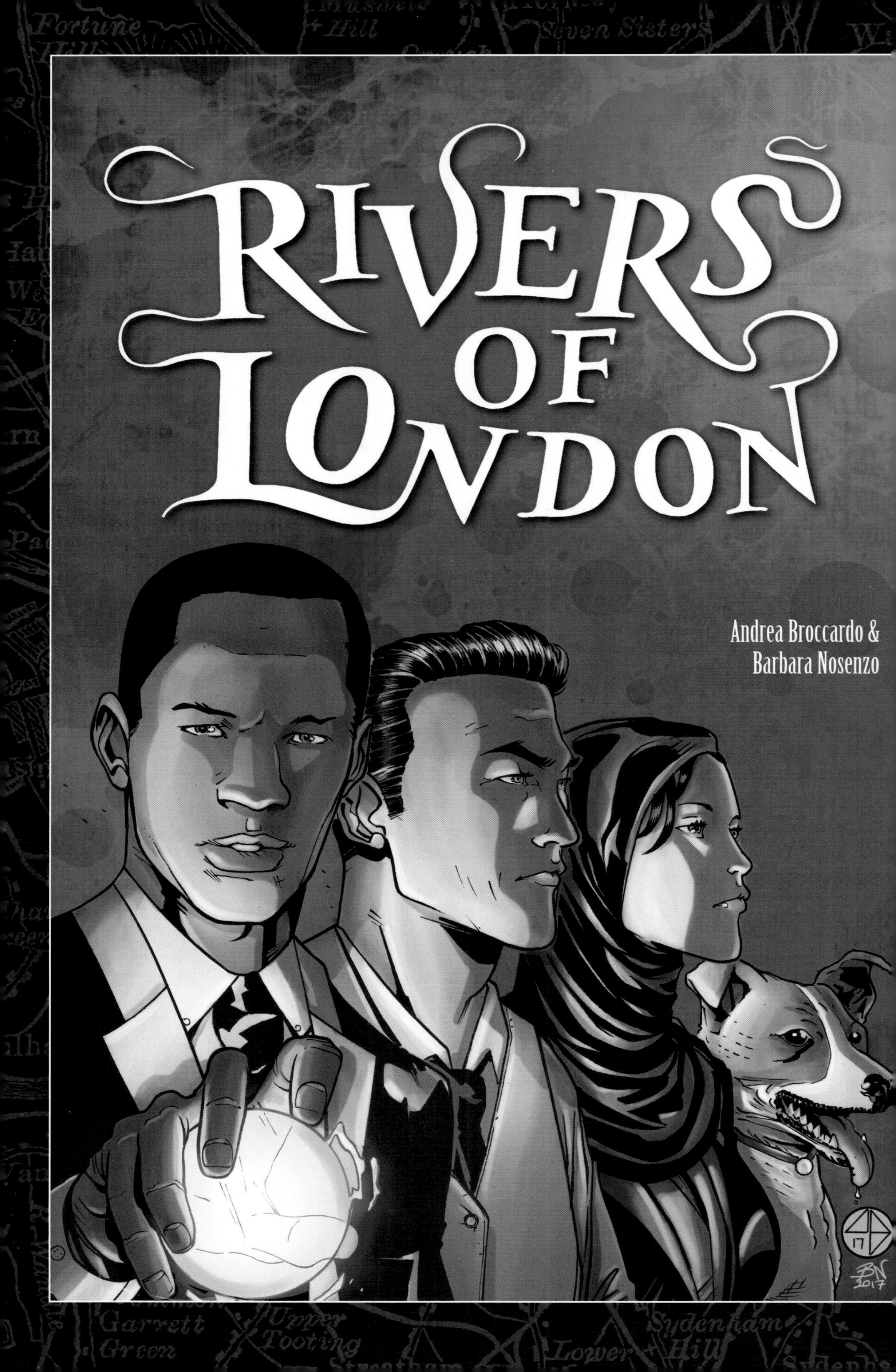

RIVERS OF LONDON
Andrea Broccardo &
Barbara Nosenzo
Fortune
Hill
Seven Sisters
Garrett
Green
Upper
Tooting
Sydenham
Lower
Hill

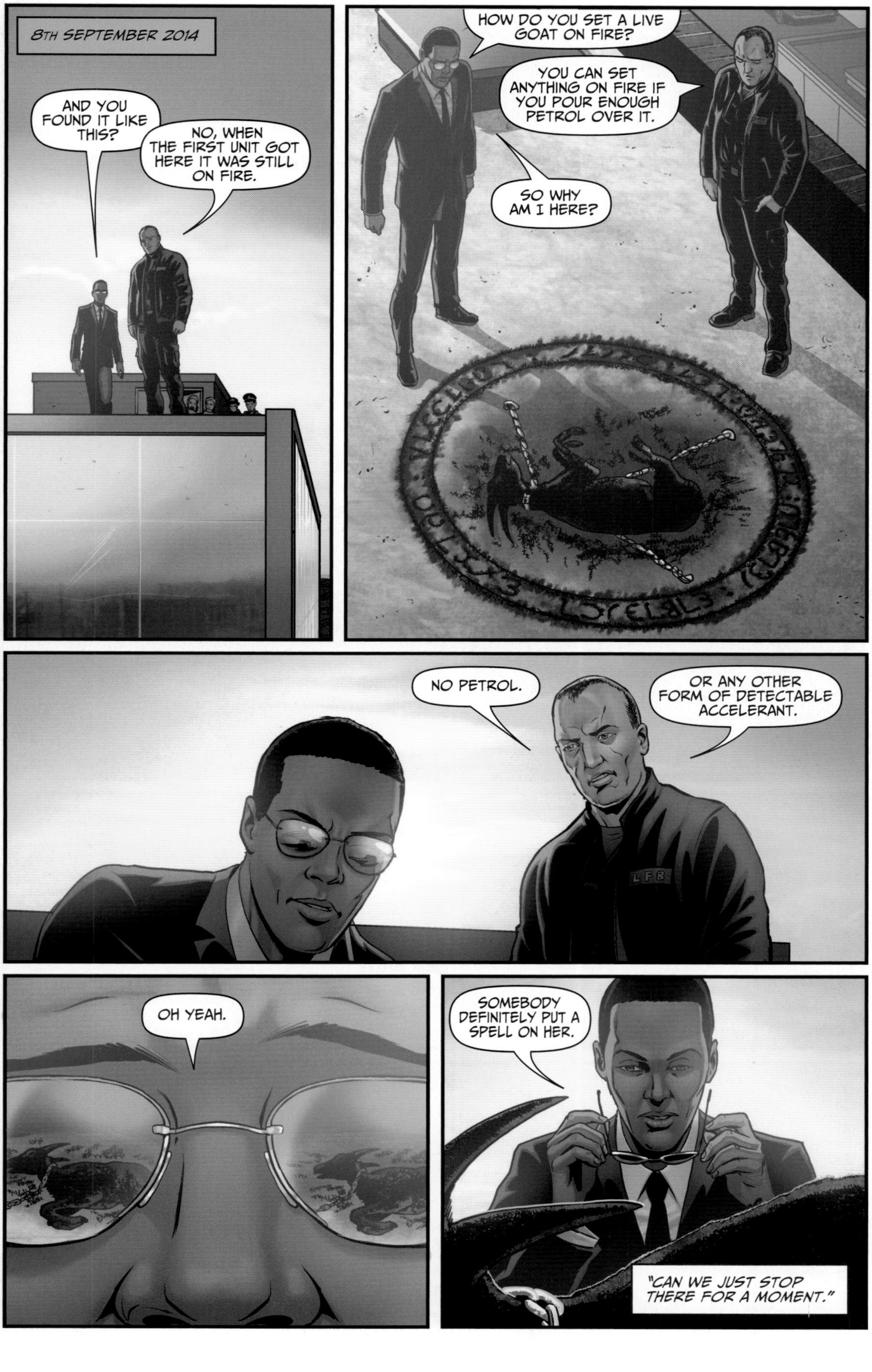
8TH SEPTEMBER 2014
AND YOU FOUND IT LIKE THIS?
NO, WHEN THE FIRST UNIT GOT HERE IT WAS STILL ON FIRE.
HOW DO YOU SET A LIVE GOAT ON FIRE?
YOU CAN SET ANYTHING ON FIRE IF YOU POUR ENOUGH PETROL OVER IT.
SO WHY AM I HERE?
NO PETROL.
OR ANY OTHER FORM OF DETECTABLE ACCELERANT.
LFB
OH YEAH.
SOMEBODY DEFINITELY PUT A SPELL ON HER.
"CAN WE JUST STOP THERE FOR A MOMENT."

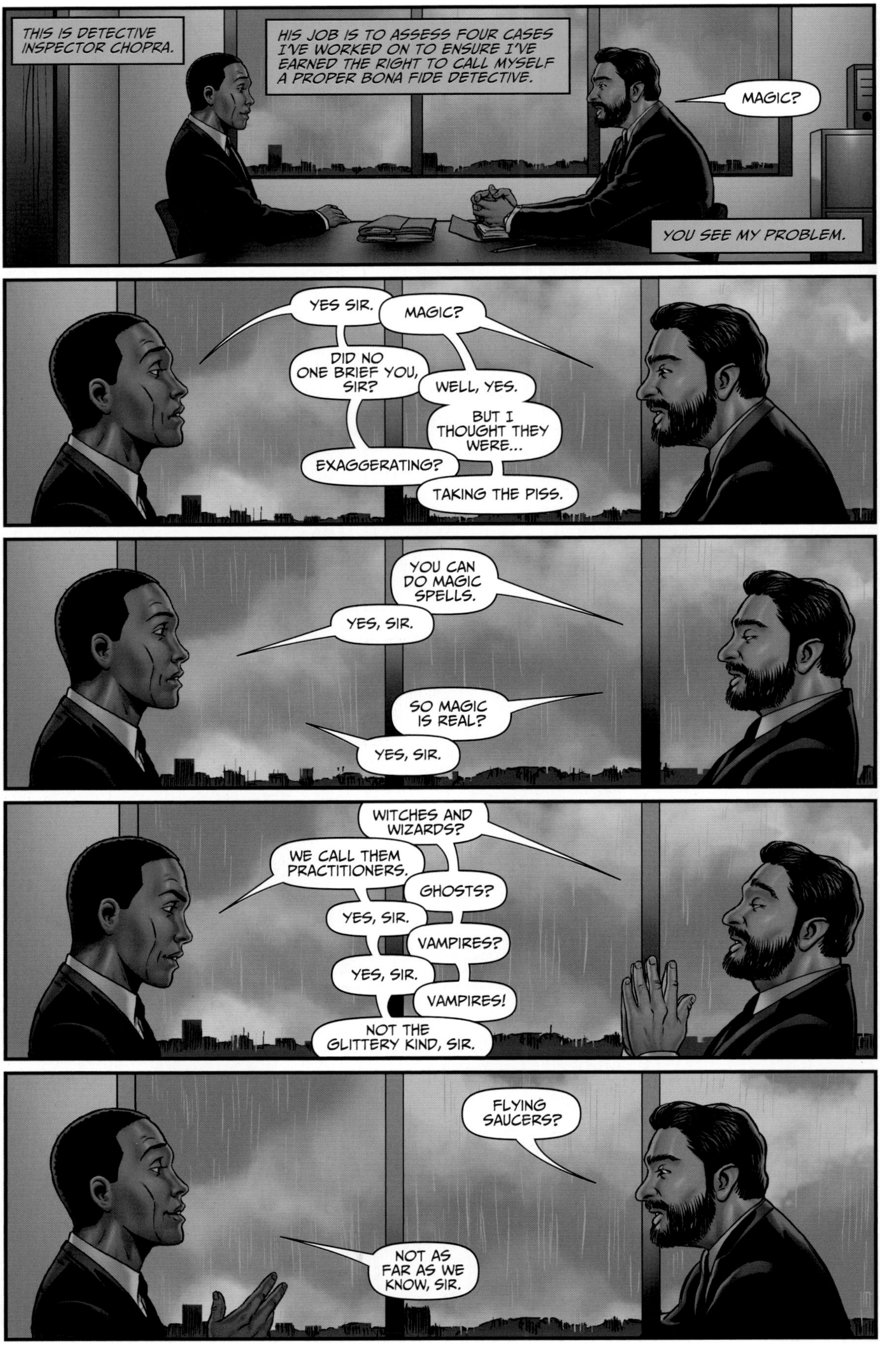

THIS IS DETECTIVE INSPECTOR CHOPRA.
HIS JOB IS TO ASSESS FOUR CASES I'VE WORKED ON TO ENSURE I'VE EARNED THE RIGHT TO CALL MYSELF A PROPER BONA FIDE DETECTIVE.
MAGIC?
YOU SEE MY PROBLEM.
YES SIR.
MAGIC?
DID NO ONE BRIEF YOU, SIR?
WELL, YES.
BUT I THOUGHT THEY WERE...
EXAGGERATING?
TAKING THE PISS.
YOU CAN DO MAGIC SPELLS.
YES, SIR.
SO MAGIC IS REAL?
YES, SIR.
WITCHES AND WIZARDS?
WE CALL THEM PRACTITIONERS.
GHOSTS?
YES, SIR.
VAMPIRES?
YES, SIR.
VAMPIRES!
NOT THE GLITTERY KIND, SIR.
FLYING SAUCERS?
NOT AS FAR AS WE KNOW, SIR.

THIS IS THE FOLLY.

SCIENTIA POTESTAS EST

HOME OF BRITISH WIZARDRY SINCE 1775.

THIS IS SIR ISAAC NEWTON.

WHO FIRST SYSTEMATISED THE PRACTISE OF MAGIC.

THAT WE KNOW OF, ANYWAY...

NATURE AND NATURE'S LAWS LAY HID IN NIGHT; GOD SAID 'LET NEWTON BE' AND ALL WAS LIGHT.

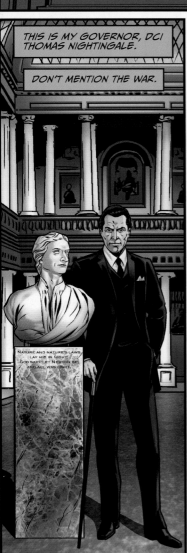

THIS IS MY GOVERNOR, DCI THOMAS NIGHTINGALE.

DON'T MENTION THE WAR.

NATURE AND NATURE'S LAWS LAY HID IN NIGHT; GOD SAID 'LET NEWTON BE' AND ALL WAS LIGHT.

AND THAT'S THE FULL COMPLEMENT OF YOUR UNIT?

THAT'S THE POLICING COMPLEMENT.

THERE ARE OTHERS...

FRANK CAFFREY, FOR EXAMPLE.

FIRE INVESTIGATION OFFICER, LONDON FIRE BRIGADE.

RESERVE PARA.

AND PART-TIME VAMPIRE EXTERMINATOR.

AND HE NOTIFIED YOU AS TO THE 'UNUSUAL' NATURE OF THE CASE?

HE'S ONE OF A NUMBER OF SUITABLY QUALIFIED INDIVIDUALS AMONGST PROFESSIONAL PARTNERS AND STAKEHOLDERS WHO ALERT US TO INCIDENTS THAT POTENTIALLY FALL WITHIN OUR SPHERE OF RESPONSIBILITY.

'PARTNERS' AND 'STAKEHOLDERS' IN THE SAME SENTENCE FOR DOUBLE WORD SCORE.

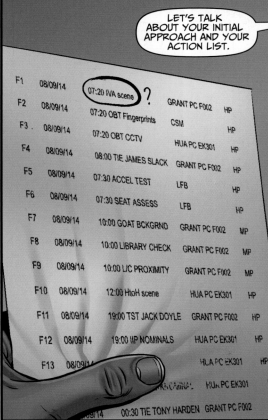

LET'S TALK ABOUT YOUR INITIAL APPROACH AND YOUR ACTION LIST.

F1   08/09/14   07:20 IVA scene   ?   GRANT PC F002   HP

F2   08/09/14   07:20 OBT Fingerprints   CSM   HP

F3   08/09/14   07:20 OBT CCTV   HUA PC EK301   HP

F4   08/09/14   08:00 TIE JAMES SLACK   GRANT PC F002   HP

F5   08/09/14   07:30 ACCEL TEST   LFB   HP

F6   08/09/14   07:30 SEAT ASSESS   LFB   HP

F7   08/09/14   10:00 GOAT BCKGRND   GRANT PC F002   MP

F8   08/09/14   10:00 LIBRARY CHECK   GRANT PC F002   MP

F9   08/09/14   10:00 L/C PROXIMITY   GRANT PC F002   MP

F10   08/09/14   12:00 HtoH scene   HUA PC EK301   HP

F11   08/09/14   19:00 TST JACK DOYLE   GRANT PC F002   HP

F12   08/09/14   19:00 IIP NOMINALS   HUA PC EK301   HP

F13   08/09/14   HLA PC EK301   HP

   HUA PC EK301   HP

   00:30 TIE TONY HARDEN   GRANT PC F002   HP

I'M ALMOST AFRAID TO ASK BUT...

WHAT EXACTLY IS AN IVA?

08/09/14   07:20 IVA scene   ?   GRANT PC F002

08/09/14   07:20 OBT Fingerprints   CSM

08/09/14   07:20 OBT CCTV   HUA PC EK301

08/09/14   08:00 TIE JAMES SLACK   GRANT PC F002

F5   08/09/14   07:30 ACCEL TEST   LFB

F6   08/09/14   07:30 SEAT ASSESS

F7   08/09/14   10:00 GOAT BCKGRND

F8   08/09/14   10:00 LIBRARY CHECK

   10:00 L/C PROXIMITY   GRANT PC F002

THAT WOULD BE AN INITIAL VESTIGIUM ASSESSMENT, SIR.

F1 08/09/14 IVA SCENE PC GRANT HP

IT'S BASICALLY THE SAME AS THE LOCARD'S THEORY OF TRANSFER.

IF YOU USE MAGIC TO DO SOMETHING, IT NEARLY ALWAYS LEAVES A TRACE BEHIND.

WHICH IS ACTUALLY QUITE EASY TO SPOT.

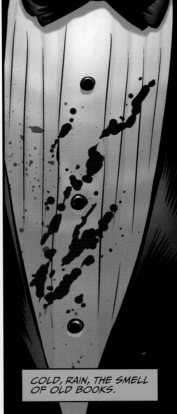

COLD, RAIN, THE SMELL OF OLD BOOKS.

IF YOU KNOW WHAT YOU'RE LOOKING FOR.

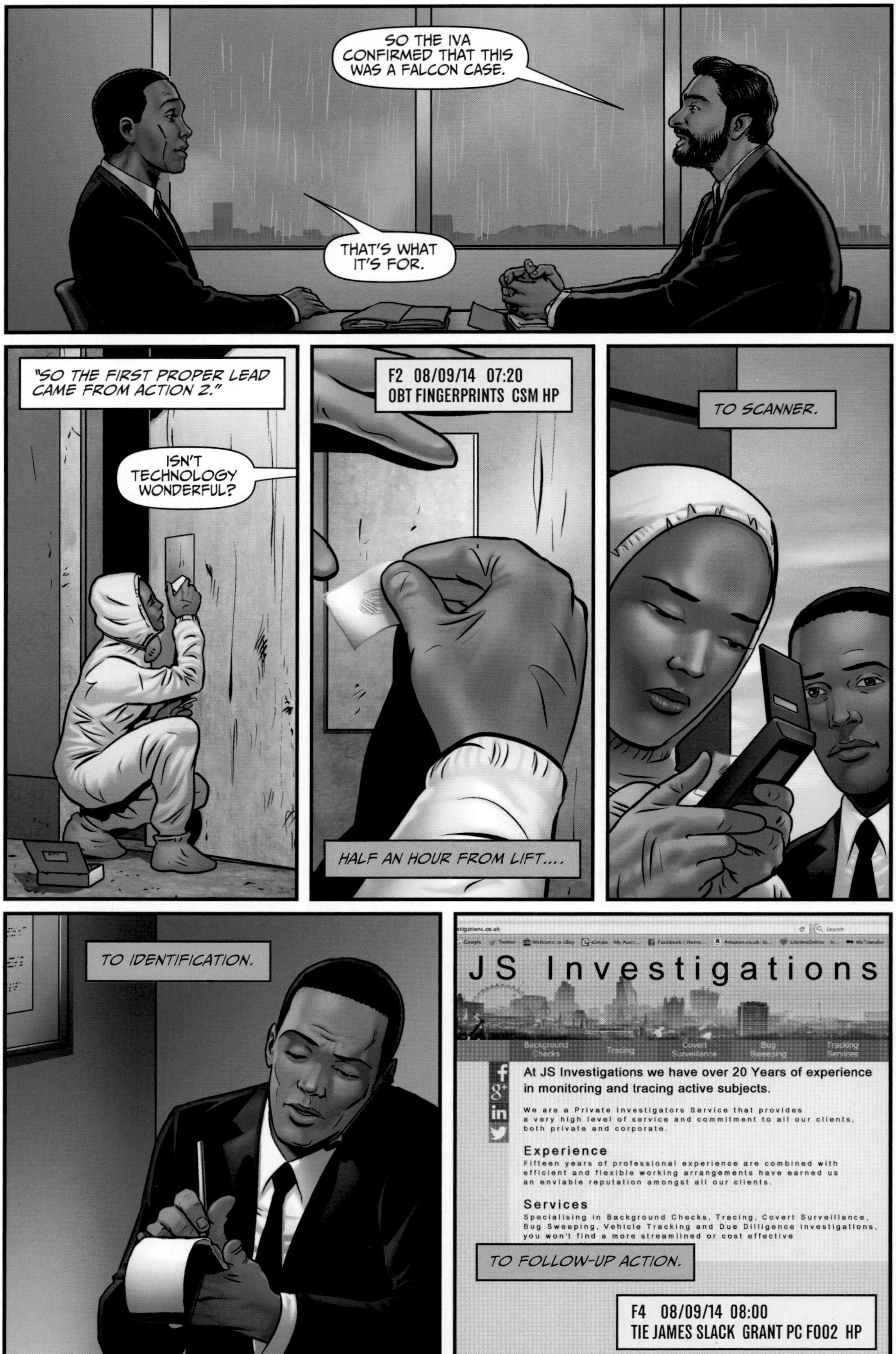
SO THE IVA CONFIRMED THAT THIS WAS A FALCON CASE.
THAT'S WHAT IT'S FOR.
"SO THE FIRST PROPER LEAD CAME FROM ACTION 2."
ISN'T TECHNOLOGY WONDERFUL?
F2 08/09/14 07:20
OBT FINGERPRINTS CSM HP
HALF AN HOUR FROM LIFT....
TO SCANNER.
TO IDENTIFICATION.
stigations.co.uk
JS Investigations
Background Checks
Tracing
Covert Surveillance
Bug Sweeping
Tracking Services
At JS Investigations we have over 20 Years of experience in monitoring and tracing active subjects.
We are a Private Investigators Service that provides a very high level of service and commitment to all our clients, both private and corporate.
Experience
Fifteen years of professional experience are combined with efficient and flexible working arrangements have earned us an enviable reputation amongst all our clients.
Services
Specialising in Background Checks, Tracing, Covert Surveillance, Bug Sweeping, Vehicle Tracking and Due Dilligence investigations, you won't find a more streamlined or cost effective
TO FOLLOW-UP ACTION.
F4 08/09/14 08:00
TIE JAMES SLACK GRANT PC F002 HP

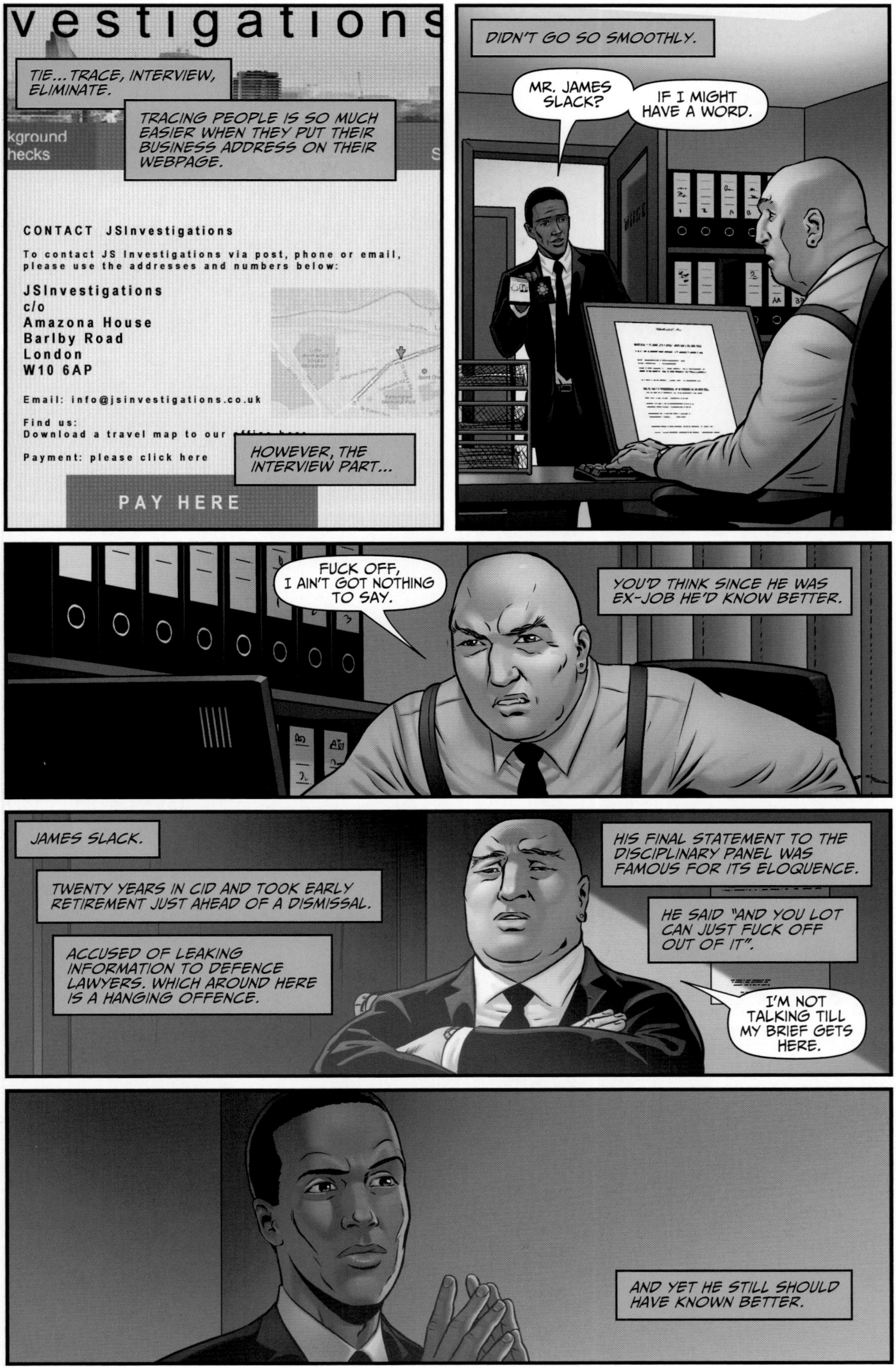
vestigations
TIE...TRACE, INTERVIEW, ELIMINATE.
TRACING PEOPLE IS SO MUCH EASIER WHEN THEY PUT THEIR BUSINESS ADDRESS ON THEIR WEBPAGE.
kground
hecks
CONTACT JSInvestigations
To contact JS Investigations via post, phone or email, please use the addresses and numbers below:
JSInvestigations
c/o
Amazona House
Barlby Road
London
W10 6AP
Email: info@jsinvestigations.co.uk
Find us:
Payment: please click here
HOWEVER, THE INTERVIEW PART...
PAY HERE
DIDN'T GO SO SMOOTHLY.
MR. JAMES SLACK?
IF I MIGHT HAVE A WORD.
FUCK OFF, I AIN'T GOT NOTHING TO SAY.
YOU'D THINK SINCE HE WAS EX-JOB HE'D KNOW BETTER.
JAMES SLACK.
TWENTY YEARS IN CID AND TOOK EARLY RETIREMENT JUST AHEAD OF A DISMISSAL.
ACCUSED OF LEAKING INFORMATION TO DEFENCE LAWYERS. WHICH AROUND HERE IS A HANGING OFFENCE.
HIS FINAL STATEMENT TO THE DISCIPLINARY PANEL WAS FAMOUS FOR ITS ELOQUENCE.
HE SAID "AND YOU LOT CAN JUST FUCK OFF OUT OF IT".
I'M NOT TALKING TILL MY BRIEF GETS HERE.
AND YET HE STILL SHOULD HAVE KNOWN BETTER.

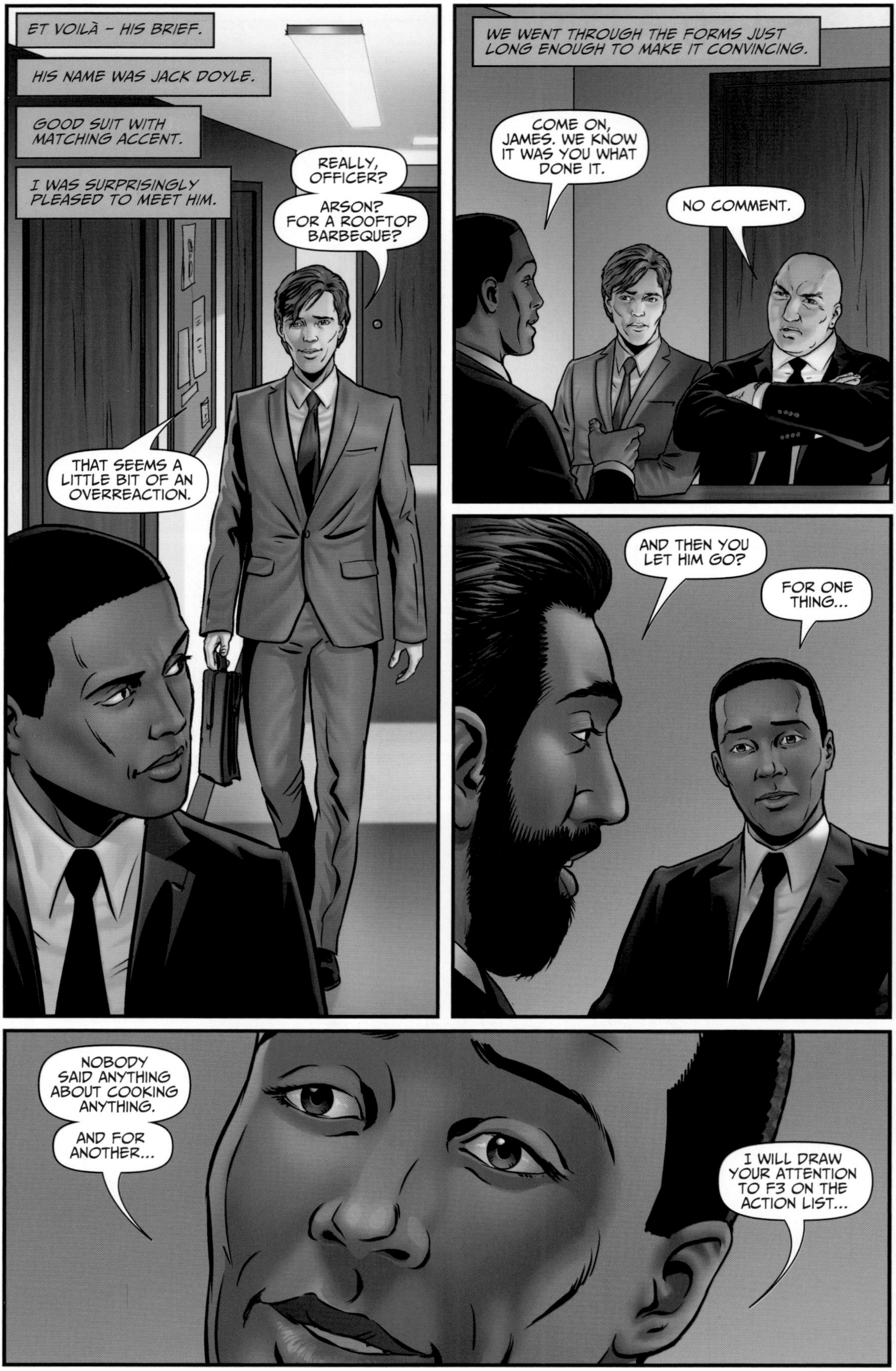

ET VOILÀ – HIS BRIEF.
HIS NAME WAS JACK DOYLE.
GOOD SUIT WITH MATCHING ACCENT.
I WAS SURPRISINGLY PLEASED TO MEET HIM.
REALLY, OFFICER?
ARSON? FOR A ROOFTOP BARBEQUE?
THAT SEEMS A LITTLE BIT OF AN OVERREACTION.
WE WENT THROUGH THE FORMS JUST LONG ENOUGH TO MAKE IT CONVINCING.
COME ON, JAMES. WE KNOW IT WAS YOU WHAT DONE IT.
NO COMMENT.
AND THEN YOU LET HIM GO?
FOR ONE THING...
NOBODY SAID ANYTHING ABOUT COOKING ANYTHING.
AND FOR ANOTHER...
I WILL DRAW YOUR ATTENTION TO F3 ON THE ACTION LIST...

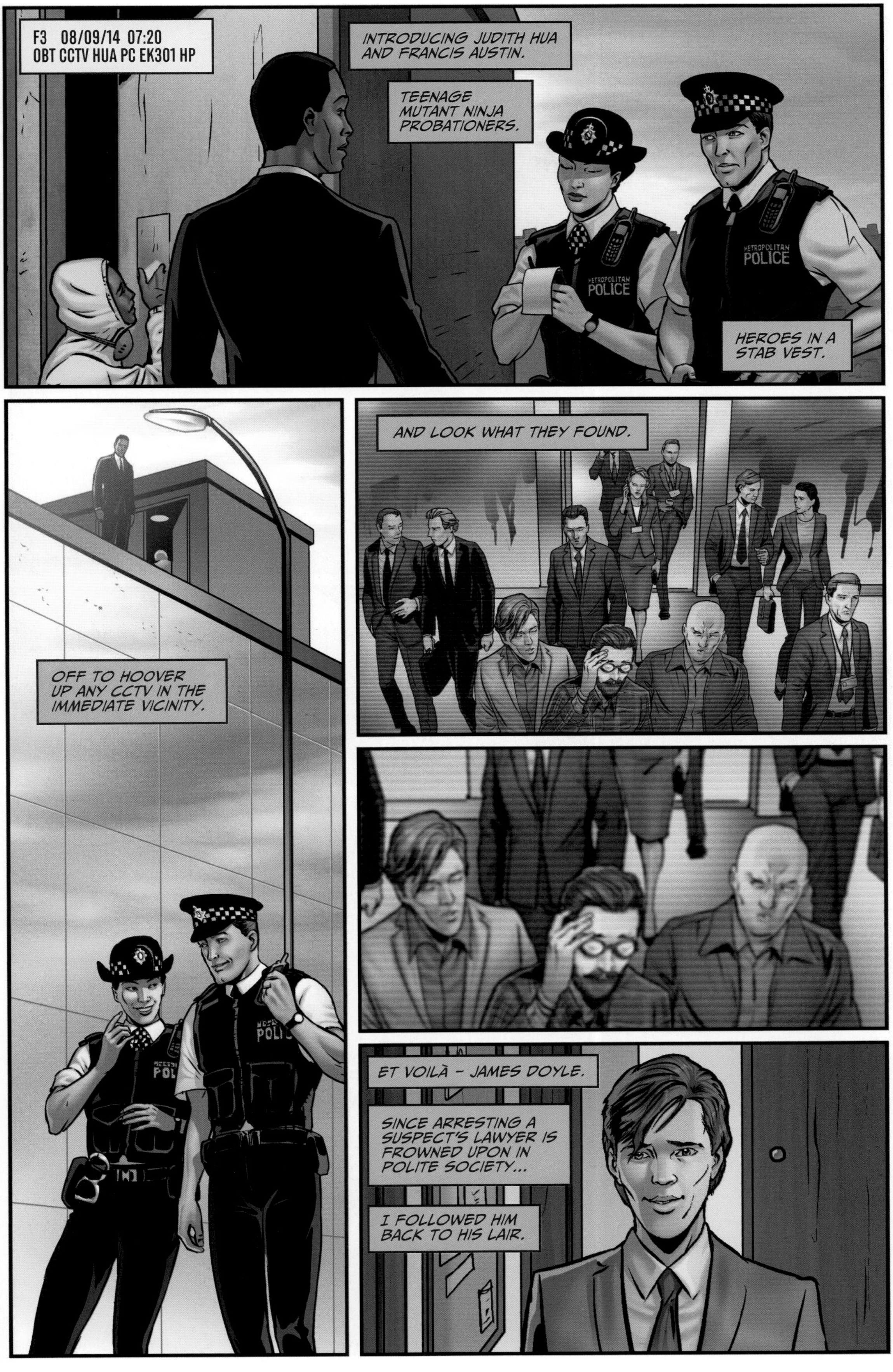
F3 08/09/14 07:20
OBT CCTV HUA PC EK301 HP
INTRODUCING JUDITH HUA AND FRANCIS AUSTIN.
TEENAGE MUTANT NINJA PROBATIONERS.
METROPOLITAN POLICE
METROPOLITAN POLICE
HEROES IN A STAB VEST.
OFF TO HOOVER UP ANY CCTV IN THE IMMEDIATE VICINITY.
AND LOOK WHAT THEY FOUND.
ET VOILÀ – JAMES DOYLE.
SINCE ARRESTING A SUSPECT'S LAWYER IS FROWNED UPON IN POLITE SOCIETY...
I FOLLOWED HIM BACK TO HIS LAIR.

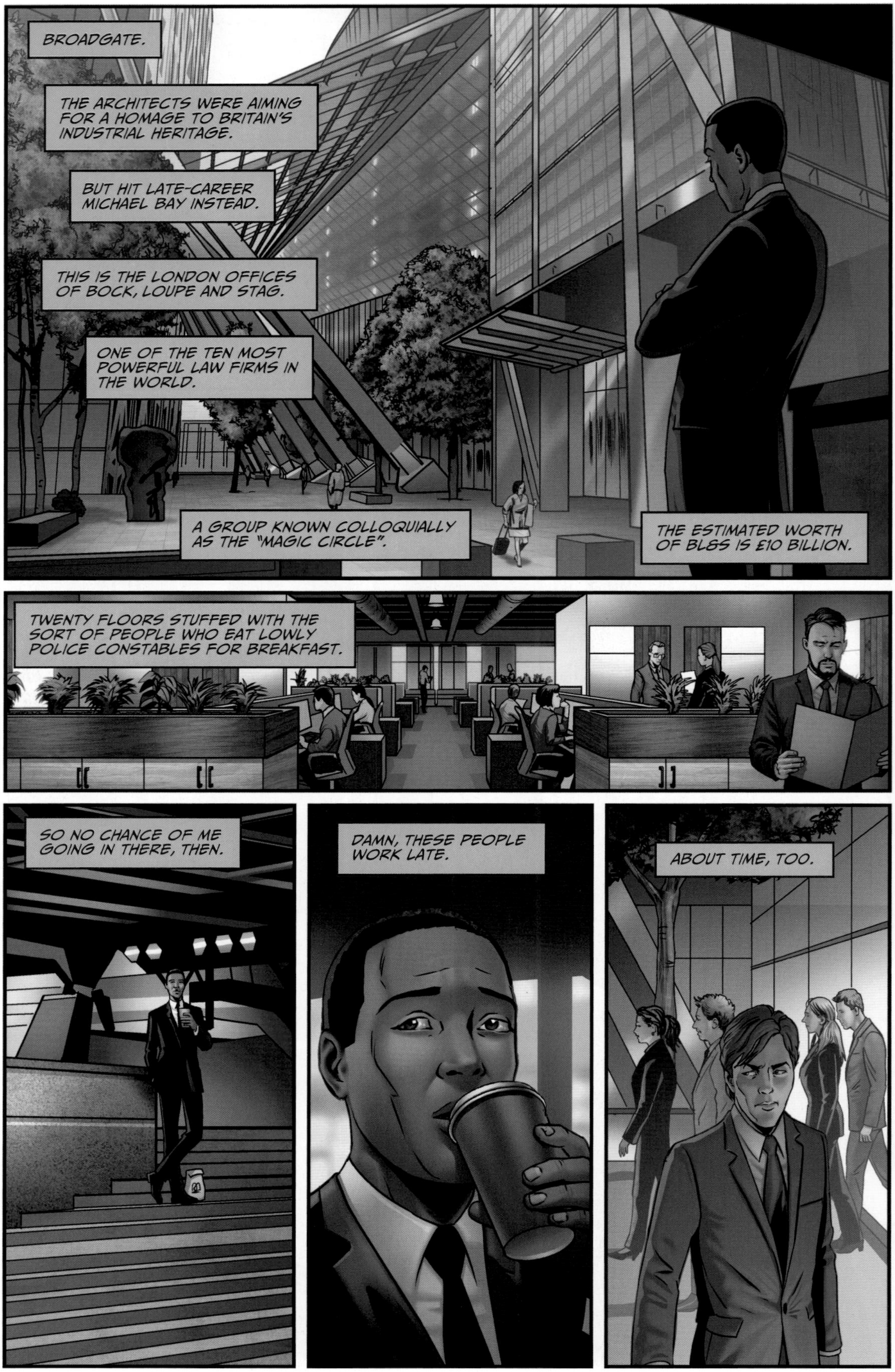
BROADGATE.
THE ARCHITECTS WERE AIMING FOR A HOMAGE TO BRITAIN'S INDUSTRIAL HERITAGE.
BUT HIT LATE-CAREER MICHAEL BAY INSTEAD.
THIS IS THE LONDON OFFICES OF BOCK, LOUPE AND STAG.
ONE OF THE TEN MOST POWERFUL LAW FIRMS IN THE WORLD.
A GROUP KNOWN COLLOQUIALLY AS THE "MAGIC CIRCLE".
THE ESTIMATED WORTH OF BL&S IS £10 BILLION.
TWENTY FLOORS STUFFED WITH THE SORT OF PEOPLE WHO EAT LOWLY POLICE CONSTABLES FOR BREAKFAST.
SO NO CHANCE OF ME GOING IN THERE, THEN.
DAMN, THESE PEOPLE WORK LATE.
ABOUT TIME, TOO.

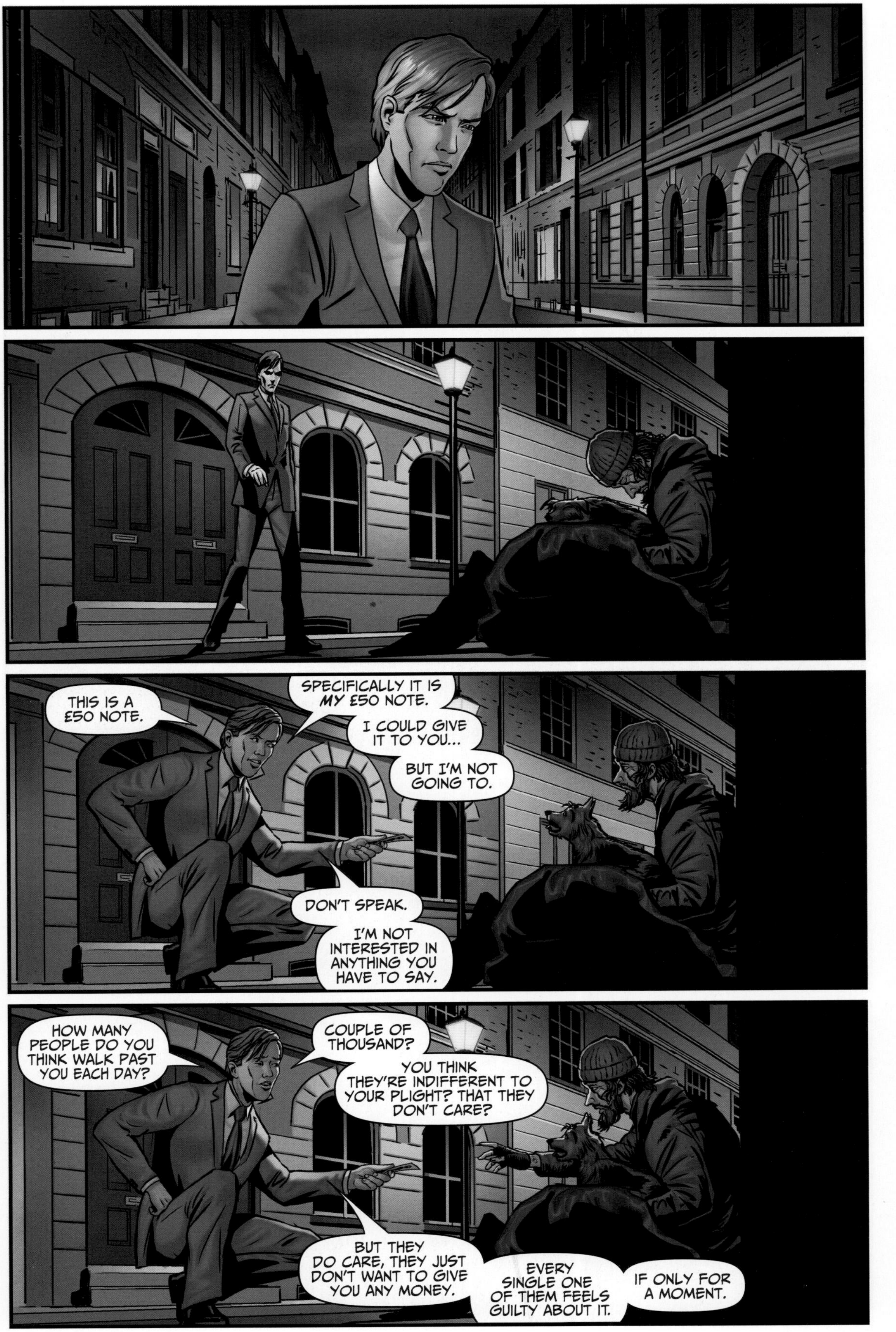
THIS IS A £50 NOTE.
SPECIFICALLY IT IS MY £50 NOTE.
I COULD GIVE IT TO YOU...
BUT I'M NOT GOING TO.
DON'T SPEAK.
I'M NOT INTERESTED IN ANYTHING YOU HAVE TO SAY.
HOW MANY PEOPLE DO YOU THINK WALK PAST YOU EACH DAY?
COUPLE OF THOUSAND?
YOU THINK THEY'RE INDIFFERENT TO YOUR PLIGHT? THAT THEY DON'T CARE?
BUT THEY DO CARE, THEY JUST DON'T WANT TO GIVE YOU ANY MONEY.
EVERY SINGLE ONE OF THEM FEELS GUILTY ABOUT IT.
IF ONLY FOR A MOMENT.

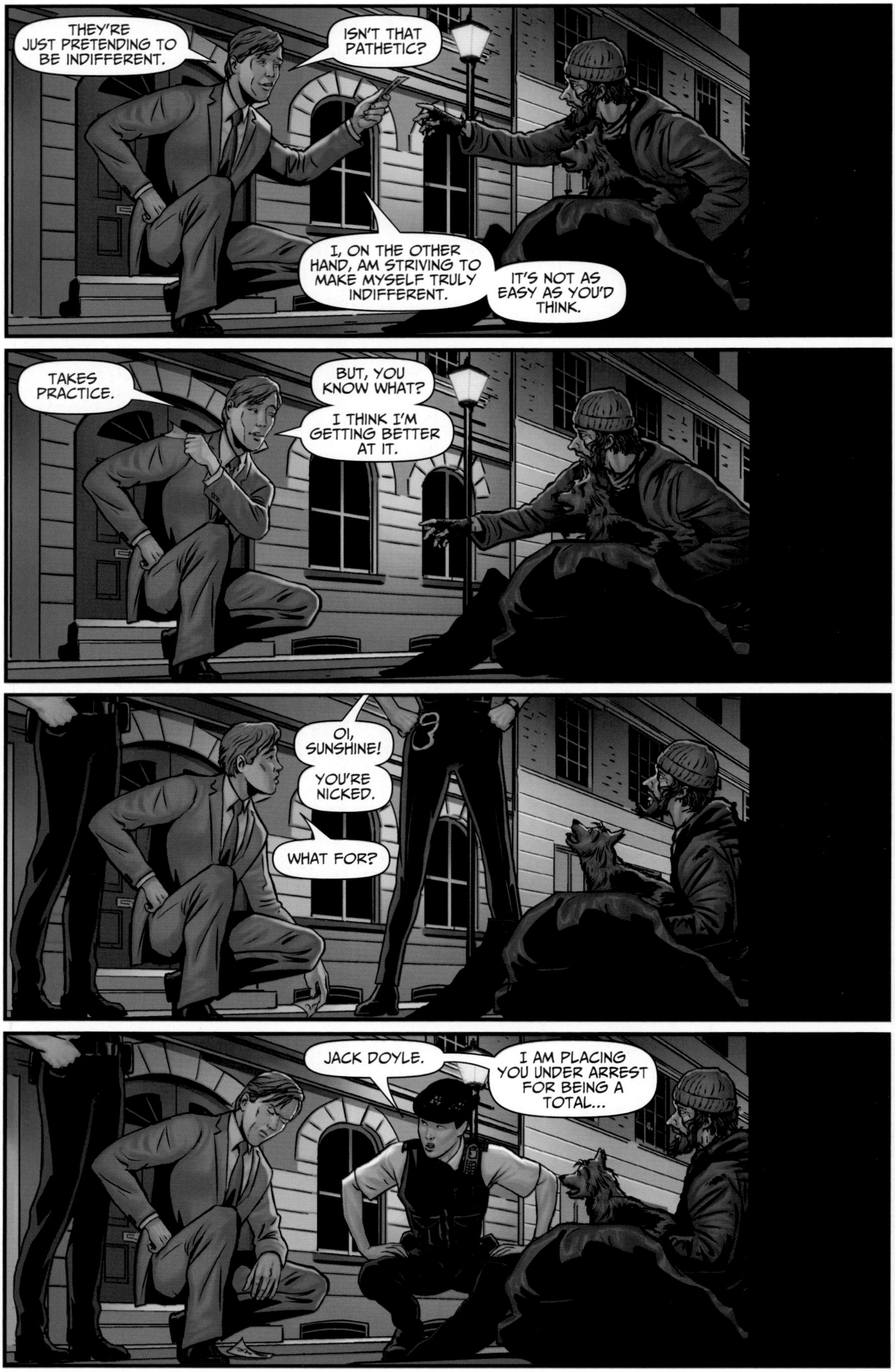
THEY'RE JUST PRETENDING TO BE INDIFFERENT.
ISN'T THAT PATHETIC?
I, ON THE OTHER HAND, AM STRIVING TO MAKE MYSELF TRULY INDIFFERENT.
IT'S NOT AS EASY AS YOU'D THINK.
TAKES PRACTICE.
BUT, YOU KNOW WHAT?
I THINK I'M GETTING BETTER AT IT.
OI, SUNSHINE!
YOU'RE NICKED.
WHAT FOR?
JACK DOYLE.
I AM PLACING YOU UNDER ARREST FOR BEING A TOTAL...

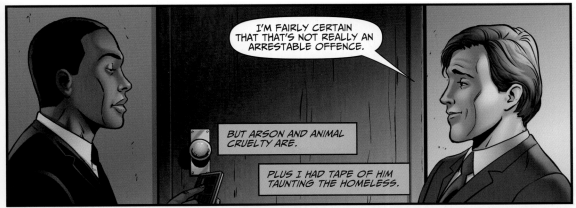

I'M FAIRLY CERTAIN THAT THAT'S NOT REALLY AN ARRESTABLE OFFENCE.

BUT ARSON AND ANIMAL CRUELTY ARE.

PLUS I HAD TAPE OF HIM TAUNTING THE HOMELESS.

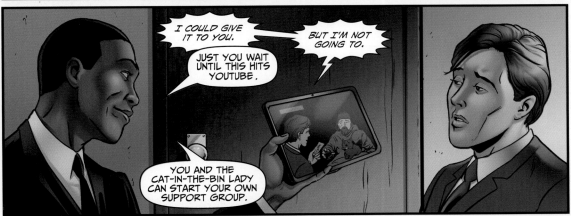

I COULD GIVE IT TO YOU.

BUT I'M NOT GOING TO.

JUST YOU WAIT UNTIL THIS HITS YOUTUBE.

YOU AND THE CAT-IN-THE-BIN LADY CAN START YOUR OWN SUPPORT GROUP.

YOU JUST HAPPENED TO HAVE A DIGITAL CAMERA WITH A ZOOM LENS ABOUT YOUR PERSON?

I LIKE TO BE PREPARED.

YOU NEVER *KNOW* WHAT A SUSPECT IS GOING TO DO.

THE TRICK IS TO MAKE IT SO THAT WHATEVER THEY DO, YOU CAN USE IT AGAINST THEM.

SUN TZU?

LORD VETINARI.

AND DID MR. DOYLE SING?

LIKE A TONE DEAF CONTESTANT ON *BRITAIN'S GOT TALENT.*

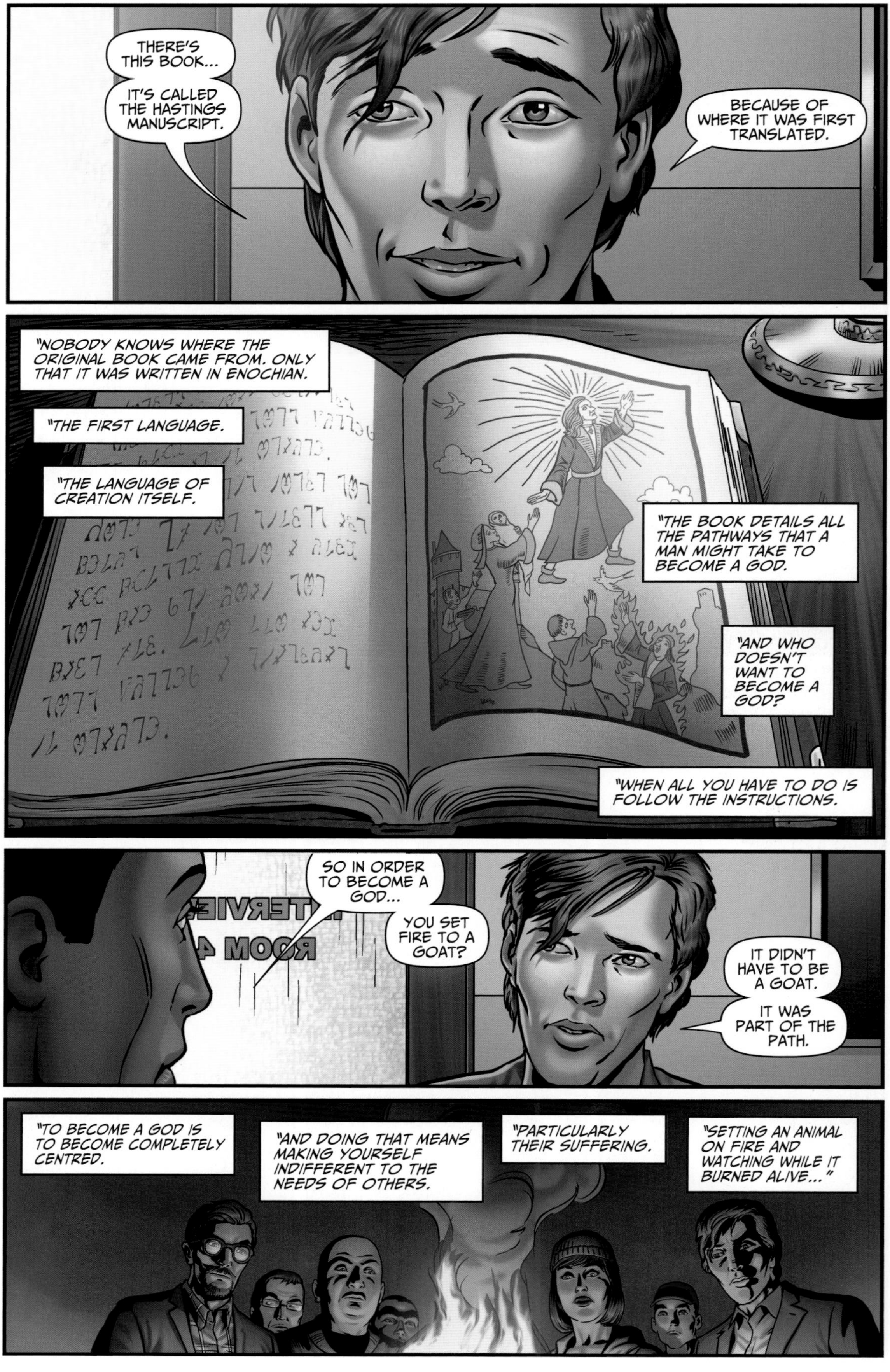
THERE'S THIS BOOK...
IT'S CALLED THE HASTINGS MANUSCRIPT.
BECAUSE OF WHERE IT WAS FIRST TRANSLATED.
"NOBODY KNOWS WHERE THE ORIGINAL BOOK CAME FROM. ONLY THAT IT WAS WRITTEN IN ENOCHIAN.
"THE FIRST LANGUAGE.
"THE LANGUAGE OF CREATION ITSELF.
"THE BOOK DETAILS ALL THE PATHWAYS THAT A MAN MIGHT TAKE TO BECOME A GOD.
"AND WHO DOESN'T WANT TO BECOME A GOD?
"WHEN ALL YOU HAVE TO DO IS FOLLOW THE INSTRUCTIONS.
SO IN ORDER TO BECOME A GOD...
YOU SET FIRE TO A GOAT?
IT DIDN'T HAVE TO BE A GOAT.
IT WAS PART OF THE PATH.
"TO BECOME A GOD IS TO BECOME COMPLETELY CENTRED.
"AND DOING THAT MEANS MAKING YOURSELF INDIFFERENT TO THE NEEDS OF OTHERS.
"PARTICULARLY THEIR SUFFERING.
"SETTING AN ANIMAL ON FIRE AND WATCHING WHILE IT BURNED ALIVE..."

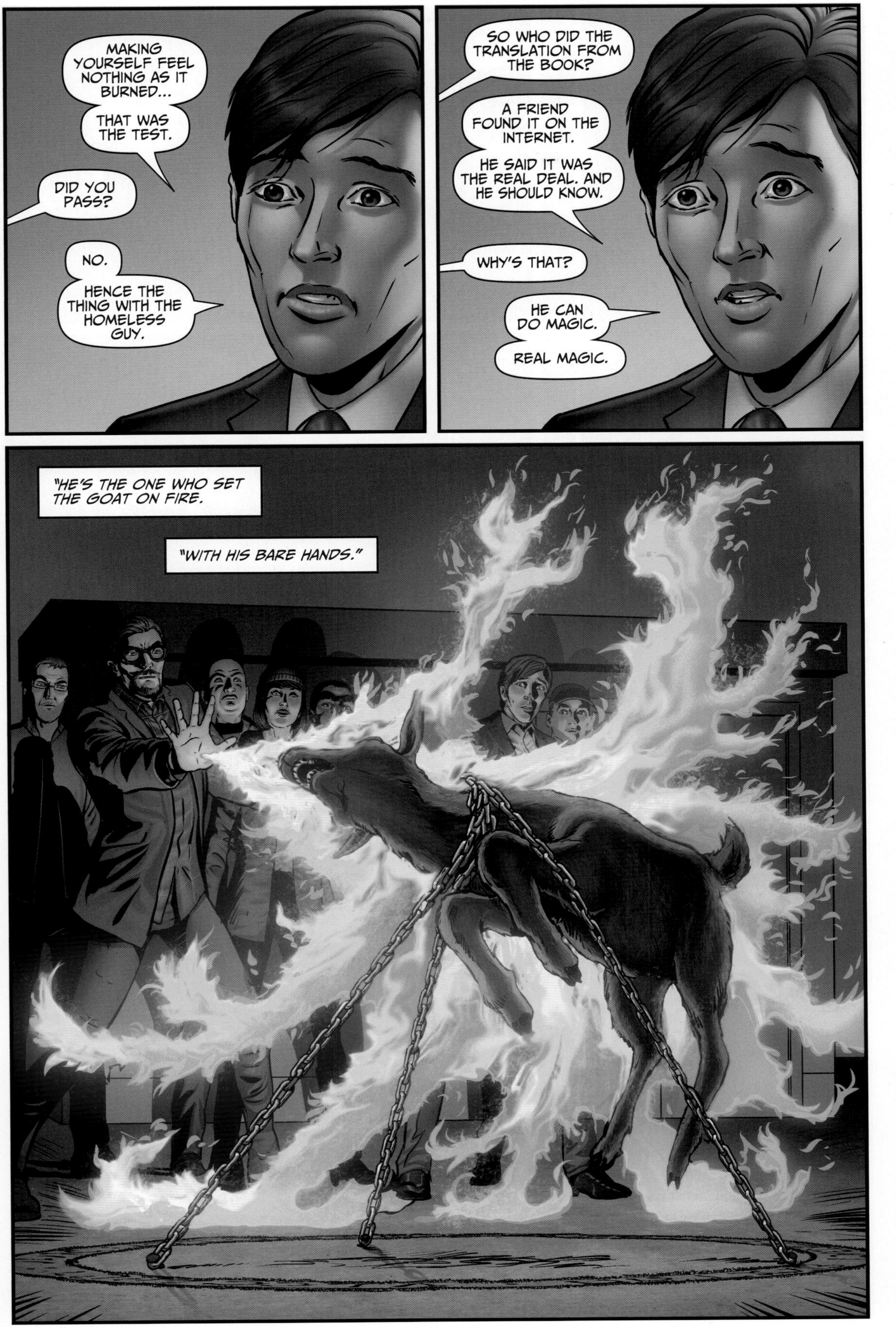
MAKING YOURSELF FEEL NOTHING AS IT BURNED...
THAT WAS THE TEST.
DID YOU PASS?
NO.
HENCE THE THING WITH THE HOMELESS GUY.
SO WHO DID THE TRANSLATION FROM THE BOOK?
A FRIEND FOUND IT ON THE INTERNET.
HE SAID IT WAS THE REAL DEAL. AND HE SHOULD KNOW.
WHY'S THAT?
HE CAN DO MAGIC.
REAL MAGIC.
"HE'S THE ONE WHO SET THE GOAT ON FIRE.
"WITH HIS BARE HANDS."

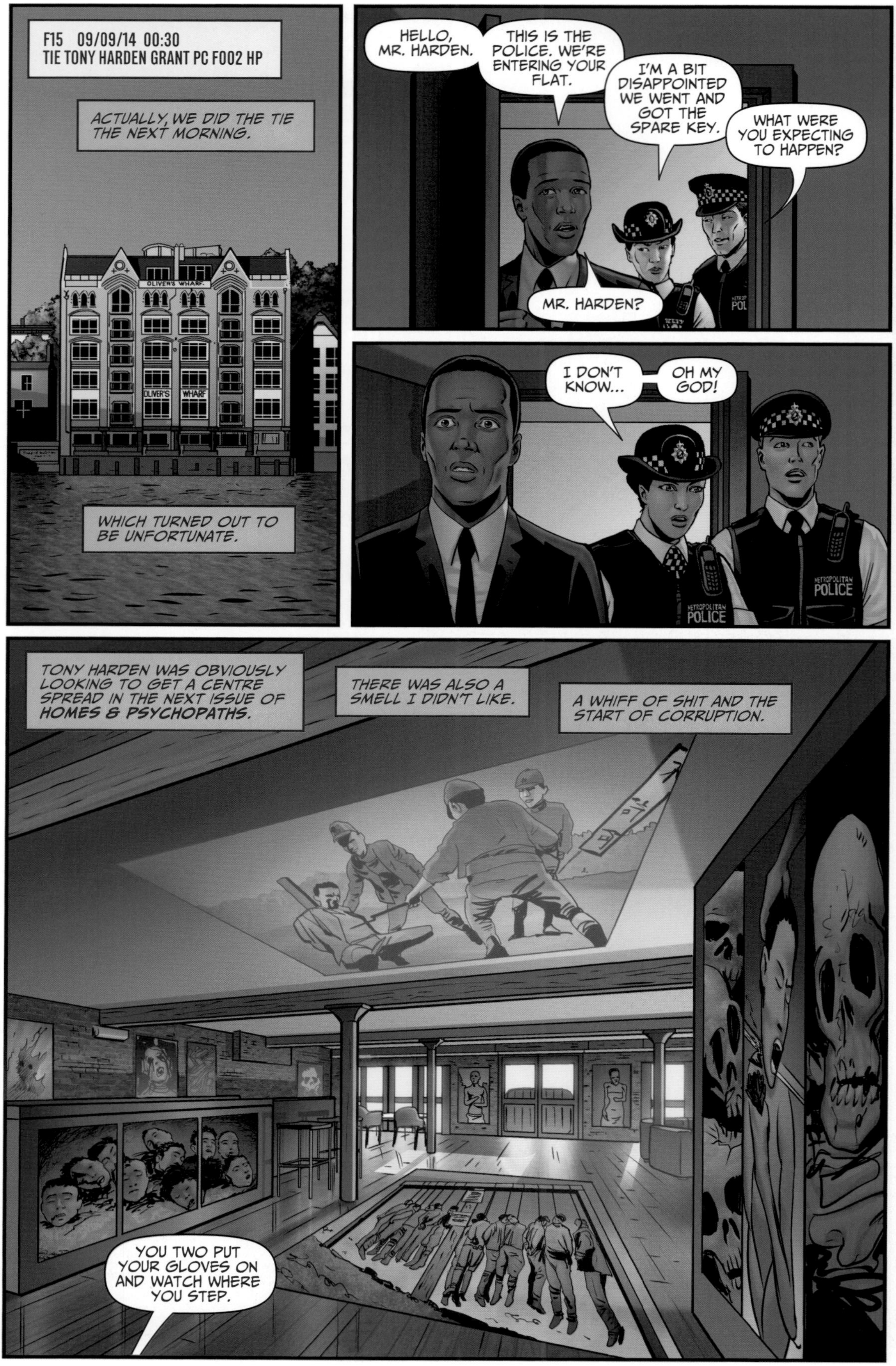
F15 09/09/14 00:30
TIE TONY HARDEN GRANT PC F002 HP
ACTUALLY, WE DID THE TIE THE NEXT MORNING.
OLIVER'S WHARF.
OLIVER'S WHARF
WHICH TURNED OUT TO BE UNFORTUNATE.
HELLO, MR. HARDEN.
THIS IS THE POLICE. WE'RE ENTERING YOUR FLAT.
I'M A BIT DISAPPOINTED WE WENT AND GOT THE SPARE KEY.
WHAT WERE YOU EXPECTING TO HAPPEN?
MR. HARDEN?
I DON'T KNOW...
OH MY GOD!
METROPOLITAN POLICE
METROPOLITAN POLICE
TONY HARDEN WAS OBVIOUSLY LOOKING TO GET A CENTRE SPREAD IN THE NEXT ISSUE OF HOMES & PSYCHOPATHS.
THERE WAS ALSO A SMELL I DIDN'T LIKE.
A WHIFF OF SHIT AND THE START OF CORRUPTION.
YOU TWO PUT YOUR GLOVES ON AND WATCH WHERE YOU STEP.

TONY HARDEN.

WORK MATE OF JACK DOYLE AND ANOTHER RISING STAR AT BOCK, LOUPE AND STAG.

DEADER THAN BROWN BREAD.

IT'S HARD TO DO AN INTERVIEW WHEN YOUR NOMINAL HAS BEEN ELIMINATED.

ACCORDING TO YOUR MEDICAL REPORT HE DIED OF NATURAL CAUSES.

"INTRACRANIAL BLEEDING, WHICH I RECOGNISE...

"AND SOMETHING LISTED ONLY AS HTD."

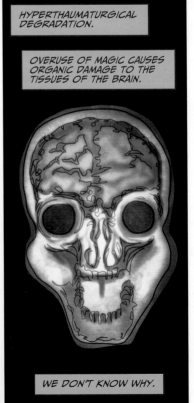

HYPERTHAUMATURGICAL DEGRADATION.

OVERUSE OF MAGIC CAUSES ORGANIC DAMAGE TO THE TISSUES OF THE BRAIN.

WE DON'T KNOW WHY.

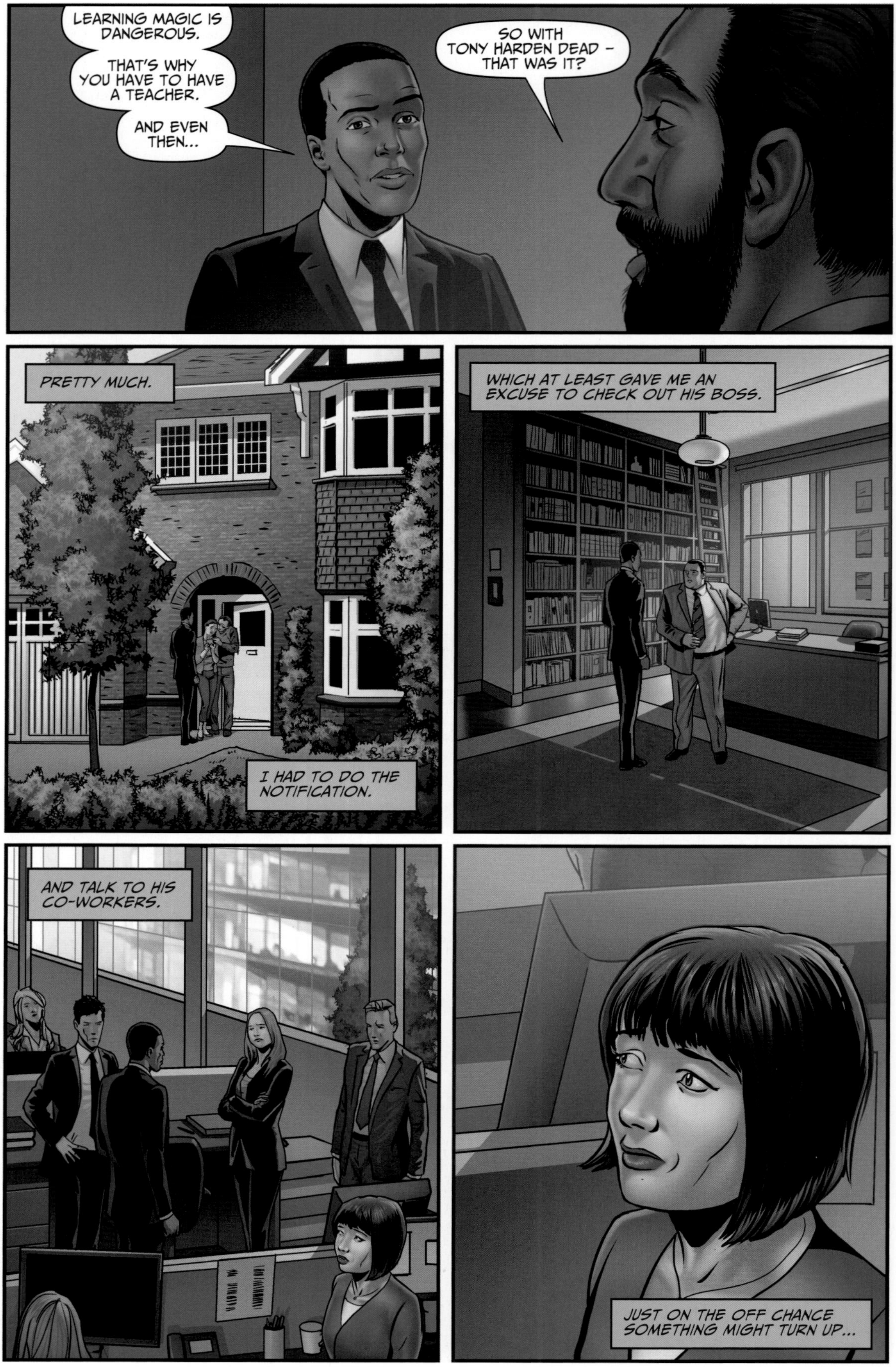
LEARNING MAGIC IS DANGEROUS.
THAT'S WHY YOU HAVE TO HAVE A TEACHER.
AND EVEN THEN...
SO WITH TONY HARDEN DEAD – THAT WAS IT?
PRETTY MUCH.
I HAD TO DO THE NOTIFICATION.
WHICH AT LEAST GAVE ME AN EXCUSE TO CHECK OUT HIS BOSS.
AND TALK TO HIS CO-WORKERS.
JUST ON THE OFF CHANCE SOMETHING MIGHT TURN UP...

WE DID FOLLOW UP ON THE HOUSE TO HOUSE AND CCTV, AND IDENTIFIED A COUPLE MORE POTENTIAL WITNESSES THAT HAD BEEN ON THE ROOF.

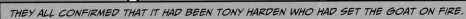

THEY ALL CONFIRMED THAT IT HAD BEEN TONY HARDEN WHO HAD SET THE GOAT ON FIRE.

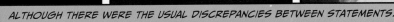

ALTHOUGH THERE WERE THE USUAL DISCREPANCIES BETWEEN STATEMENTS.

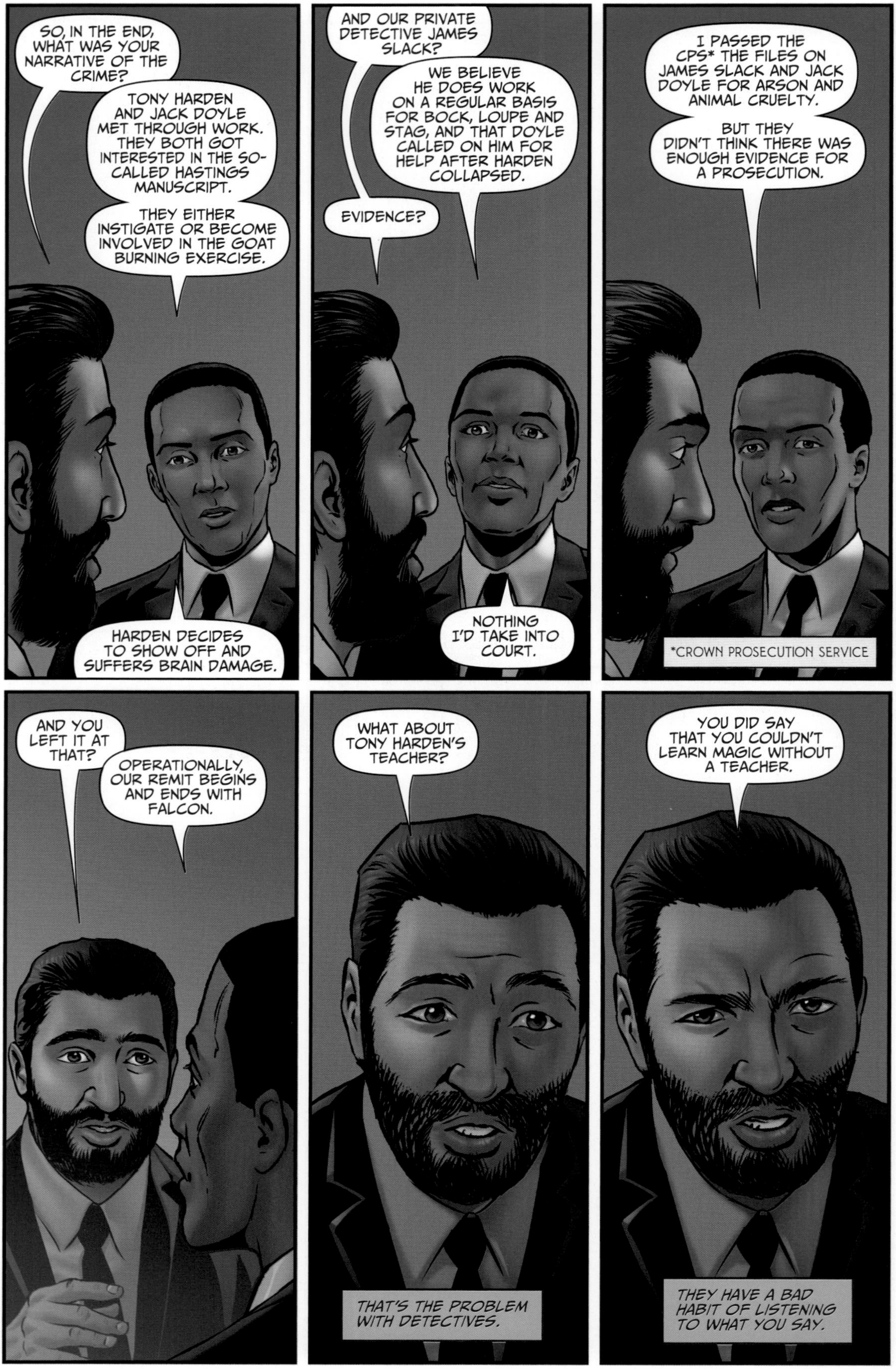
SO, IN THE END, WHAT WAS YOUR NARRATIVE OF THE CRIME?
TONY HARDEN AND JACK DOYLE MET THROUGH WORK. THEY BOTH GOT INTERESTED IN THE SO-CALLED HASTINGS MANUSCRIPT.
THEY EITHER INSTIGATE OR BECOME INVOLVED IN THE GOAT BURNING EXERCISE.
HARDEN DECIDES TO SHOW OFF AND SUFFERS BRAIN DAMAGE.
AND OUR PRIVATE DETECTIVE JAMES SLACK?
WE BELIEVE HE DOES WORK ON A REGULAR BASIS FOR BOCK, LOUPE AND STAG, AND THAT DOYLE CALLED ON HIM FOR HELP AFTER HARDEN COLLAPSED.
EVIDENCE?
NOTHING I'D TAKE INTO COURT.
I PASSED THE CPS* THE FILES ON JAMES SLACK AND JACK DOYLE FOR ARSON AND ANIMAL CRUELTY.
BUT THEY DIDN'T THINK THERE WAS ENOUGH EVIDENCE FOR A PROSECUTION.
*CROWN PROSECUTION SERVICE
AND YOU LEFT IT AT THAT?
OPERATIONALLY, OUR REMIT BEGINS AND ENDS WITH FALCON.
WHAT ABOUT TONY HARDEN'S TEACHER?
THAT'S THE PROBLEM WITH DETECTIVES.
YOU DID SAY THAT YOU COULDN'T LEARN MAGIC WITHOUT A TEACHER.
THEY HAVE A BAD HABIT OF LISTENING TO WHAT YOU SAY.

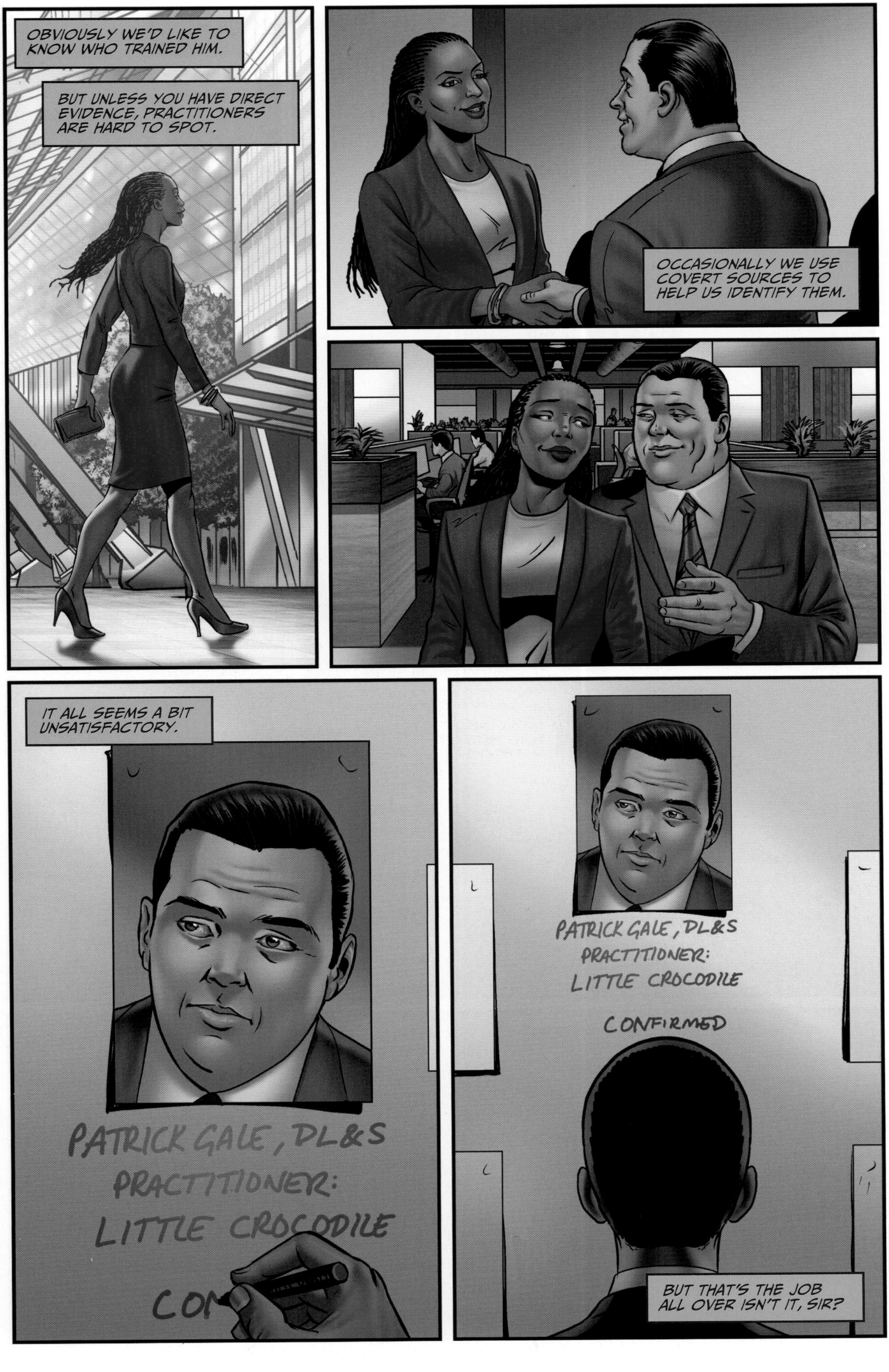
OBVIOUSLY WE'D LIKE TO KNOW WHO TRAINED HIM.
BUT UNLESS YOU HAVE DIRECT EVIDENCE, PRACTITIONERS ARE HARD TO SPOT.
OCCASIONALLY WE USE COVERT SOURCES TO HELP US IDENTIFY THEM.
IT ALL SEEMS A BIT UNSATISFACTORY.
PATRICK GALE, DL&S
PRACTITIONER:
LITTLE CROCODILE
CON
PATRICK GALE, DL&S
PRACTITIONER:
LITTLE CROCODILE
CONFIRMED
BUT THAT'S THE JOB ALL OVER ISN'T IT, SIR?

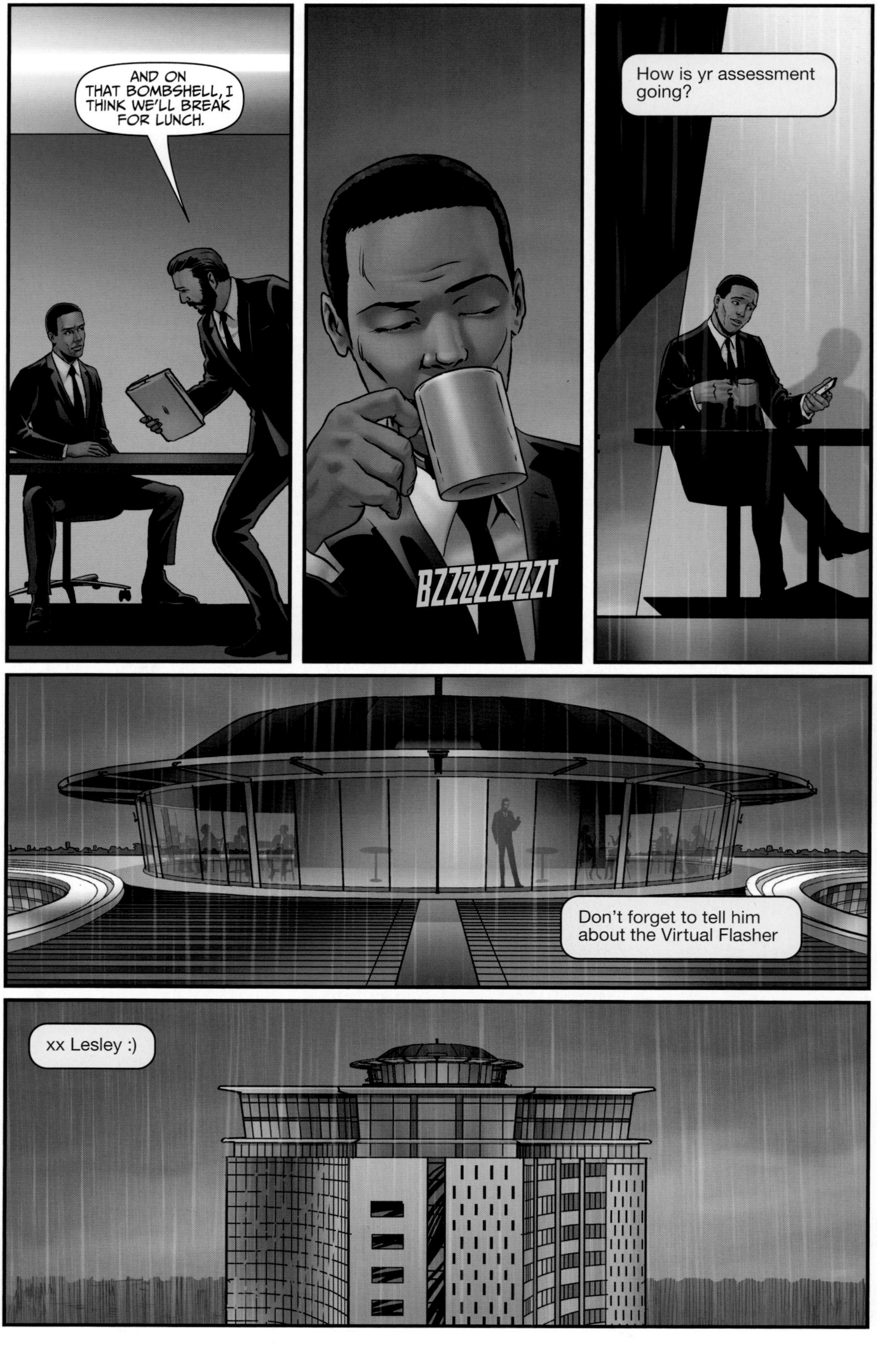
AND ON THAT BOMBSHELL, I THINK WE'LL BREAK FOR LUNCH.
BZZZZZZZZT
How is yr assessment going?
Don't forget to tell him about the Virtual Flasher
xx Lesley :)

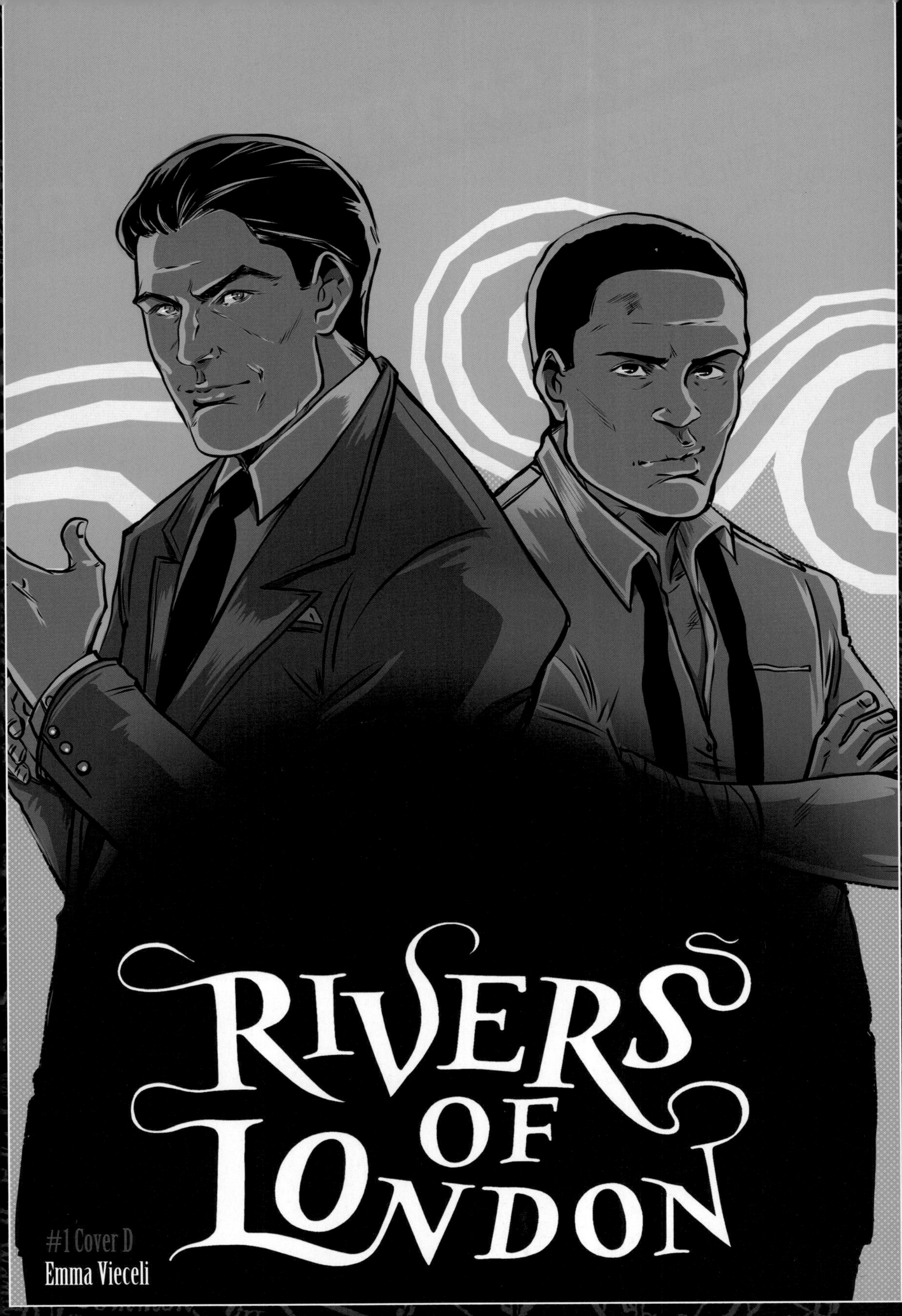
RIVERS OF LONDON
#1 Cover D
Emma Vieceli

PIFFLE: A SPOTTER'S GUIDE

BY PROFESSOR HAROLD POSTMARTIN, DPHIL, FRS, FHSW

THE HASTINGS MANUSCRIPT

If only arcane documents came with mandatory contents labelling such as adorn the back of packets of sandwiches and whatnot. How much easier would life as an archivist be if they were labelled as being 22% Piffle, 8% Balderdash, with trace amounts of Veracity. A standardised system covering the whole of the EU would no doubt facilitate trade and force the *Bibliothèque de la Sorbonne* to admit its inferior place in the hierarchy of great libraries. Alas, however, no such labelling standards exist, and the humble archivist is forced to fall back on his knowledge, his tenacity, and his guile. None of this applies to the Hastings Manuscript which is, of course, obvious piffle from start to finish.

The manuscript is attributed to George Cecil Jones, a man famous for being an associate of Aleister Crowley and nothing else whatsoever. A member of the Hermetic Order of the Golden Dawn, he is reputed to have introduced Crowley to that organisation and together they later formed the A∴A∴ which I categorically refuse to acknowledge with more than half a sentence.

The Hastings Manuscript itself surfaced in the 1960s and has been passed around the more credulous fringes of occult society ever since. All the editions I have traced so far have originated with various well-known vanity presses – some of them quite beautifully illustrated. The manuscript purports to describe the true paths a human being may take to godhood. The wrinkle is that the aspirant deity must translate the ▶

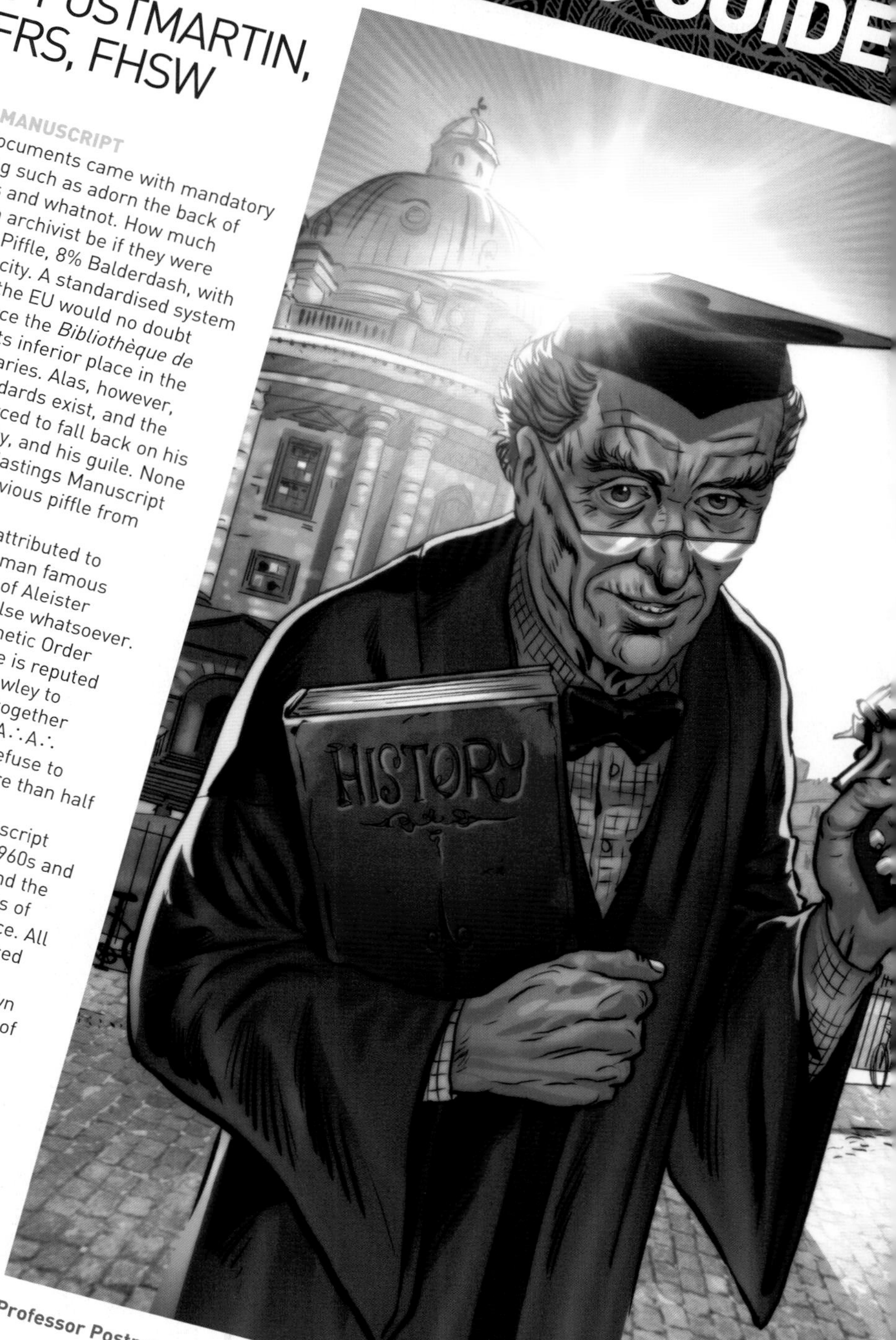
HISTORY

Professor Postmartin

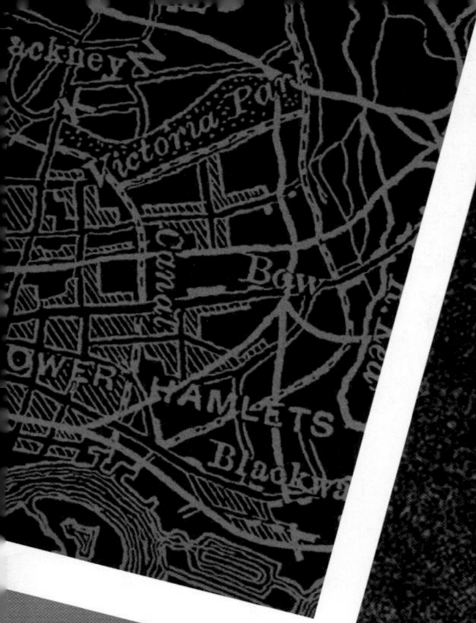
Victoria Park
Canal
Bow

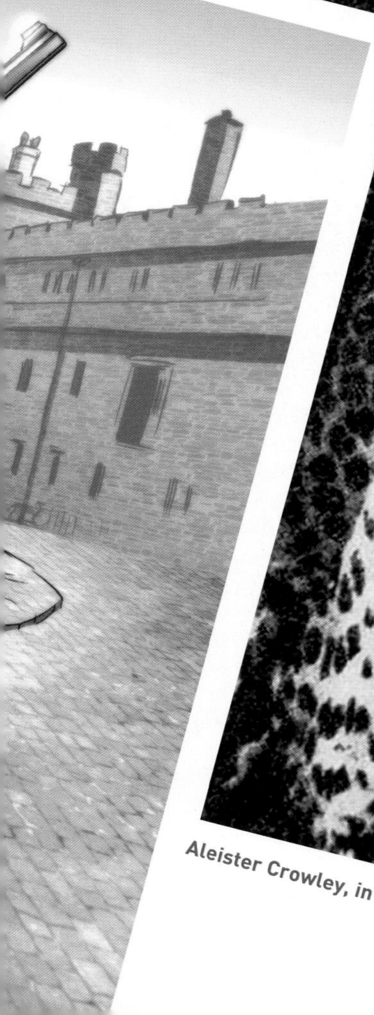

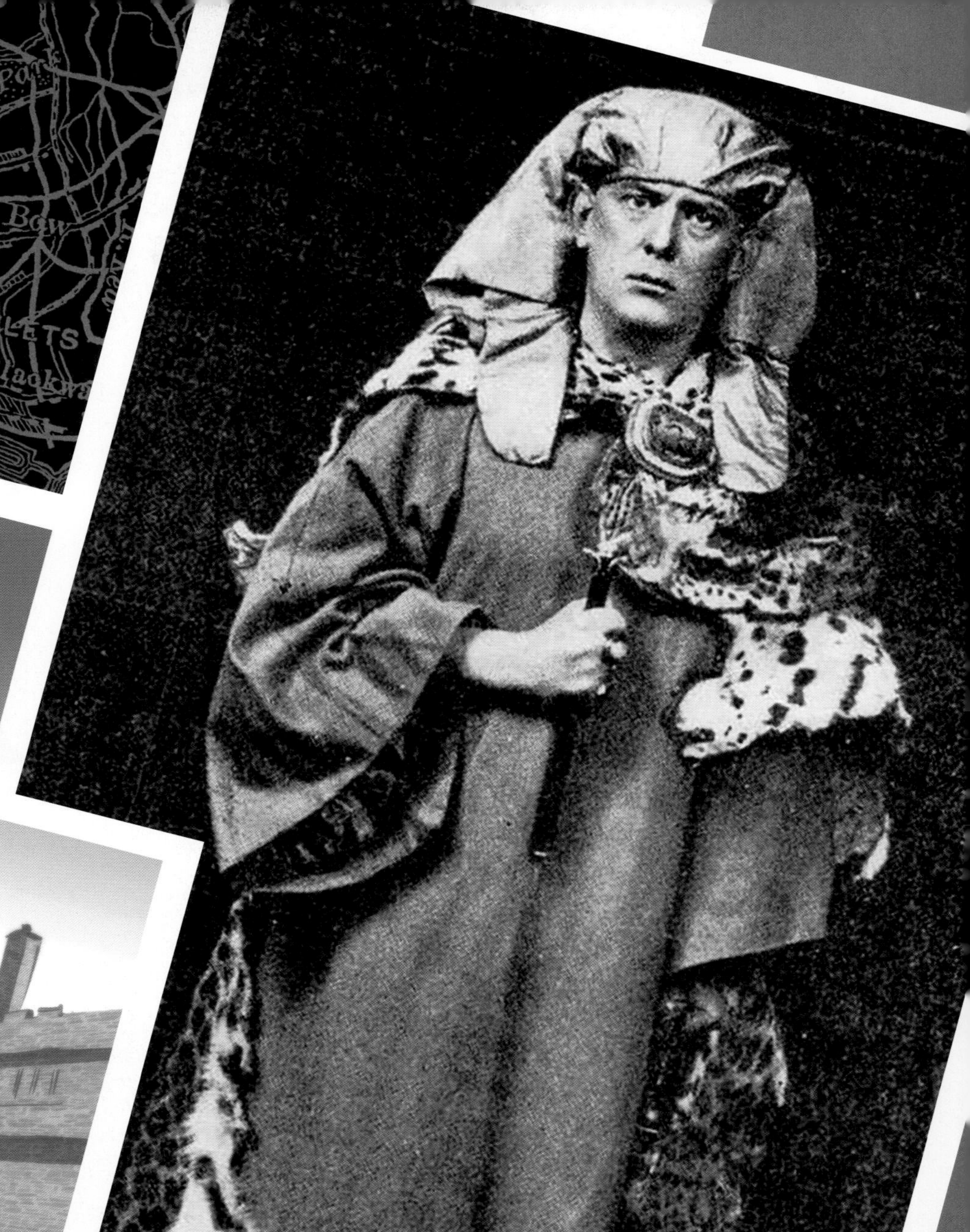

Aleister Crowley, in Golden Dawn garb

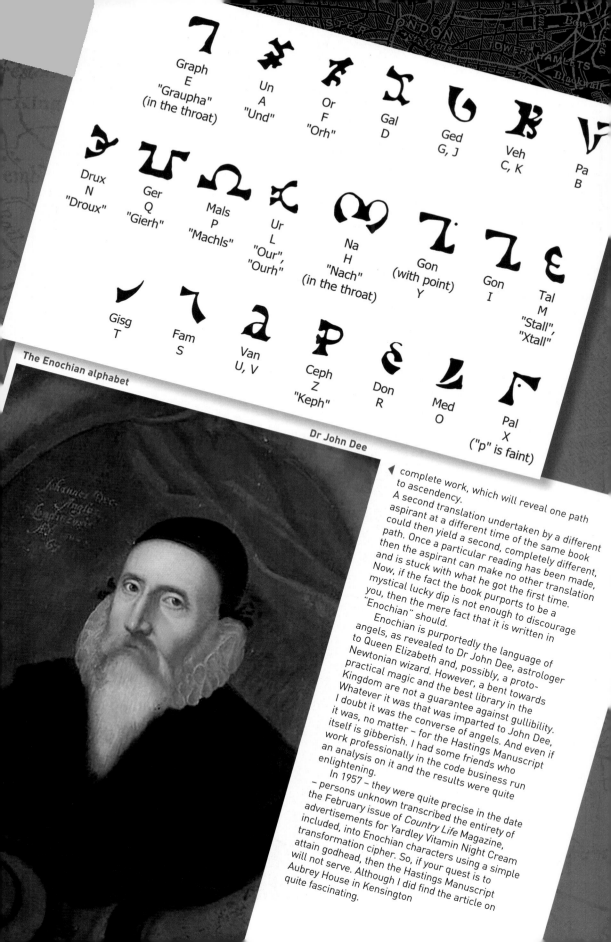

The Enochian alphabet

Graph E "Graupha" (in the throat)	Un A "Und"	Or F "Orh"
Gal D	Ged G, J	Veh C, K
Pa B	Drux N "Droux"	Ger Q "Gierh"
Mals P "Machls"	Ur L "Our", "Ourh"	Na H "Nach" (in the throat)
Gon (with point) Y	Gon I	Tal M "Stall", "Xtall"
Gisg T	Fam S	Van U, V
Ceph Z "Keph"	Don R	Med O
Pal X ("p" is faint)		

Dr John Dee

complete work, which will reveal one path to ascendency.

A second translation undertaken by a different aspirant at a different time of the same book could then yield a second, completely different, path. Once a particular reading has been made, then the aspirant can make no other translation and is stuck with what he got the first time. Now, if the fact the book purports to be a mystical lucky dip is not enough to discourage you, then the mere fact that it is written in "Enochian" should.

Enochian is purportedly the language of angels, as revealed to Dr John Dee, astrologer to Queen Elizabeth and, possibly, a proto-Newtonian wizard. However, a bent towards practical magic and the best library in the Kingdom are not a guarantee against gullibility. Whatever it was that was imparted to John Dee, I doubt it was the converse of angels. And even if it was, no matter – for the Hastings Manuscript itself is gibberish. I had some friends who work professionally in the code business run an analysis on it and the results were quite enlightening.

In 1957 – they were quite precise in the date – persons unknown transcribed the entirety of the February issue of *Country Life* Magazine, advertisements for Yardley Vitamin Night Cream included, into Enochian characters using a simple transformation cipher. So, if your quest is to attain godhead, then the Hastings Manuscript will not serve. Although I did find the article on Aubrey House in Kensington quite fascinating.

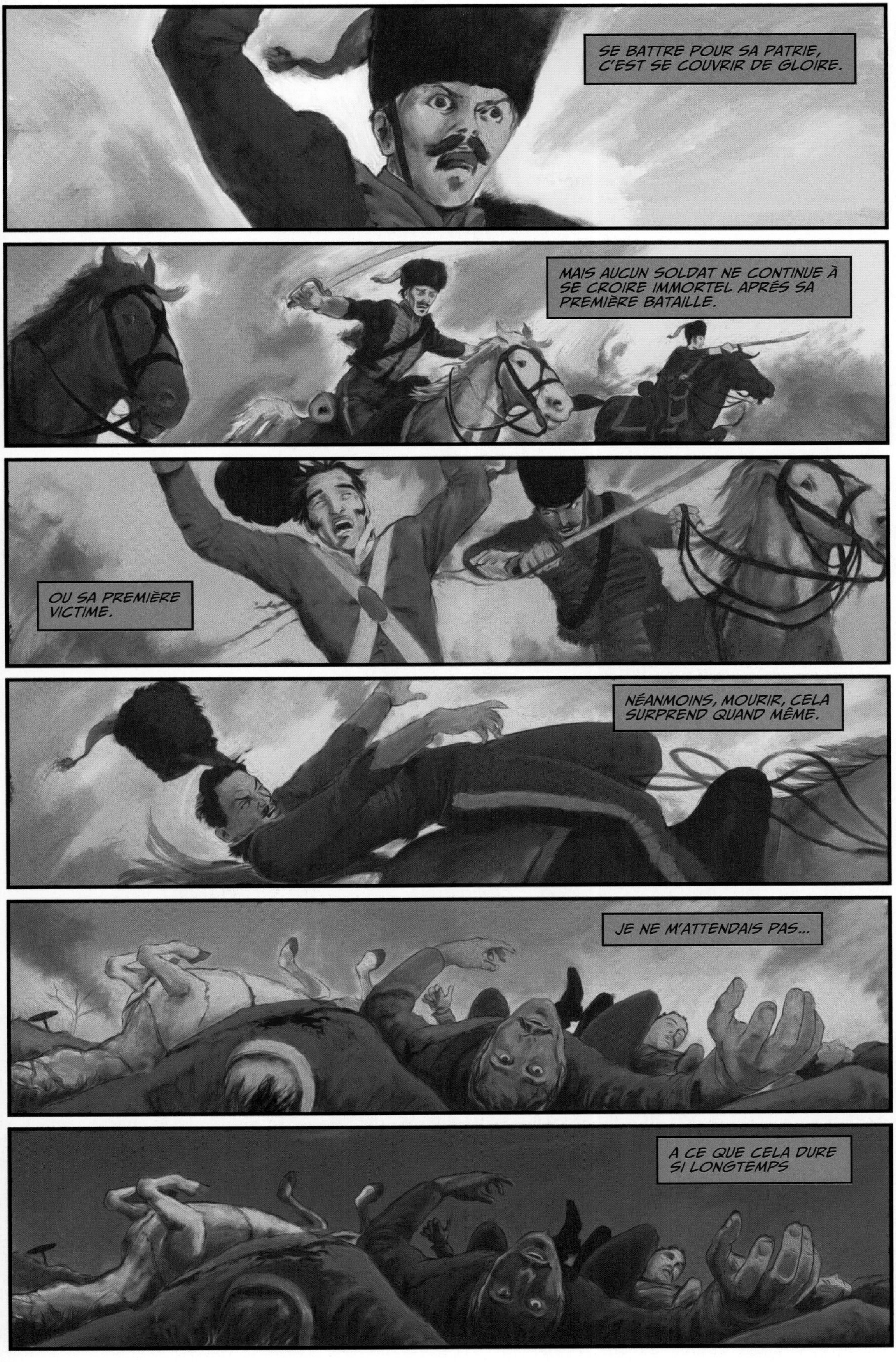
SE BATTRE POUR SA PATRIE, C'EST SE COUVRIR DE GLOIRE.
MAIS AUCUN SOLDAT NE CONTINUE À SE CROIRE IMMORTEL APRÈS SA PREMIÈRE BATAILLE.
OU SA PREMIÈRE VICTIME.
NÉANMOINS, MOURIR, CELA SURPREND QUAND MÊME.
JE NE M'ATTENDAIS PAS...
A CE QUE CELA DURE SI LONGTEMPS

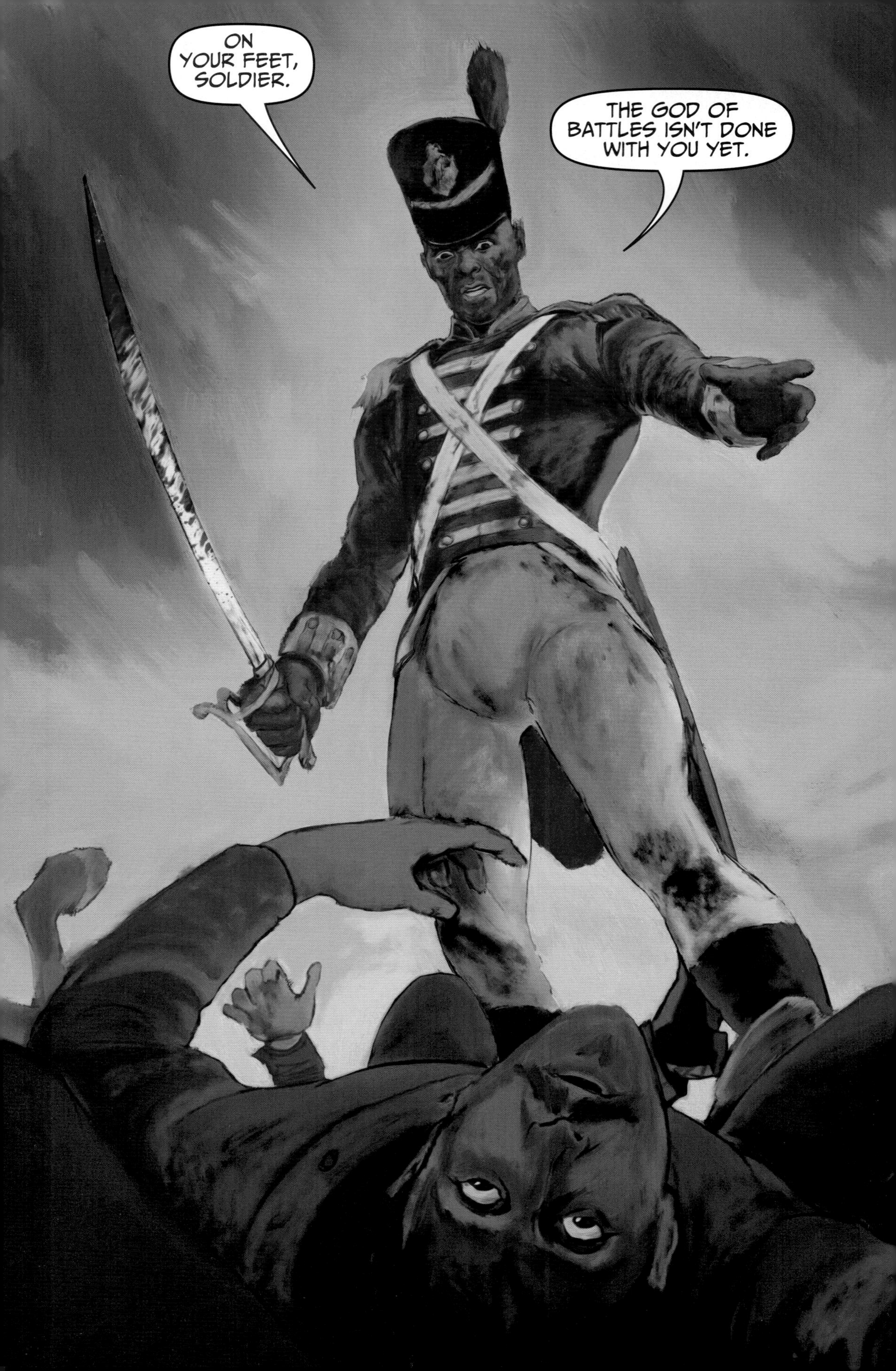
ON YOUR FEET, SOLDIER.
THE GOD OF BATTLES ISN'T DONE WITH YOU YET.

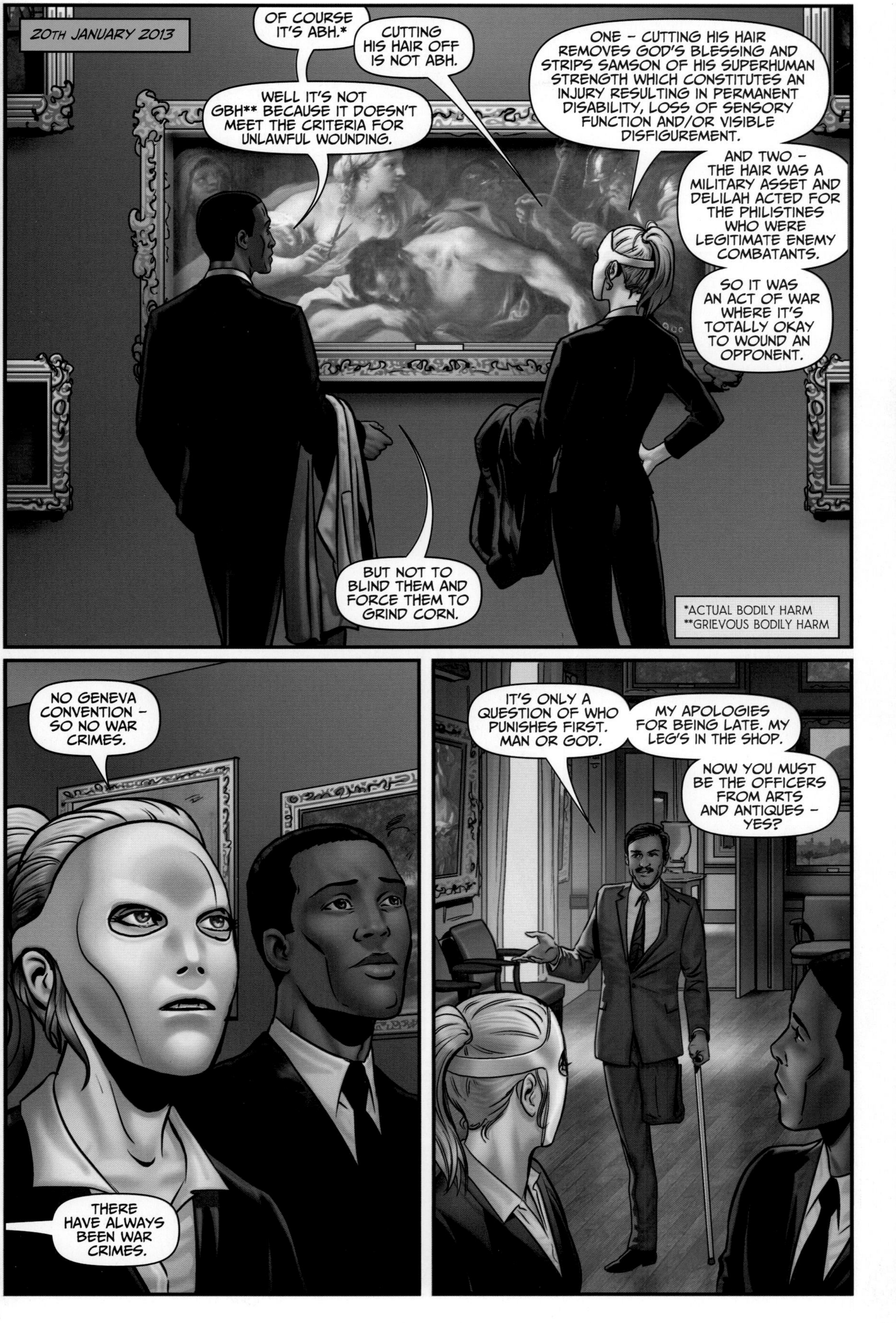
20TH JANUARY 2013
OF COURSE IT'S ABH.*
CUTTING HIS HAIR OFF IS NOT ABH.
WELL IT'S NOT GBH** BECAUSE IT DOESN'T MEET THE CRITERIA FOR UNLAWFUL WOUNDING.
ONE – CUTTING HIS HAIR REMOVES GOD'S BLESSING AND STRIPS SAMSON OF HIS SUPERHUMAN STRENGTH WHICH CONSTITUTES AN INJURY RESULTING IN PERMANENT DISABILITY, LOSS OF SENSORY FUNCTION AND/OR VISIBLE DISFIGUREMENT.
AND TWO – THE HAIR WAS A MILITARY ASSET AND DELILAH ACTED FOR THE PHILISTINES WHO WERE LEGITIMATE ENEMY COMBATANTS.
SO IT WAS AN ACT OF WAR WHERE IT'S TOTALLY OKAY TO WOUND AN OPPONENT.
BUT NOT TO BLIND THEM AND FORCE THEM TO GRIND CORN.
*ACTUAL BODILY HARM
**GRIEVOUS BODILY HARM
NO GENEVA CONVENTION – SO NO WAR CRIMES.
THERE HAVE ALWAYS BEEN WAR CRIMES.
IT'S ONLY A QUESTION OF WHO PUNISHES FIRST. MAN OR GOD.
MY APOLOGIES FOR BEING LATE. MY LEG'S IN THE SHOP.
NOW YOU MUST BE THE OFFICERS FROM ARTS AND ANTIQUES – YES?

I WAS WONDERING ABOUT THIS.

THIS IS DETECTIVE INSPECTOR CHOPRA, WHOSE JOB IS TO ASSESS A SELECTION OF MY CASES AS PART OF MY LEVEL 2 PIP* ACCREDITATION.

*PROFESSIONALISM IN POLICING.

THE EXAM BIT WAS EASY ENOUGH.

SO WERE THE SEMINARS.

BUT SOME OF THE INVESTIGATIONS...

RISK AND CONTROL STRATEGY MODELS

Remove
Avoid
Reduce
A

WORLD'S FIRST ANGLO-AMERICAN SEWER LUGE TEAM – CHRISTMAS 2012

CAN BE DIFFICULT TO EXPLAIN.

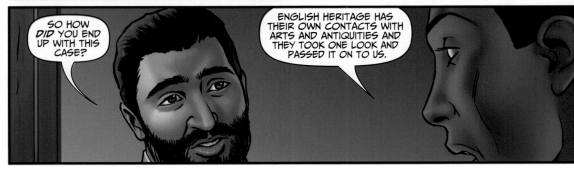

SO HOW *DID* YOU END UP WITH THIS CASE?

ENGLISH HERITAGE HAS THEIR OWN CONTACTS WITH ARTS AND ANTIQUITIES AND THEY TOOK ONE LOOK AND PASSED IT ON TO US.

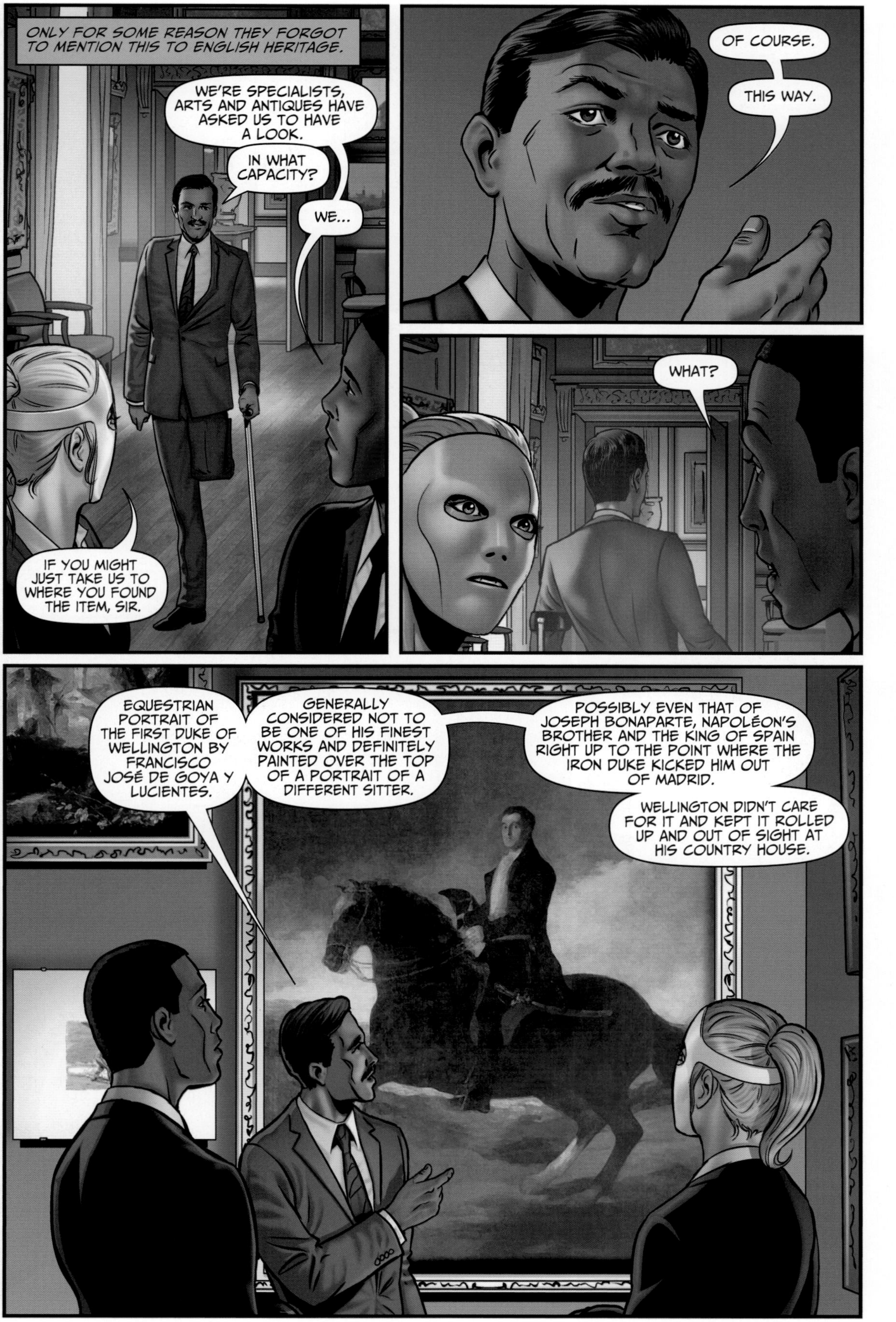
ONLY FOR SOME REASON THEY FORGOT TO MENTION THIS TO ENGLISH HERITAGE.
WE'RE SPECIALISTS, ARTS AND ANTIQUES HAVE ASKED US TO HAVE A LOOK.
IN WHAT CAPACITY?
WE...
IF YOU MIGHT JUST TAKE US TO WHERE YOU FOUND THE ITEM, SIR.
OF COURSE.
THIS WAY.
WHAT?
EQUESTRIAN PORTRAIT OF THE FIRST DUKE OF WELLINGTON BY FRANCISCO JOSÉ DE GOYA Y LUCIENTES.
GENERALLY CONSIDERED NOT TO BE ONE OF HIS FINEST WORKS AND DEFINITELY PAINTED OVER THE TOP OF A PORTRAIT OF A DIFFERENT SITTER.
POSSIBLY EVEN THAT OF JOSEPH BONAPARTE, NAPOLÉON'S BROTHER AND THE KING OF SPAIN RIGHT UP TO THE POINT WHERE THE IRON DUKE KICKED HIM OUT OF MADRID.
WELLINGTON DIDN'T CARE FOR IT AND KEPT IT ROLLED UP AND OUT OF SIGHT AT HIS COUNTRY HOUSE.

AND THE REASON WE'RE HERE?

YES...

THAT'S OVER HERE.

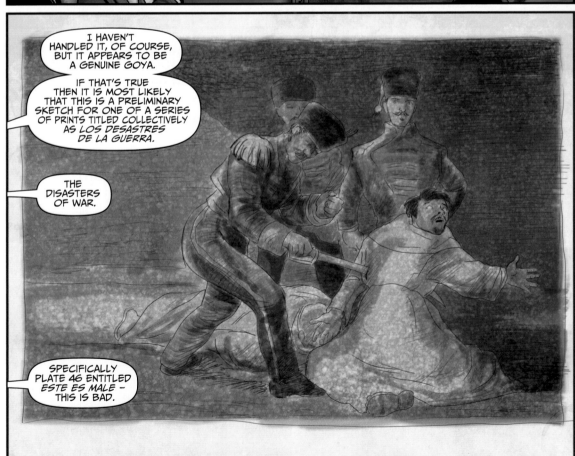

I HAVEN'T HANDLED IT, OF COURSE, BUT IT APPEARS TO BE A GENUINE GOYA.

IF THAT'S TRUE THEN IT IS MOST LIKELY THAT THIS IS A PRELIMINARY SKETCH FOR ONE OF A SERIES OF PRINTS TITLED COLLECTIVELY AS *LOS DESASTRES DE LA GUERRA.*

THE DISASTERS OF WAR.

SPECIFICALLY PLATE 46 ENTITLED *ESTE ES MALE* – THIS IS BAD.

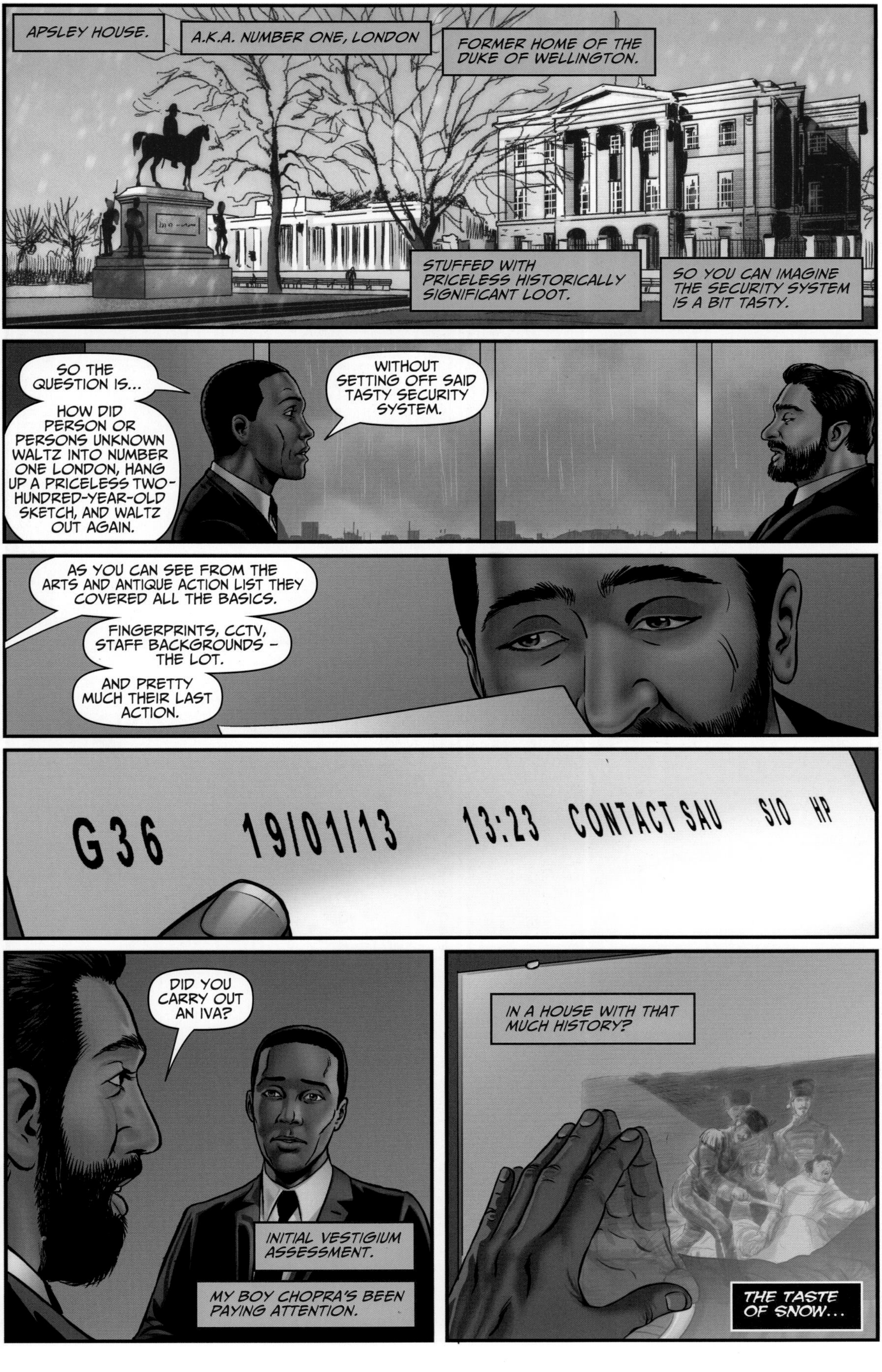
APSLEY HOUSE.
A.K.A. NUMBER ONE, LONDON
FORMER HOME OF THE DUKE OF WELLINGTON.
STUFFED WITH PRICELESS HISTORICALLY SIGNIFICANT LOOT.
SO YOU CAN IMAGINE THE SECURITY SYSTEM IS A BIT TASTY.
SO THE QUESTION IS...
HOW DID PERSON OR PERSONS UNKNOWN WALTZ INTO NUMBER ONE LONDON, HANG UP A PRICELESS TWO-HUNDRED-YEAR-OLD SKETCH, AND WALTZ OUT AGAIN.
WITHOUT SETTING OFF SAID TASTY SECURITY SYSTEM.
AS YOU CAN SEE FROM THE ARTS AND ANTIQUE ACTION LIST THEY COVERED ALL THE BASICS.
FINGERPRINTS, CCTV, STAFF BACKGROUNDS – THE LOT.
AND PRETTY MUCH THEIR LAST ACTION.
G36 19/01/13 13:23 CONTACT SAU SIO HP
DID YOU CARRY OUT AN IVA?
INITIAL VESTIGIUM ASSESSMENT.
MY BOY CHOPRA'S BEEN PAYING ATTENTION.
IN A HOUSE WITH THAT MUCH HISTORY?
THE TASTE OF SNOW...

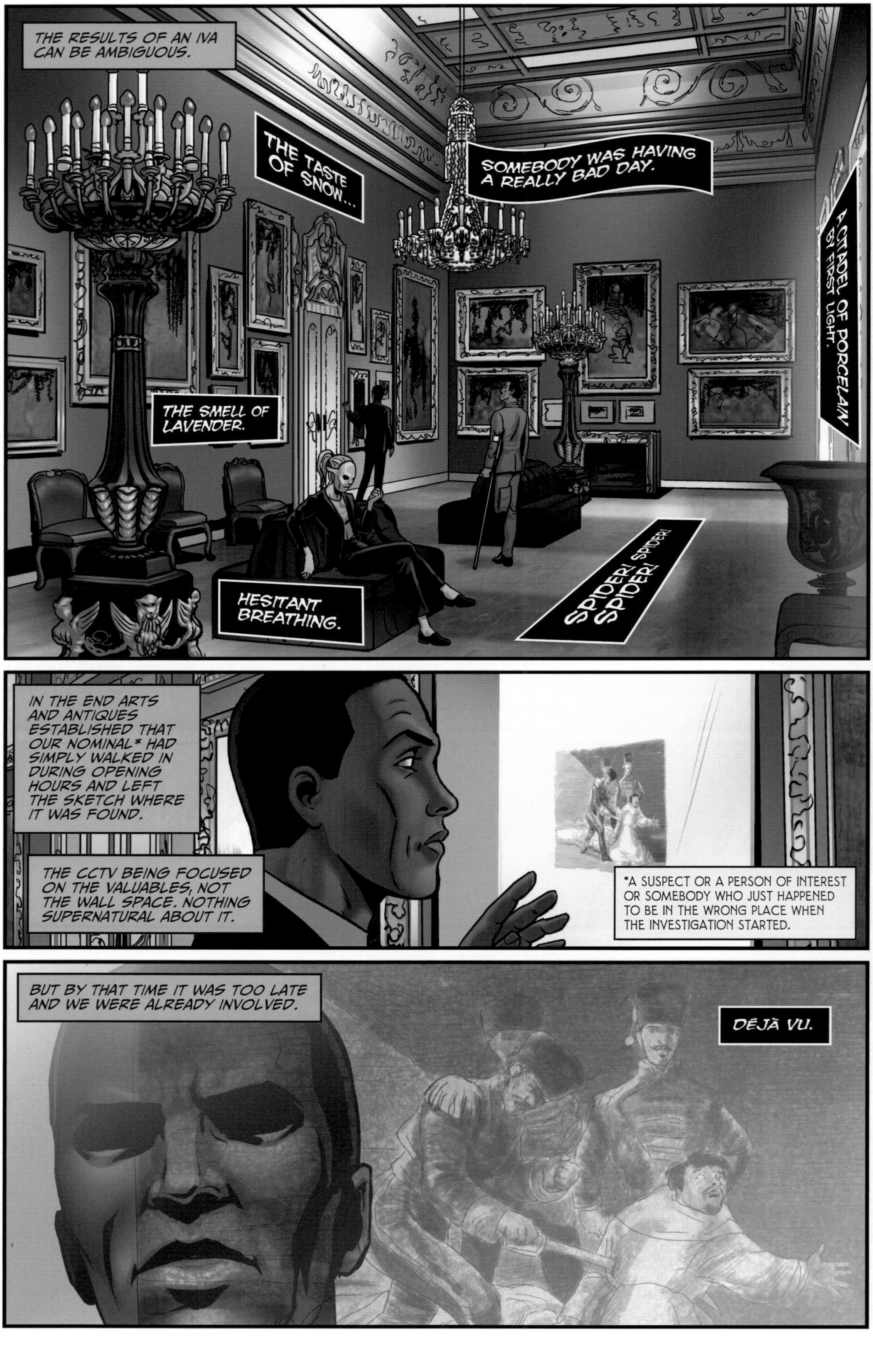
THE RESULTS OF AN IVA CAN BE AMBIGUOUS.
THE TASTE OF SNOW...
SOMEBODY WAS HAVING A REALLY BAD DAY.
A CITADEL OF PORCELAIN BY FIRST LIGHT.
THE SMELL OF LAVENDER.
HESITANT BREATHING.
SPIDER! SPIDER! SPIDER! SPIDER!
IN THE END ARTS AND ANTIQUES ESTABLISHED THAT OUR NOMINAL* HAD SIMPLY WALKED IN DURING OPENING HOURS AND LEFT THE SKETCH WHERE IT WAS FOUND.
THE CCTV BEING FOCUSED ON THE VALUABLES, NOT THE WALL SPACE. NOTHING SUPERNATURAL ABOUT IT.
*A SUSPECT OR A PERSON OF INTEREST OR SOMEBODY WHO JUST HAPPENED TO BE IN THE WRONG PLACE WHEN THE INVESTIGATION STARTED.
BUT BY THAT TIME IT WAS TOO LATE AND WE WERE ALREADY INVOLVED.
DÉJÀ VU.

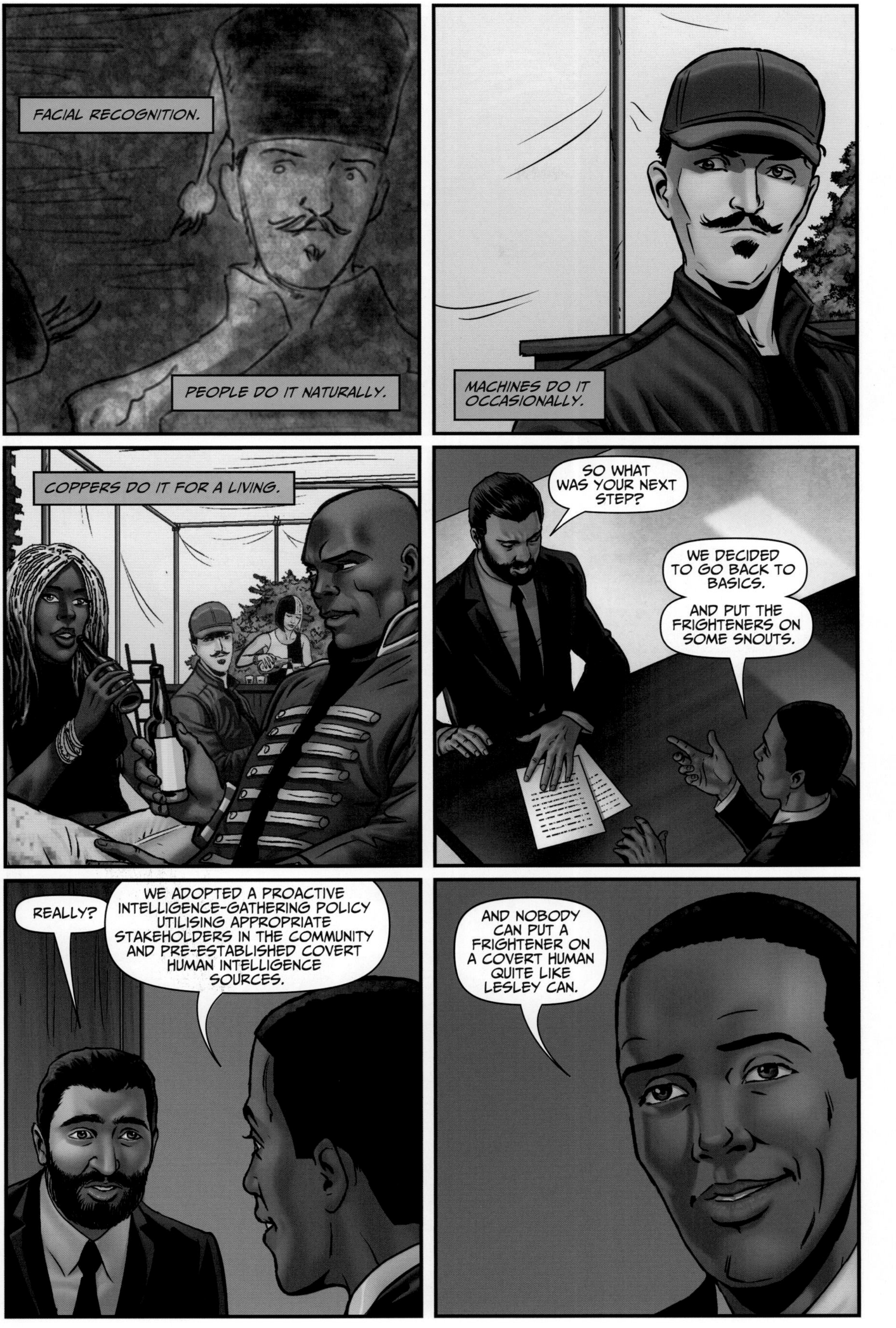
FACIAL RECOGNITION.
PEOPLE DO IT NATURALLY.
MACHINES DO IT OCCASIONALLY.
COPPERS DO IT FOR A LIVING.
SO WHAT WAS YOUR NEXT STEP?
WE DECIDED TO GO BACK TO BASICS.
AND PUT THE FRIGHTENERS ON SOME SNOUTS.
REALLY?
WE ADOPTED A PROACTIVE INTELLIGENCE-GATHERING POLICY UTILISING APPROPRIATE STAKEHOLDERS IN THE COMMUNITY AND PRE-ESTABLISHED COVERT HUMAN INTELLIGENCE SOURCES.
AND NOBODY CAN PUT A FRIGHTENER ON A COVERT HUMAN QUITE LIKE LESLEY CAN.

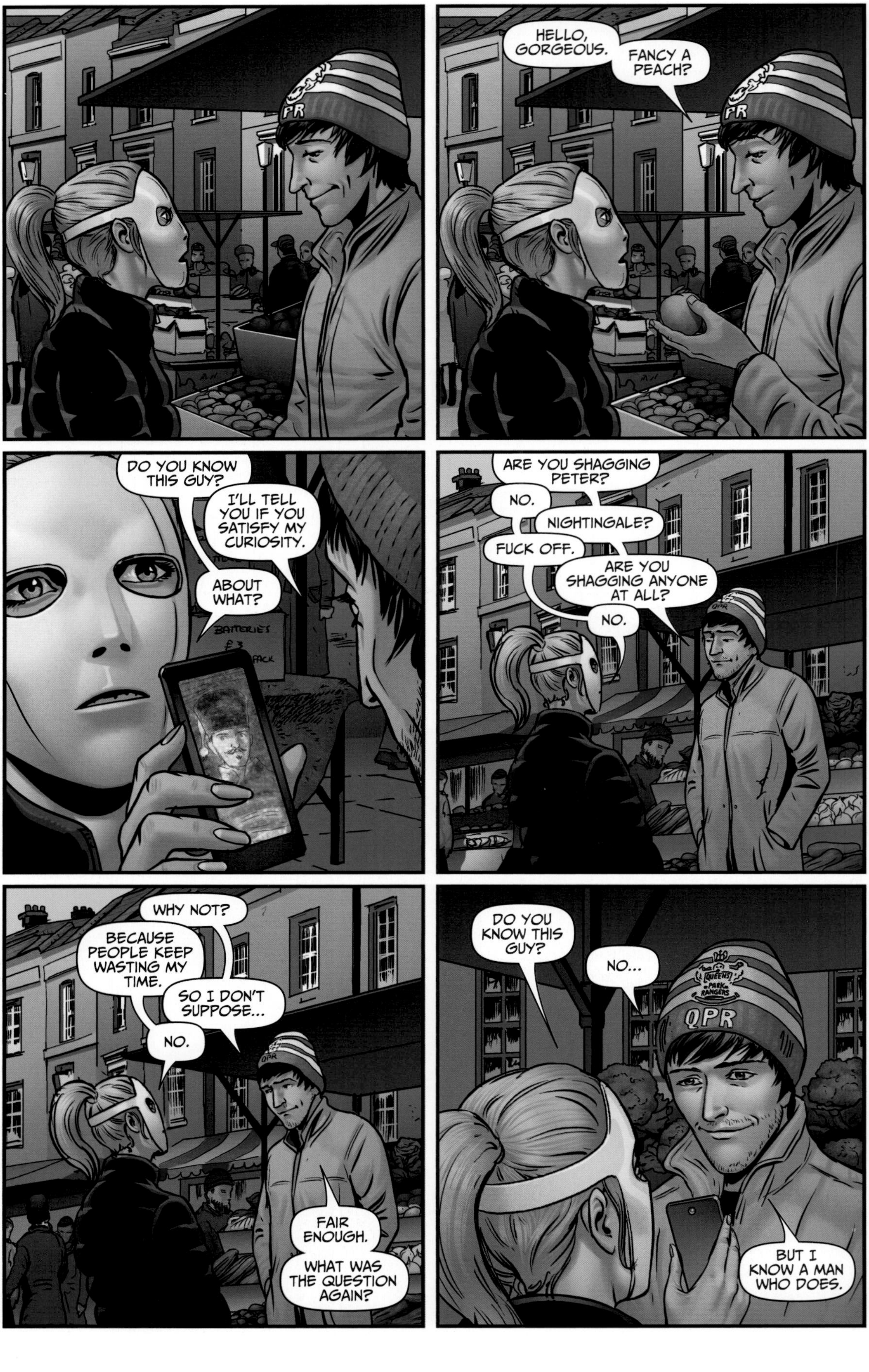
HELLO, GORGEOUS.
FANCY A PEACH?
DO YOU KNOW THIS GUY?
I'LL TELL YOU IF YOU SATISFY MY CURIOSITY.
ABOUT WHAT?
BATTERIES
£3
ARE YOU SHAGGING PETER?
NO.
NIGHTINGALE?
FUCK OFF.
ARE YOU SHAGGING ANYONE AT ALL?
NO.
WHY NOT?
BECAUSE PEOPLE KEEP WASTING MY TIME.
SO I DON'T SUPPOSE...
NO.
FAIR ENOUGH.
WHAT WAS THE QUESTION AGAIN?
DO YOU KNOW THIS GUY?
NO...
QUEENS PARK RANGERS
QPR
BUT I KNOW A MAN WHO DOES.

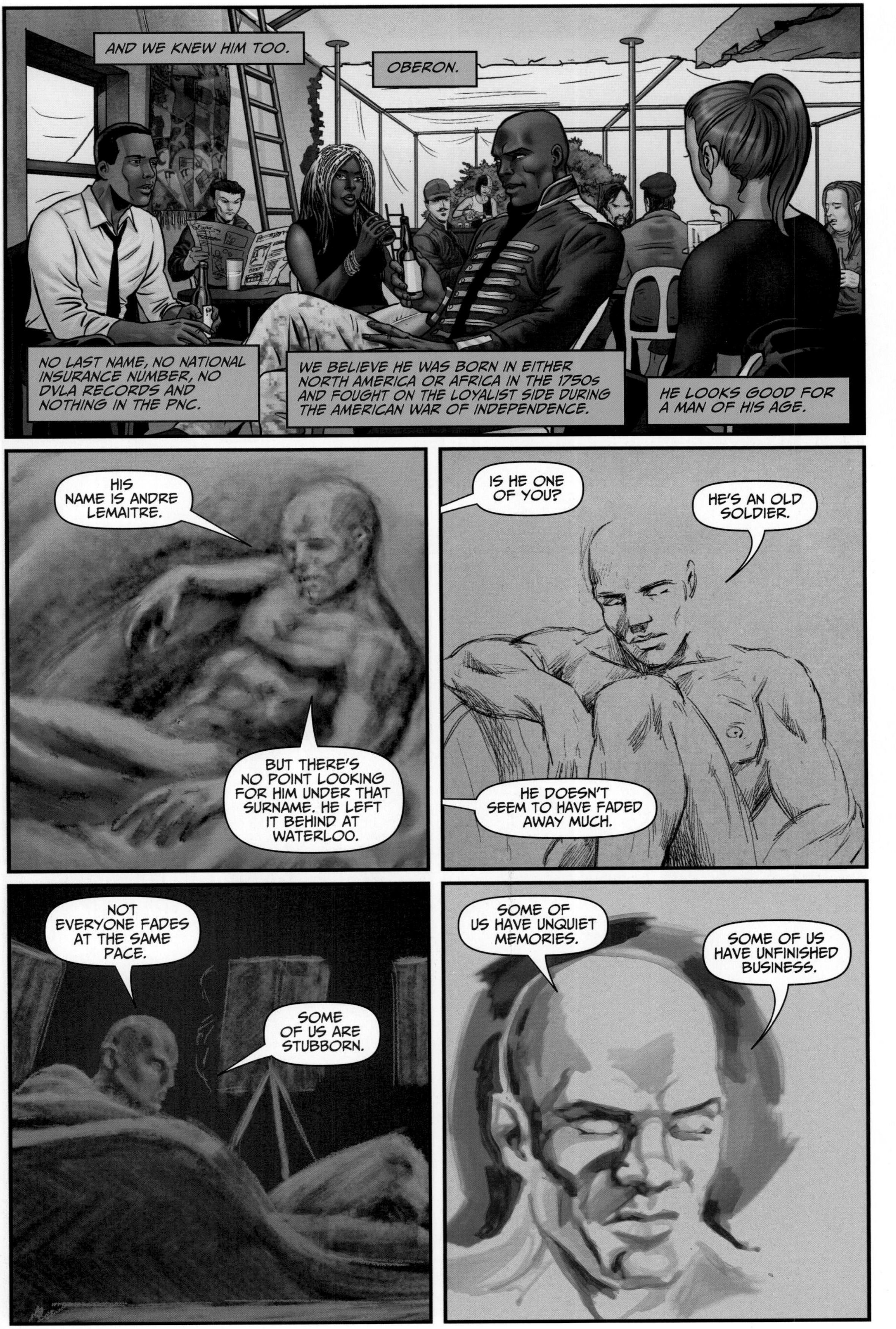
AND WE KNEW HIM TOO.
OBERON.
NO LAST NAME, NO NATIONAL INSURANCE NUMBER, NO DVLA RECORDS AND NOTHING IN THE PNC.
WE BELIEVE HE WAS BORN IN EITHER NORTH AMERICA OR AFRICA IN THE 1750s AND FOUGHT ON THE LOYALIST SIDE DURING THE AMERICAN WAR OF INDEPENDENCE.
HE LOOKS GOOD FOR A MAN OF HIS AGE.
HIS NAME IS ANDRE LEMAITRE.
BUT THERE'S NO POINT LOOKING FOR HIM UNDER THAT SURNAME. HE LEFT IT BEHIND AT WATERLOO.
IS HE ONE OF YOU?
HE'S AN OLD SOLDIER.
HE DOESN'T SEEM TO HAVE FADED AWAY MUCH.
NOT EVERYONE FADES AT THE SAME PACE.
SOME OF US ARE STUBBORN.
SOME OF US HAVE UNQUIET MEMORIES.
SOME OF US HAVE UNFINISHED BUSINESS.

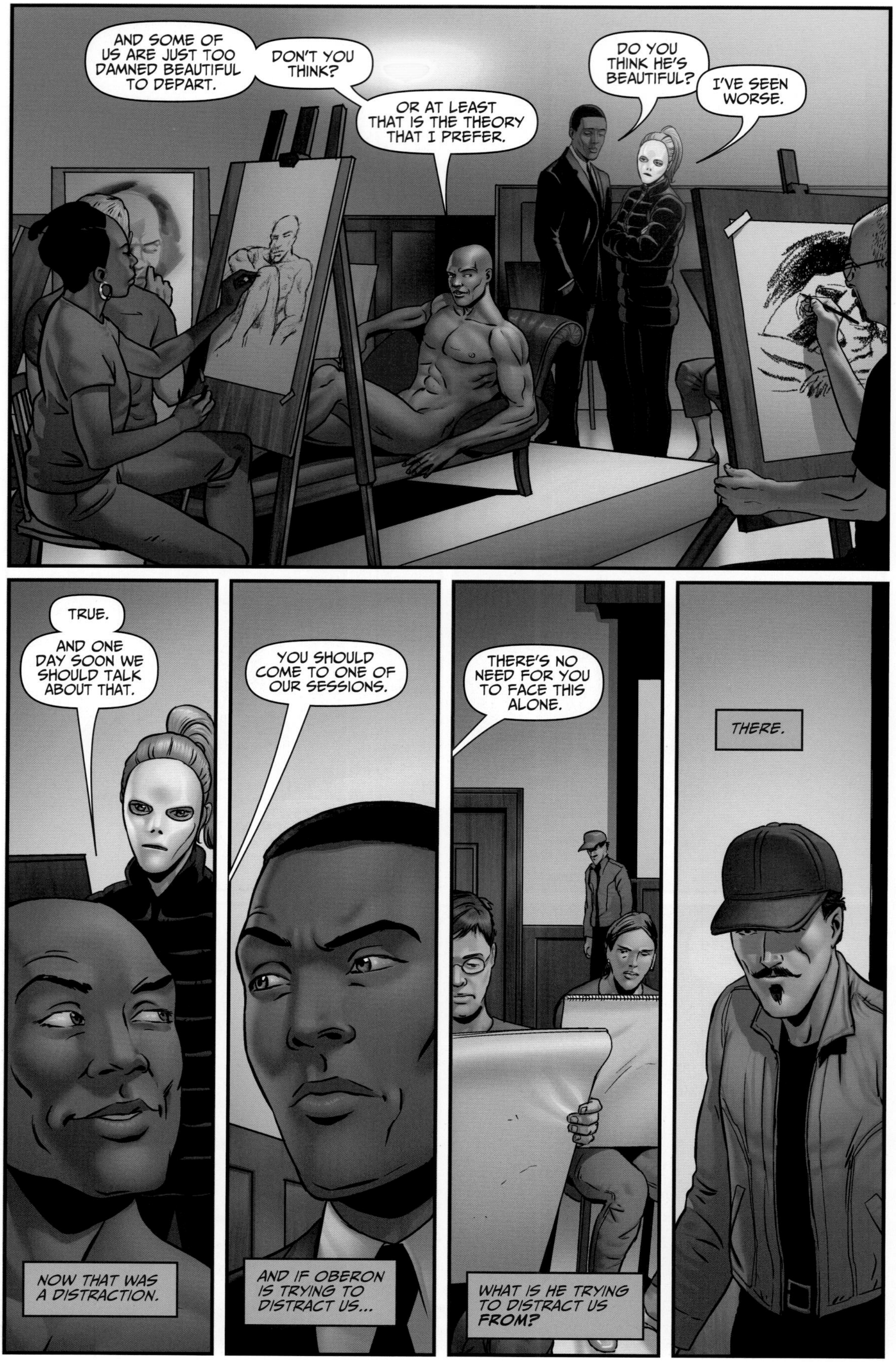

AND SOME OF US ARE JUST TOO DAMNED BEAUTIFUL TO DEPART.
DON'T YOU THINK?
OR AT LEAST THAT IS THE THEORY THAT I PREFER.
DO YOU THINK HE'S BEAUTIFUL?
I'VE SEEN WORSE.
TRUE.
AND ONE DAY SOON WE SHOULD TALK ABOUT THAT.
NOW THAT WAS A DISTRACTION.
YOU SHOULD COME TO ONE OF OUR SESSIONS.
AND IF OBERON IS TRYING TO DISTRACT US...
THERE'S NO NEED FOR YOU TO FACE THIS ALONE.
WHAT IS HE TRYING TO DISTRACT US FROM?
THERE.

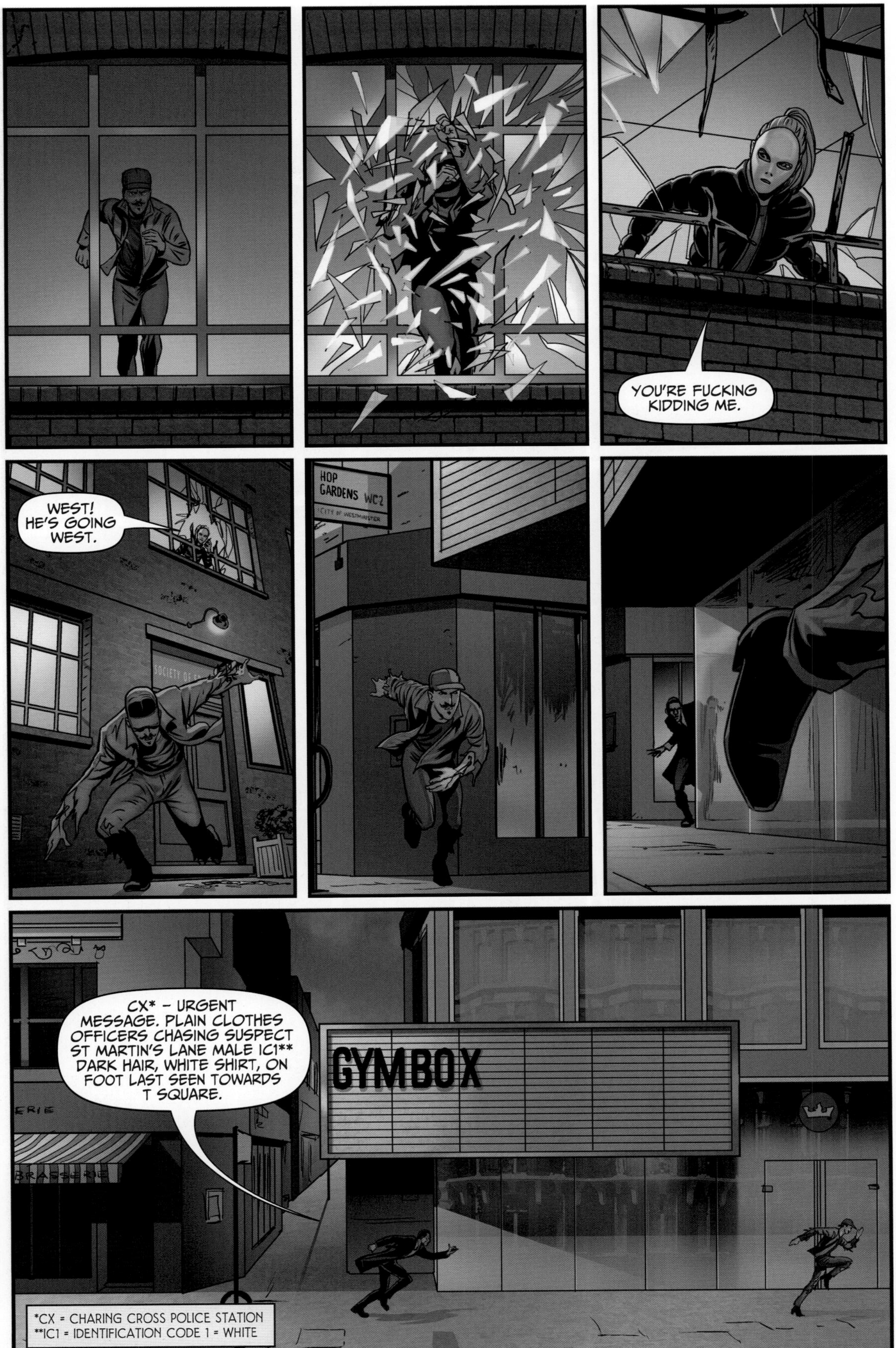
YOU'RE FUCKING KIDDING ME.
WEST! HE'S GOING WEST.
HOP GARDENS WC2
CITY OF WESTMINSTER
CX* – URGENT MESSAGE. PLAIN CLOTHES OFFICERS CHASING SUSPECT ST MARTIN'S LANE MALE IC1** DARK HAIR, WHITE SHIRT, ON FOOT LAST SEEN TOWARDS T SQUARE.
GYMBOX
BRASSERIE
*CX = CHARING CROSS POLICE STATION
**IC1 = IDENTIFICATION CODE 1 = WHITE

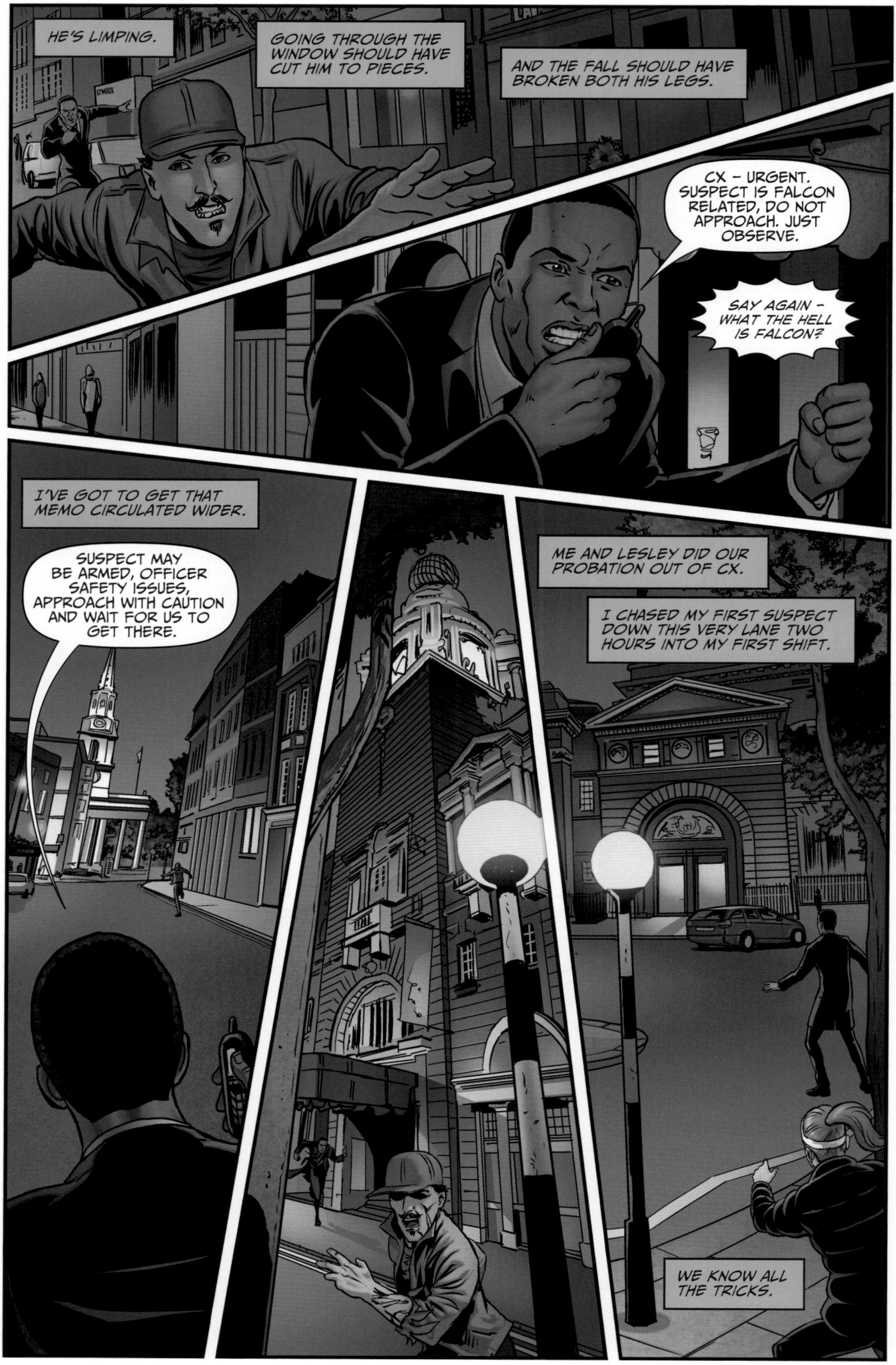
HE'S LIMPING.
GOING THROUGH THE WINDOW SHOULD HAVE CUT HIM TO PIECES.
AND THE FALL SHOULD HAVE BROKEN BOTH HIS LEGS.
CX – URGENT. SUSPECT IS FALCON RELATED, DO NOT APPROACH. JUST OBSERVE.
SAY AGAIN – WHAT THE HELL IS FALCON?
I'VE GOT TO GET THAT MEMO CIRCULATED WIDER.
SUSPECT MAY BE ARMED, OFFICER SAFETY ISSUES, APPROACH WITH CAUTION AND WAIT FOR US TO GET THERE.
ME AND LESLEY DID OUR PROBATION OUT OF CX.
I CHASED MY FIRST SUSPECT DOWN THIS VERY LANE TWO HOURS INTO MY FIRST SHIFT.
WE KNOW ALL THE TRICKS.

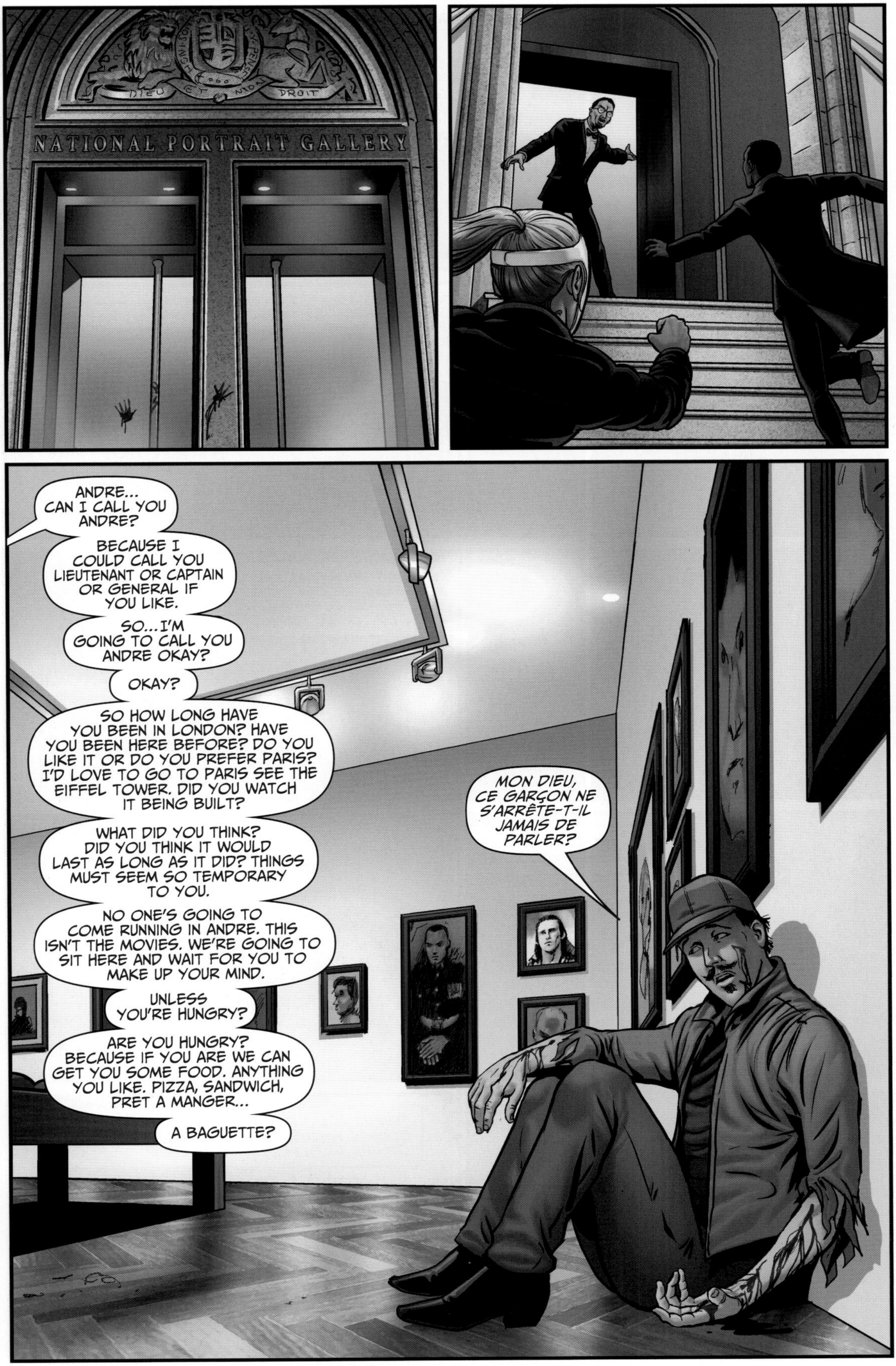
DIEU ET MON DROIT
NATIONAL PORTRAIT GALLERY
ANDRE... CAN I CALL YOU ANDRE?
BECAUSE I COULD CALL YOU LIEUTENANT OR CAPTAIN OR GENERAL IF YOU LIKE.
SO... I'M GOING TO CALL YOU ANDRE OKAY?
OKAY?
SO HOW LONG HAVE YOU BEEN IN LONDON? HAVE YOU BEEN HERE BEFORE? DO YOU LIKE IT OR DO YOU PREFER PARIS? I'D LOVE TO GO TO PARIS SEE THE EIFFEL TOWER. DID YOU WATCH IT BEING BUILT?
WHAT DID YOU THINK? DID YOU THINK IT WOULD LAST AS LONG AS IT DID? THINGS MUST SEEM SO TEMPORARY TO YOU.
NO ONE'S GOING TO COME RUNNING IN ANDRE. THIS ISN'T THE MOVIES. WE'RE GOING TO SIT HERE AND WAIT FOR YOU TO MAKE UP YOUR MIND.
UNLESS YOU'RE HUNGRY?
ARE YOU HUNGRY? BECAUSE IF YOU ARE WE CAN GET YOU SOME FOOD. ANYTHING YOU LIKE. PIZZA, SANDWICH, PRET A MANGER...
A BAGUETTE?
MON DIEU, CE GARÇON NE S'ARRÊTE-T-IL JAMAIS DE PARLER?

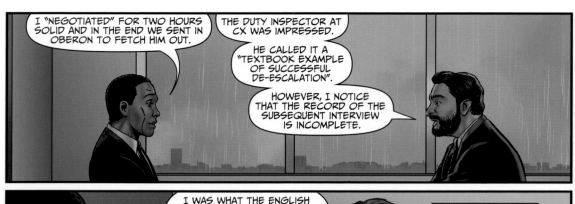

I "NEGOTIATED" FOR TWO HOURS SOLID AND IN THE END WE SENT IN OBERON TO FETCH HIM OUT.

THE DUTY INSPECTOR AT CX WAS IMPRESSED.

HE CALLED IT A "TEXTBOOK EXAMPLE OF SUCCESSFUL DE-ESCALATION".

HOWEVER, I NOTICE THAT THE RECORD OF THE SUBSEQUENT INTERVIEW IS INCOMPLETE.

I WAS WHAT THE ENGLISH CALLED A "GALLOPER" ON THE STAFF OF GENERAL SUCHET. I CAME TO KNOW FRANCISCO WHILE I WAS BILLETED IN MADRID.

THAT IS TO SAY, FRANCISCO JOSÉ DE GOYA.

WE DID WHAT ALL MEN DID IN THOSE DAYS.

"WE GOT DRUNK AND WE TALKED A LOT OF NONSENSE ABOUT POLITICS AND WOMEN AND HORSES AND DOGS AND ANYTHING ELSE THAT FLOATED TO THE TOPS OF OUR HEADS.

"HE TRUSTED ME ENOUGH TO LEAVE HIS WORK OUT.

"ON MY OATH AS A SOLDIER I NEVER DID KILL A WOMAN OR A CHILD. OR ANY MAN NOT IN UNIFORM OR ARMED AGAINST ME.

"THERE ARE MEN THAT ARE LITTLE MORE THAN BEASTS WHO THINK NOTHING OF SLAUGHTER OR THE DEFILING OF INNOCENCE.

"WHY SHOULD MY HONOUR SUFFER WHEN THOSE ANIMALS WERE REMEMBERED FONDLY?"

THIS IS A SPEECH WE'VE ALL HEARD BEFORE.

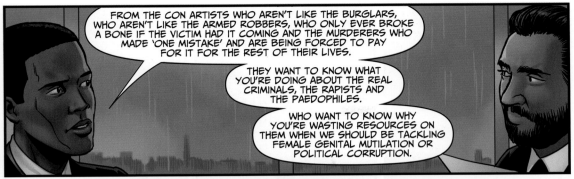

FROM THE CON ARTISTS WHO AREN'T LIKE THE BURGLARS, WHO AREN'T LIKE THE ARMED ROBBERS, WHO ONLY EVER BROKE A BONE IF THE VICTIM HAD IT COMING AND THE MURDERERS WHO MADE 'ONE MISTAKE' AND ARE BEING FORCED TO PAY FOR IT FOR THE REST OF THEIR LIVES.

THEY WANT TO KNOW WHAT YOU'RE DOING ABOUT THE REAL CRIMINALS, THE RAPISTS AND THE PAEDOPHILES.

WHO WANT TO KNOW WHY YOU'RE WASTING RESOURCES ON THEM WHEN WE SHOULD BE TACKLING FEMALE GENITAL MUTILATION OR POLITICAL CORRUPTION.

THERE'S ALWAYS A SAD STORY.

AND SOMEBODY ELSE TO BLAME.

THEY STARE.

LET THEM STARE.

THEY WHISPER.

LET THEM WHISPER.

THEY PITY.

THERE'S NONE MORE PITEOUS THAN A SLAVE.

AND I HAVE BEEN A SLAVE.

"AND TOOK MY FREEDOM AT THE POINT OF A KNIFE.

"BUT BEFORE I COULD PICK UP THAT KNIFE."

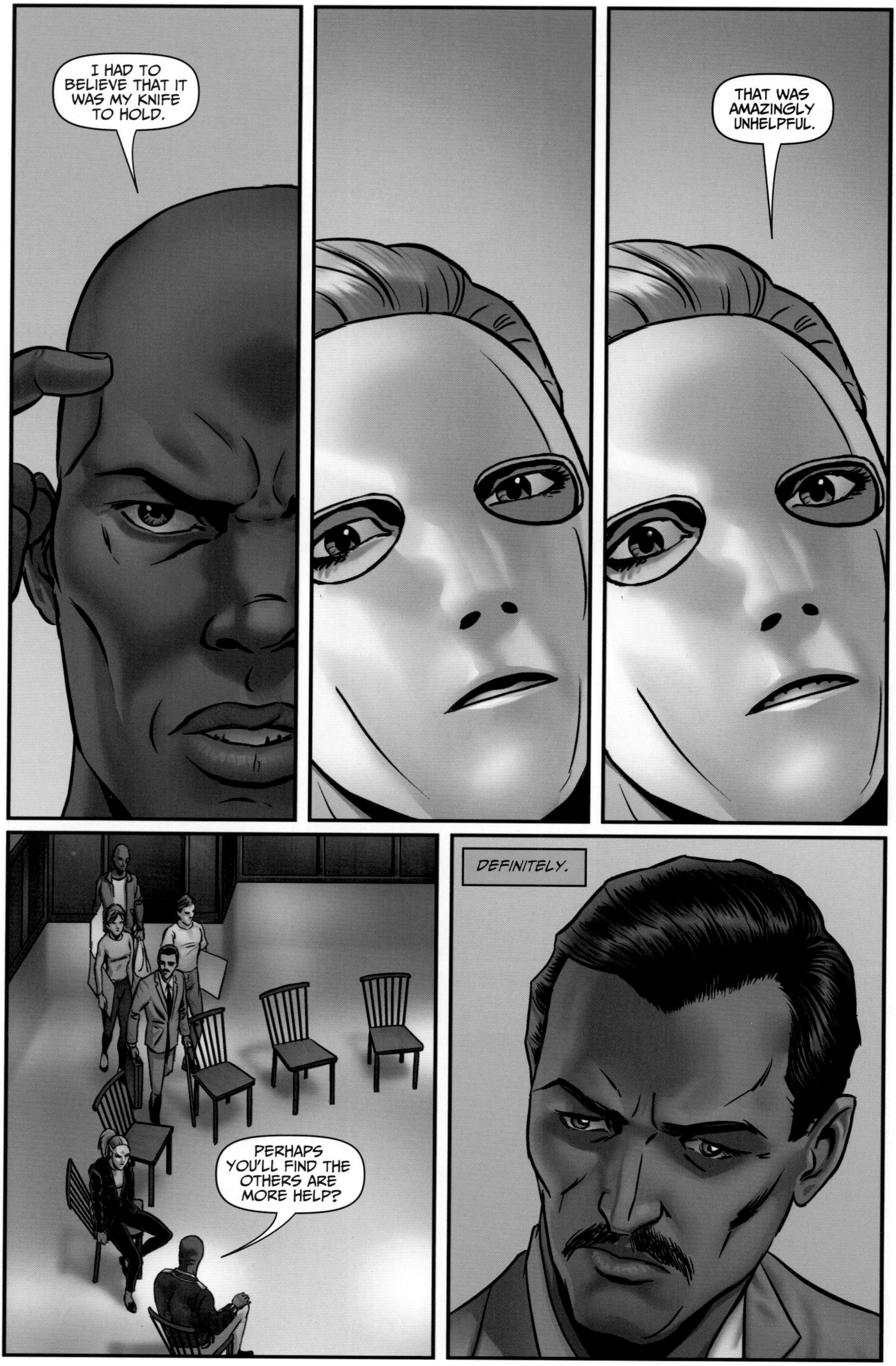
I HAD TO BELIEVE THAT IT WAS MY KNIFE TO HOLD.
THAT WAS AMAZINGLY UNHELPFUL.
PERHAPS YOU'LL FIND THE OTHERS ARE MORE HELP?
DEFINITELY.

THERE'S ALWAYS AN INSIDE MAN, ISN'T THERE?

SO ARTS AND ANTIQUES HAD ALREADY DONE A FULL IIP* CHECK ON THE RELEVANT STAFF BEFORE WE WERE EVEN CALLED IN.

INCLUDING ASIF SIDDIQI WHO, INCIDENTALLY, TURNED OUT TO BE A FORMER CAPTAIN IN THE INDIAN ARMY.

STEPPED ON AN OLD LANDMINE ON THE CHINESE BORDER.

*IIP = INTEGRATED INTELLIGENCE PLATFORM

YOU SHOULD COME TO ONE OF OUR SESSIONS.

SO WHEN WE HEARD ABOUT THE SUPPORT GROUP...

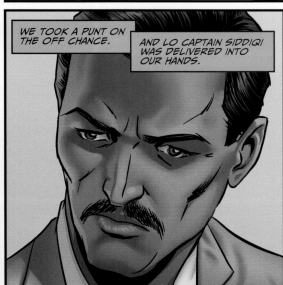

WE TOOK A PUNT ON THE OFF CHANCE.

AND LO CAPTAIN SIDDIQI WAS DELIVERED INTO OUR HANDS.

HE DIDN'T TRY AND DENY IT.

ANDRE SAID HE WANTED THE DUKE TO HAVE IT.

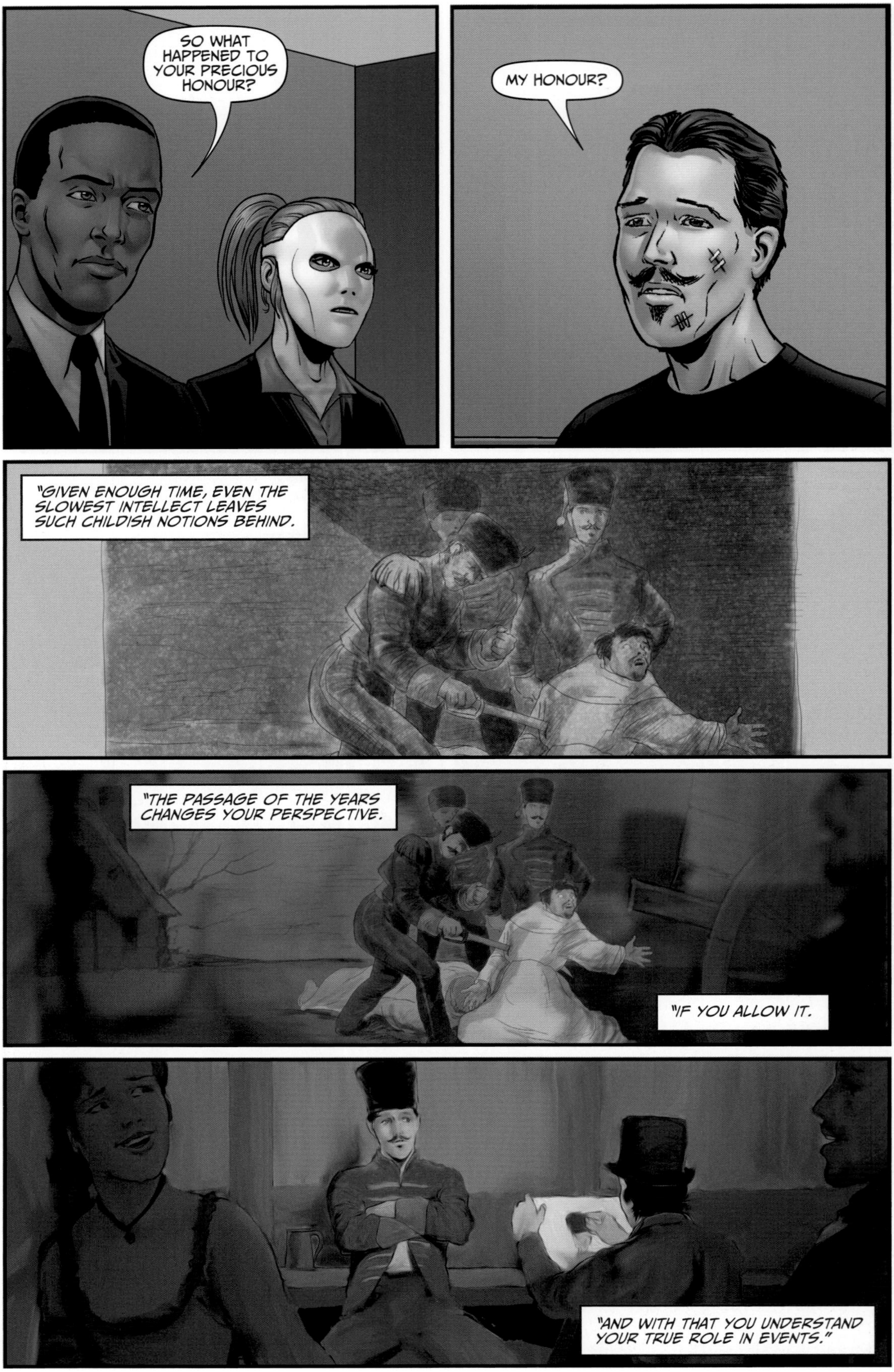
SO WHAT HAPPENED TO YOUR PRECIOUS HONOUR?
MY HONOUR?
"GIVEN ENOUGH TIME, EVEN THE SLOWEST INTELLECT LEAVES SUCH CHILDISH NOTIONS BEHIND.
"THE PASSAGE OF THE YEARS CHANGES YOUR PERSPECTIVE.
"IF YOU ALLOW IT.
"AND WITH THAT YOU UNDERSTAND YOUR TRUE ROLE IN EVENTS."

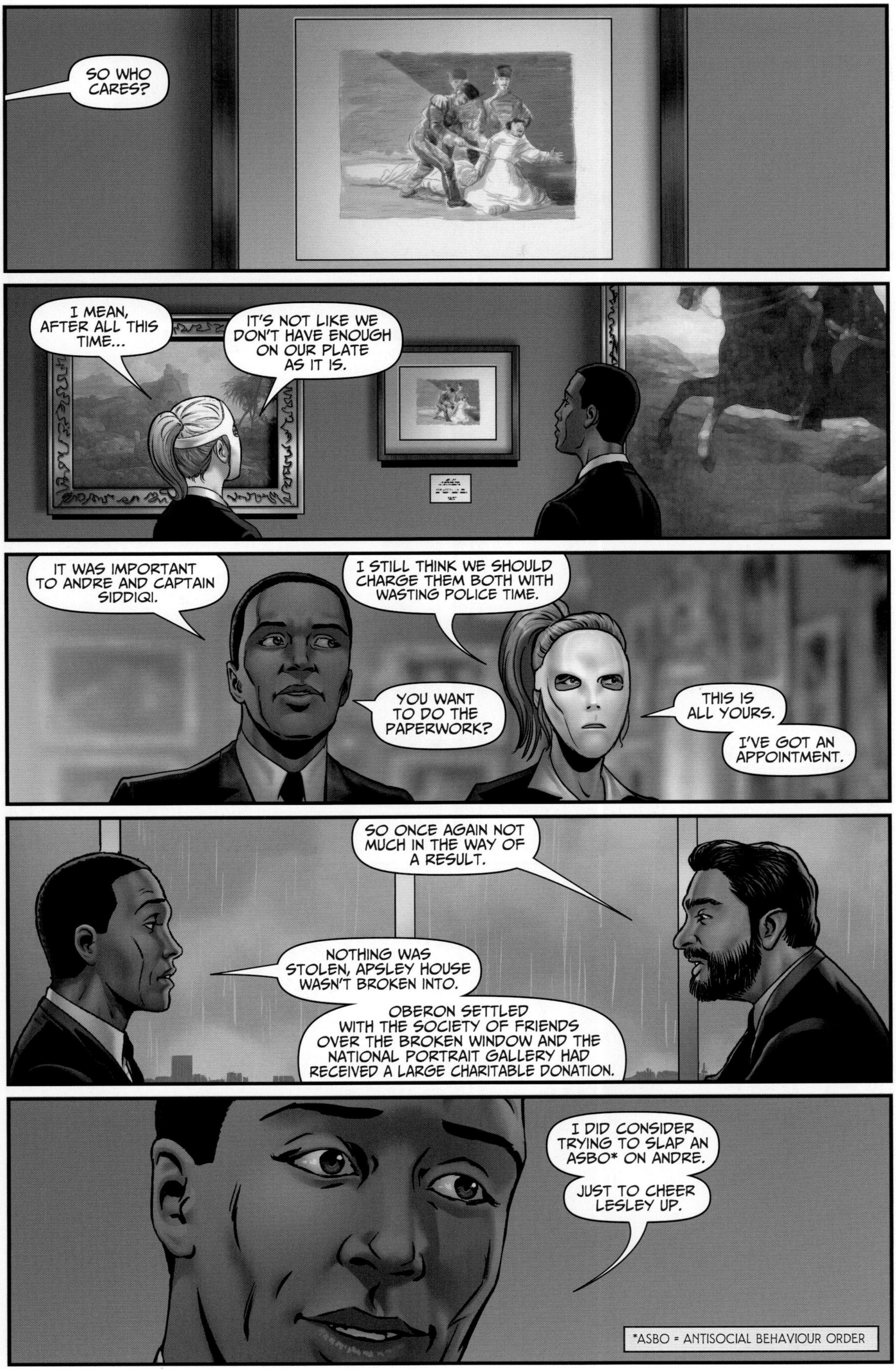

SO WHO CARES?
I MEAN, AFTER ALL THIS TIME...
IT'S NOT LIKE WE DON'T HAVE ENOUGH ON OUR PLATE AS IT IS.
IT WAS IMPORTANT TO ANDRE AND CAPTAIN SIDDIQI.
I STILL THINK WE SHOULD CHARGE THEM BOTH WITH WASTING POLICE TIME.
YOU WANT TO DO THE PAPERWORK?
THIS IS ALL YOURS.
I'VE GOT AN APPOINTMENT.
SO ONCE AGAIN NOT MUCH IN THE WAY OF A RESULT.
NOTHING WAS STOLEN, APSLEY HOUSE WASN'T BROKEN INTO.
OBERON SETTLED WITH THE SOCIETY OF FRIENDS OVER THE BROKEN WINDOW AND THE NATIONAL PORTRAIT GALLERY HAD RECEIVED A LARGE CHARITABLE DONATION.
I DID CONSIDER TRYING TO SLAP AN ASBO* ON ANDRE.
JUST TO CHEER LESLEY UP.
*ASBO = ANTISOCIAL BEHAVIOUR ORDER

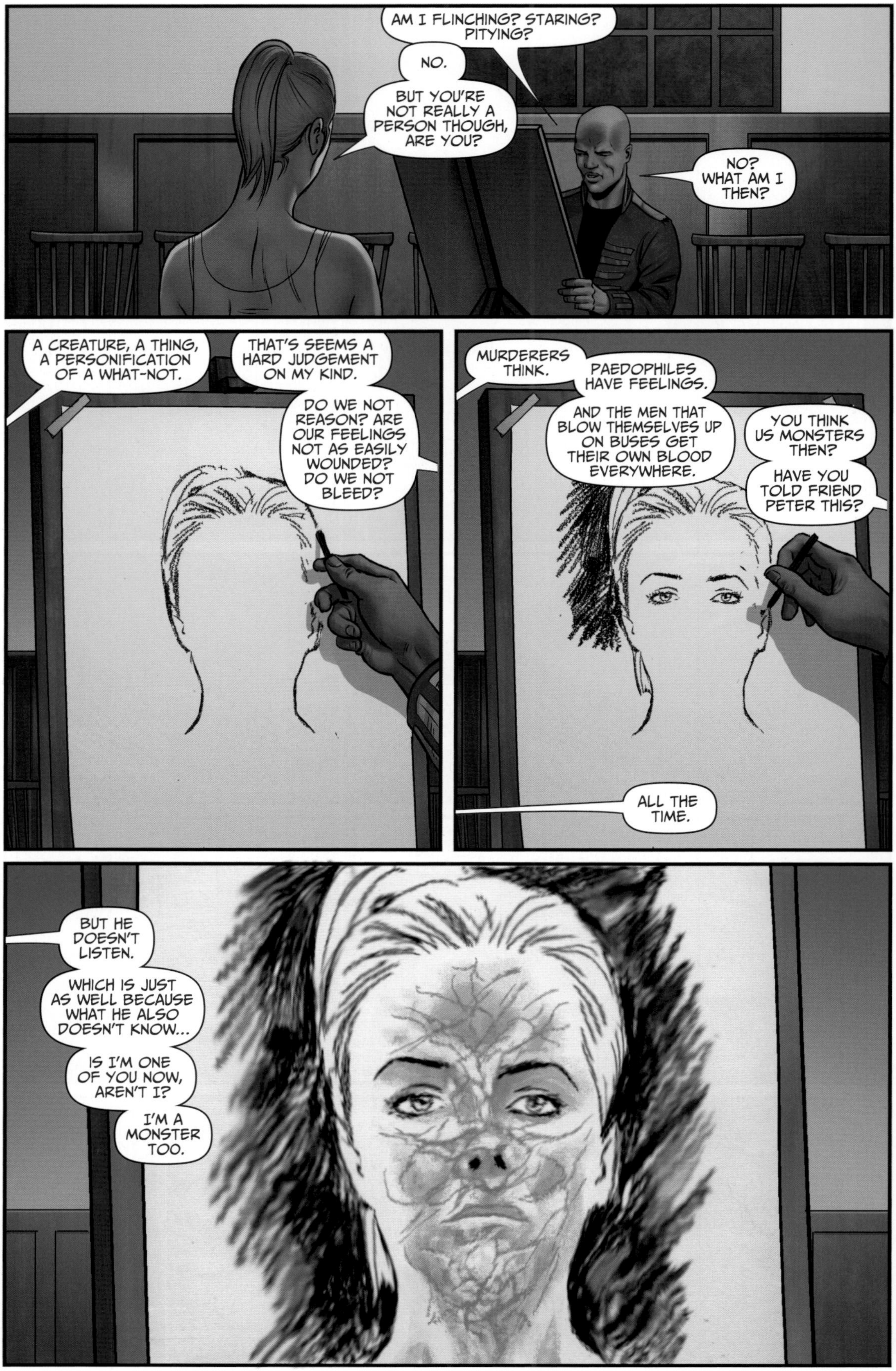
AM I FLINCHING? STARING? PITYING?
NO.
BUT YOU'RE NOT REALLY A PERSON THOUGH, ARE YOU?
NO? WHAT AM I THEN?
A CREATURE, A THING, A PERSONIFICATION OF A WHAT-NOT.
THAT'S SEEMS A HARD JUDGEMENT ON MY KIND.
DO WE NOT REASON? ARE OUR FEELINGS NOT AS EASILY WOUNDED? DO WE NOT BLEED?
MURDERERS THINK.
PAEDOPHILES HAVE FEELINGS.
AND THE MEN THAT BLOW THEMSELVES UP ON BUSES GET THEIR OWN BLOOD EVERYWHERE.
YOU THINK US MONSTERS THEN?
HAVE YOU TOLD FRIEND PETER THIS?
ALL THE TIME.
BUT HE DOESN'T LISTEN.
WHICH IS JUST AS WELL BECAUSE WHAT HE ALSO DOESN'T KNOW...
IS I'M ONE OF YOU NOW, AREN'T I?
I'M A MONSTER TOO.

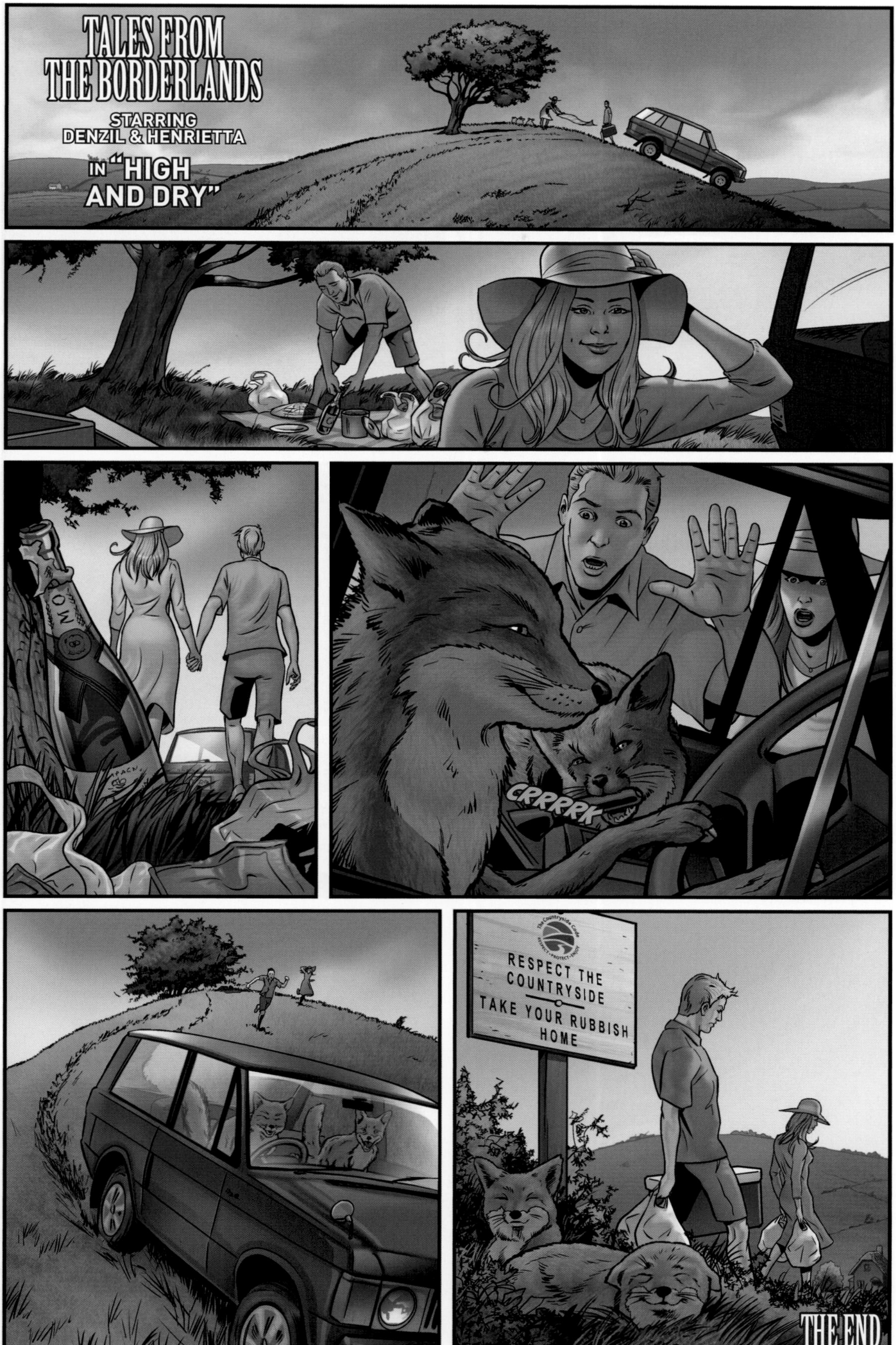
TALES FROM THE BORDERLANDS
STARRING DENZIL & HENRIETTA
IN "HIGH AND DRY"
CRRRRK
RESPECT THE COUNTRYSIDE
TAKE YOUR RUBBISH HOME
THE END

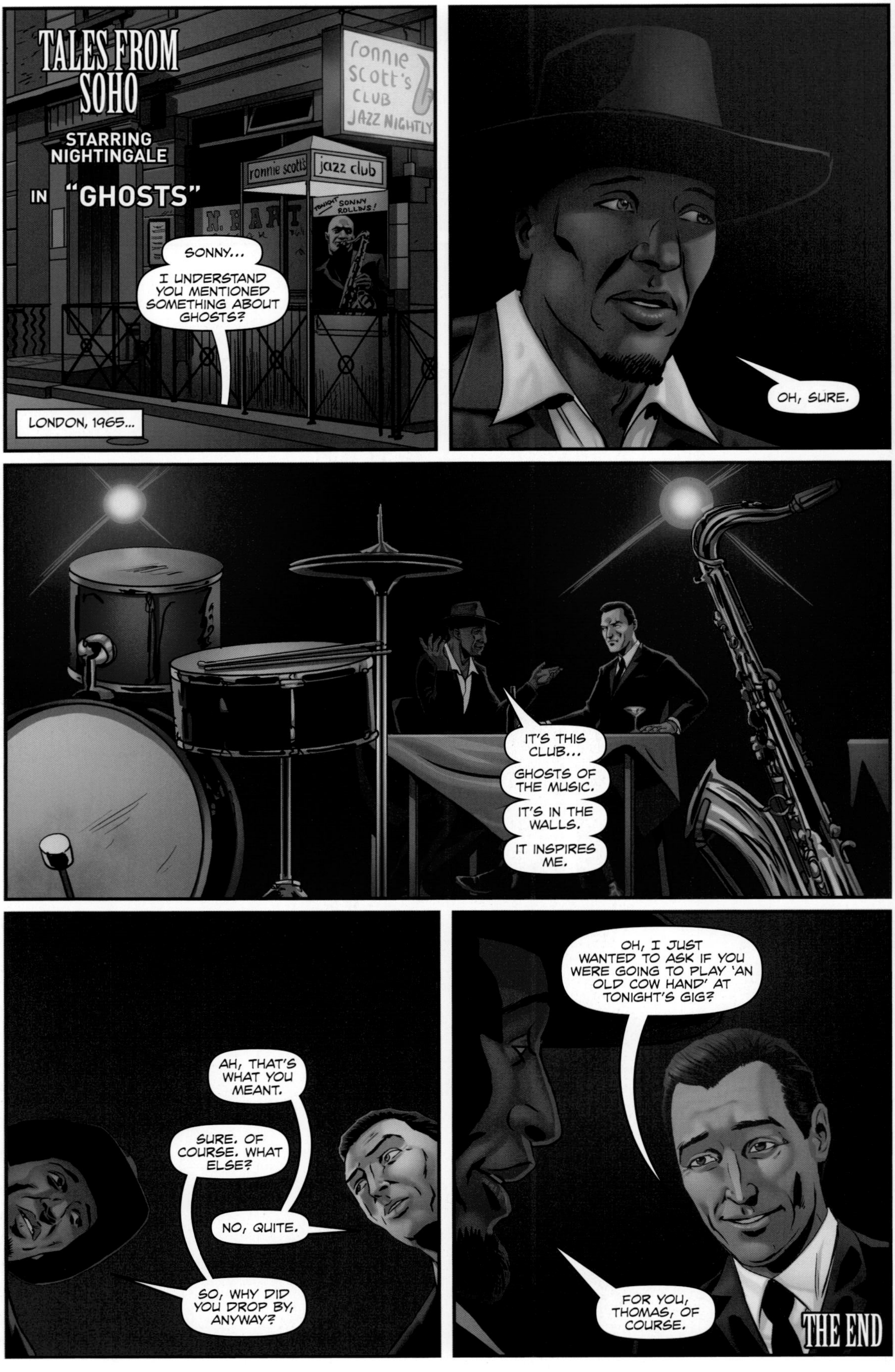
TALES FROM SOHO
STARRING NIGHTINGALE
IN "GHOSTS"
ronnie scott's CLUB JAZZ NIGHTLY
ronnie scott's
jazz club
TONIGHT SONNY ROLLINS!
SONNY...
I UNDERSTAND YOU MENTIONED SOMETHING ABOUT GHOSTS?
LONDON, 1965...
OH, SURE.
IT'S THIS CLUB...
GHOSTS OF THE MUSIC.
IT'S IN THE WALLS.
IT INSPIRES ME.
AH, THAT'S WHAT YOU MEANT.
SURE. OF COURSE. WHAT ELSE?
NO, QUITE.
SO, WHY DID YOU DROP BY, ANYWAY?
OH, I JUST WANTED TO ASK IF YOU WERE GOING TO PLAY 'AN OLD COW HAND' AT TONIGHT'S GIG?
FOR YOU, THOMAS, OF COURSE.
THE END

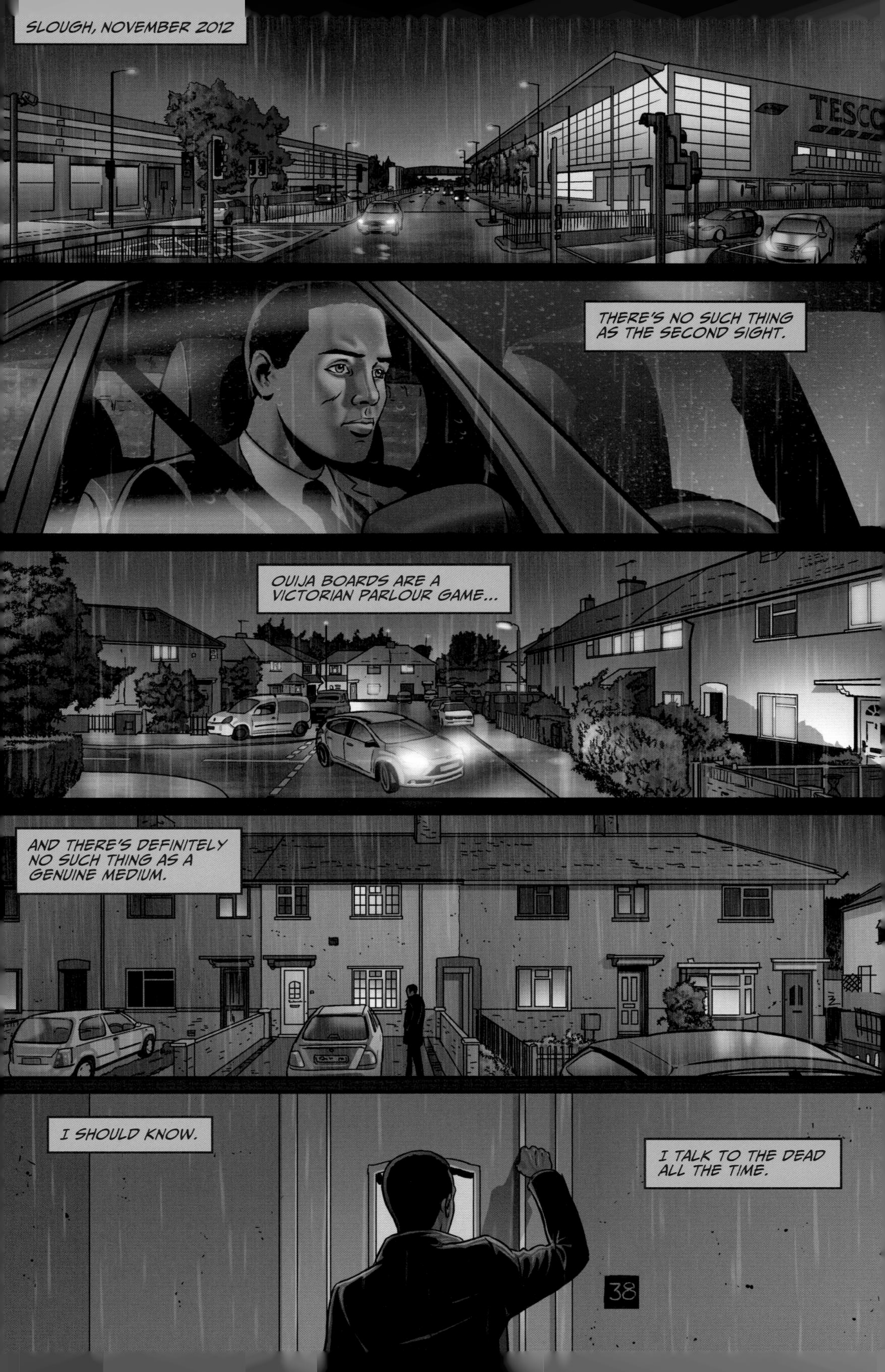
SLOUGH, NOVEMBER 2012
TESCO
THERE'S NO SUCH THING AS THE SECOND SIGHT.
OUIJA BOARDS ARE A VICTORIAN PARLOUR GAME...
AND THERE'S DEFINITELY NO SUCH THING AS A GENUINE MEDIUM.
I SHOULD KNOW.
I TALK TO THE DEAD ALL THE TIME.
38

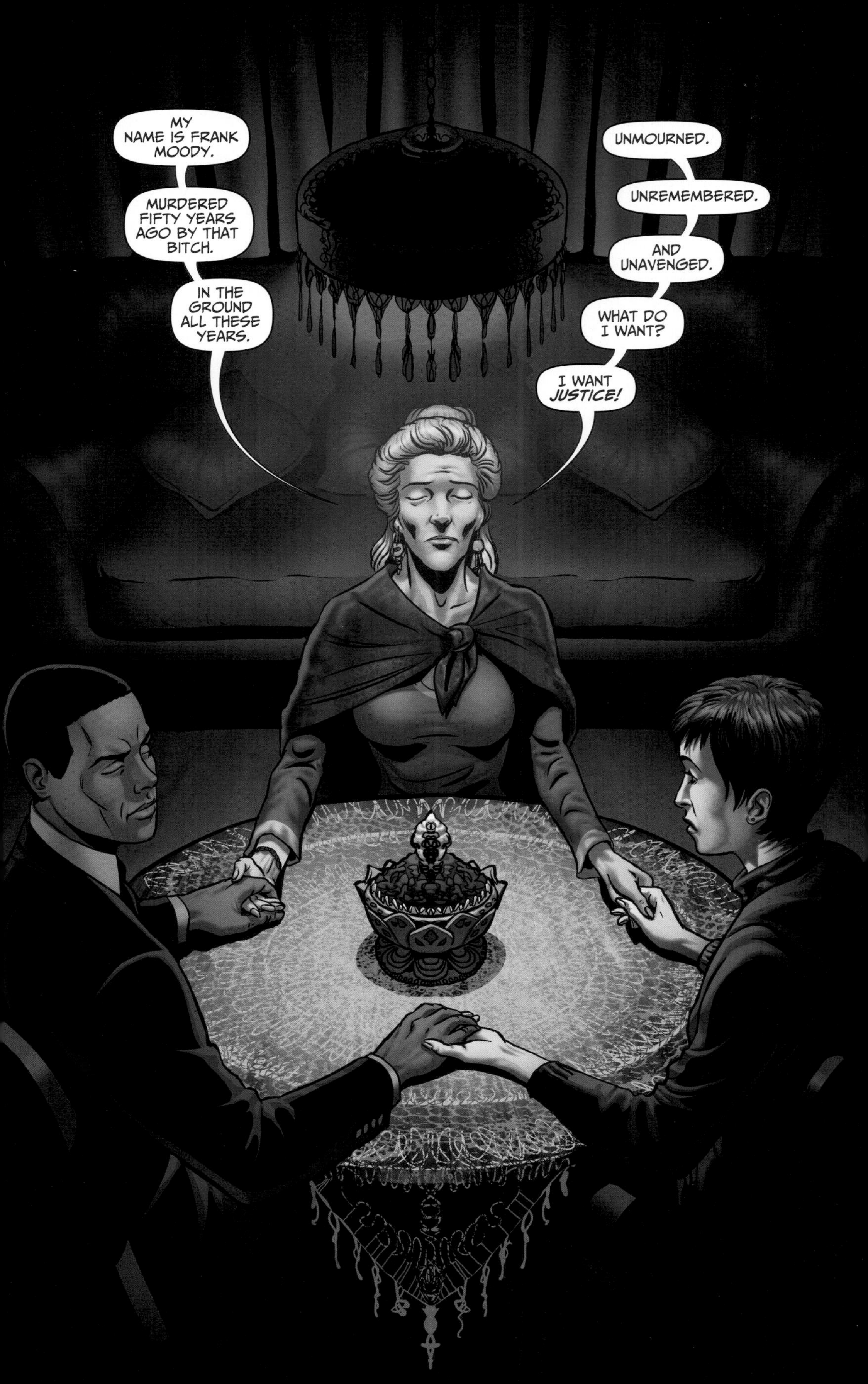
MY NAME IS FRANK MOODY.
MURDERED FIFTY YEARS AGO BY THAT BITCH.
IN THE GROUND ALL THESE YEARS.
UNMOURNED.
UNREMEMBERED.
AND UNAVENGED.
WHAT DO I WANT?
I WANT *JUSTICE!*

TO BE HONEST I'VE DECIDED TO TAKE YOUR WORD FOR THIS STUFF.

THANK YOU, SIR.

BUT NOT FOR THE POLICE WORK.

UNDERSTOOD.

SLOUGH IS THAMES VALLEY. HOW DID THIS PARTICULAR CASE COME TO YOUR ATTENTION?

THIS IS BEFORE THE NEW ACPO* GUIDELINES WERE ISSUED IN 2013 SO CHANNELS OF COMMUNICATION WERE A BIT AD HOC.

BASICALLY, THIS WOMAN WALKED INTO SLOUGH POLICE STATION AND SAID SHE WANTED TO REPORT A MURDER.

* ASSOCIATION OF CHIEF POLICE OFFICERS**

** NOW THE NATIONAL POLICE CHIEFS' COUNCIL***

*** DON'T ASK ME WHY – I JUST WORK HERE.

WILHELMINA TRIMBLE, AGED 46.

FORMER NURSE, FORMER DINNER LADY, NOW PART-TIME SPIRITUALIST.

QUITE A SUCCESSFUL ONE AS IT HAPPENS.

IF YOU COUNT UP ALL THE MONEY THAT PASSES UNDER HER TABLE.

SAYS THAT A GHOST PASSED ON INFORMATION ABOUT A MURDER THAT HAPPENED IN 1966.

SHE MUST HAVE BEEN CONVINCING, BECAUSE THE INTERVIEWING OFFICER LOOKS THE CASE UP IN HER OWN TIME...

RECOVERED FROM CANAL.

FINDS THAT THE CASE NOTES NOT ONLY CORROBORATE THE ALLEGED GHOST'S STORY...

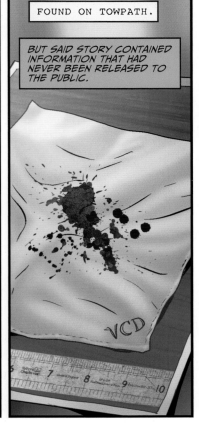

FOUND ON TOWPATH.

BUT SAID STORY CONTAINED INFORMATION THAT HAD NEVER BEEN RELEASED TO THE PUBLIC.

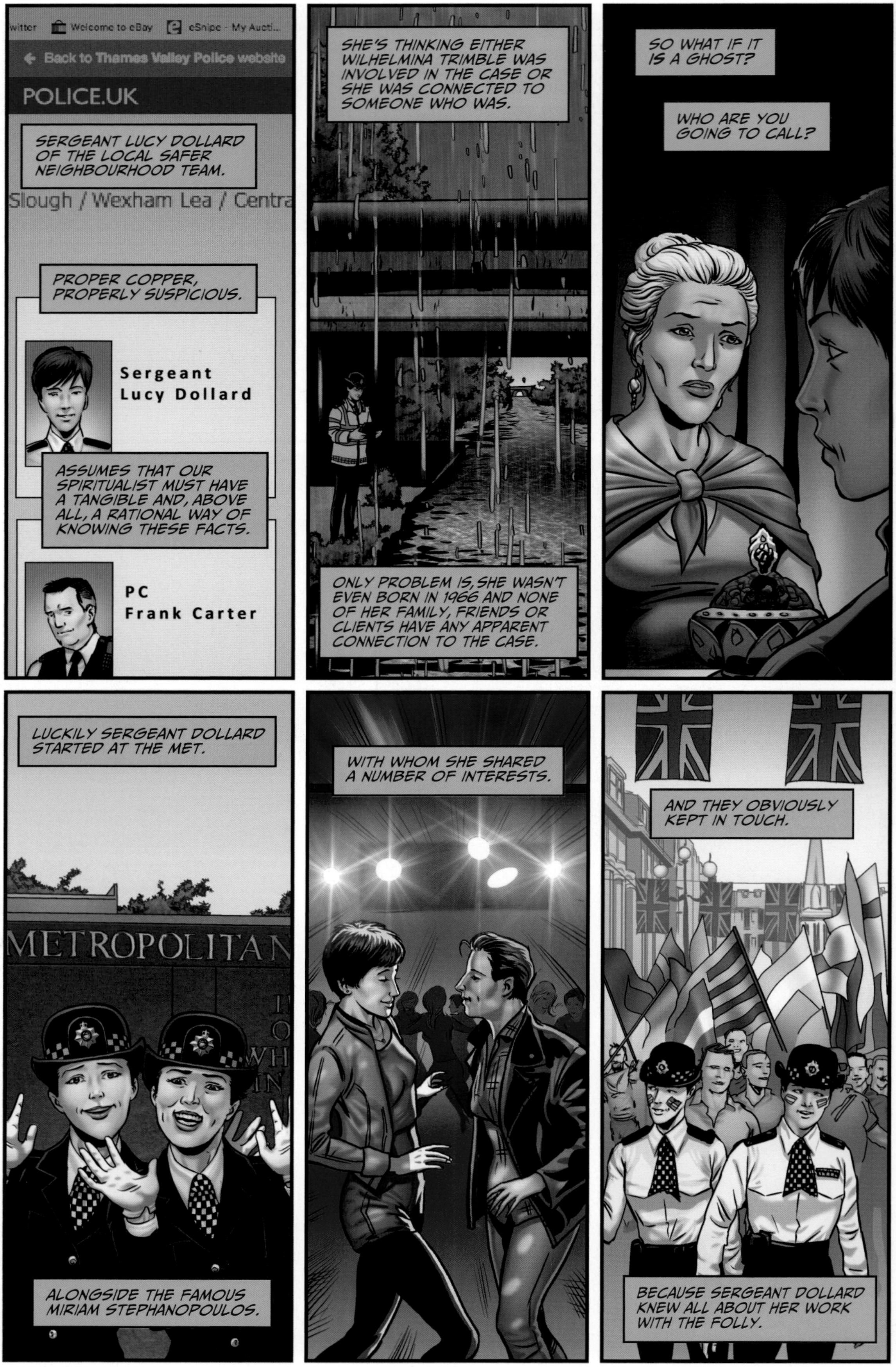
witter
Welcome to eBay
eSnipe - My Aucti...
Back to Thames Valley Police website
POLICE.UK
SERGEANT LUCY DOLLARD OF THE LOCAL SAFER NEIGHBOURHOOD TEAM.
Slough / Wexham Lea / Centra
PROPER COPPER, PROPERLY SUSPICIOUS.
Sergeant Lucy Dollard
ASSUMES THAT OUR SPIRITUALIST MUST HAVE A TANGIBLE AND, ABOVE ALL, A RATIONAL WAY OF KNOWING THESE FACTS.
PC Frank Carter
SHE'S THINKING EITHER WILHELMINA TRIMBLE WAS INVOLVED IN THE CASE OR SHE WAS CONNECTED TO SOMEONE WHO WAS.
ONLY PROBLEM IS, SHE WASN'T EVEN BORN IN 1966 AND NONE OF HER FAMILY, FRIENDS OR CLIENTS HAVE ANY APPARENT CONNECTION TO THE CASE.
SO WHAT IF IT IS A GHOST?
WHO ARE YOU GOING TO CALL?
LUCKILY SERGEANT DOLLARD STARTED AT THE MET.
METROPOLITAN
ALONGSIDE THE FAMOUS MIRIAM STEPHANOPOULOS.
WITH WHOM SHE SHARED A NUMBER OF INTERESTS.
AND THEY OBVIOUSLY KEPT IN TOUCH.
BECAUSE SERGEANT DOLLARD KNEW ALL ABOUT HER WORK WITH THE FOLLY.

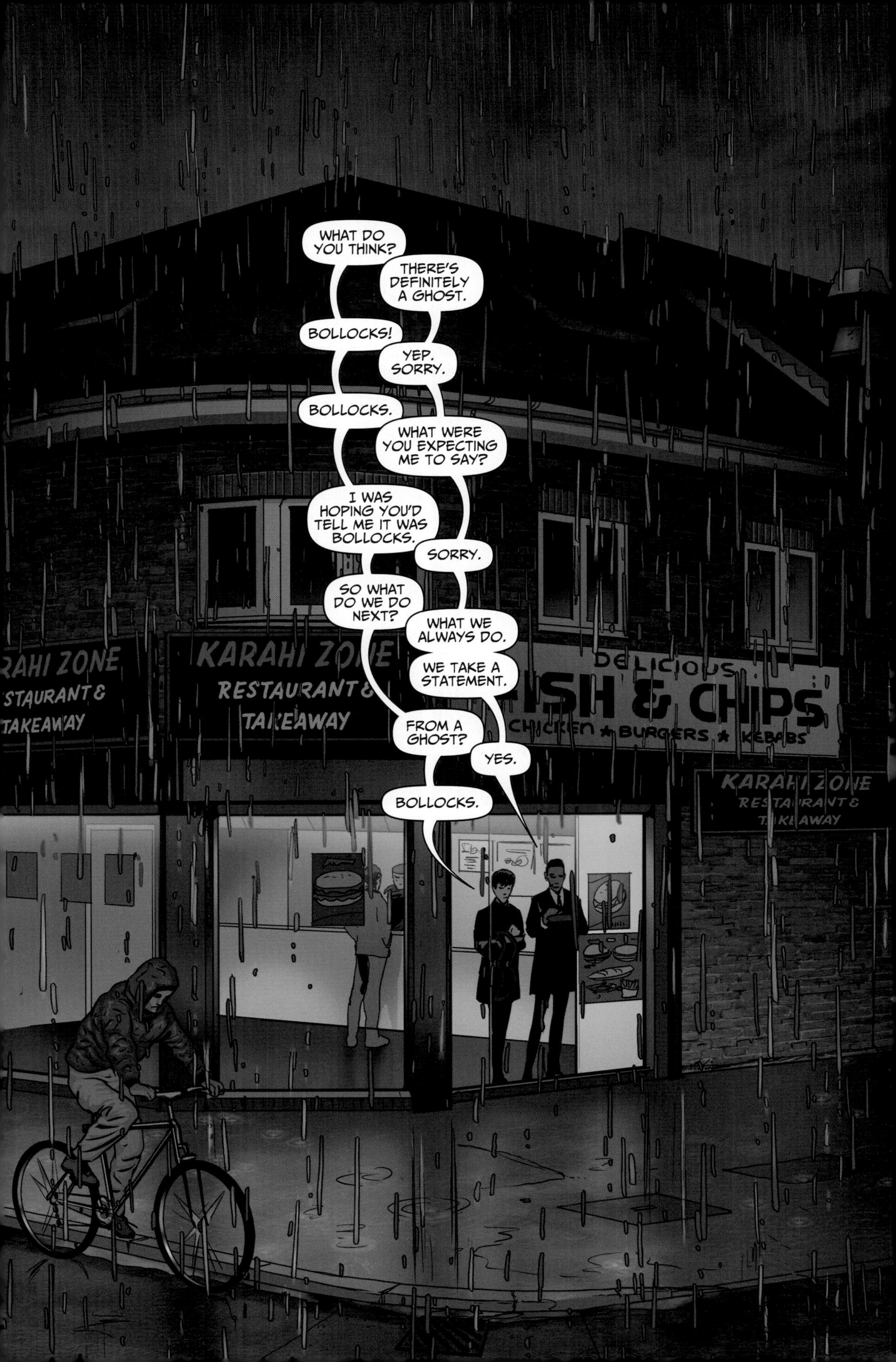
WHAT DO YOU THINK?
THERE'S DEFINITELY A GHOST.
BOLLOCKS!
YEP. SORRY.
BOLLOCKS.
WHAT WERE YOU EXPECTING ME TO SAY?
I WAS HOPING YOU'D TELL ME IT WAS BOLLOCKS.
SORRY.
SO WHAT DO WE DO NEXT?
WHAT WE ALWAYS DO.
WE TAKE A STATEMENT.
FROM A GHOST?
YES.
BOLLOCKS.
KARAHI ZONE RESTAURANT & TAKEAWAY
DELICIOUS
CHICKEN ★ BURGERS ★

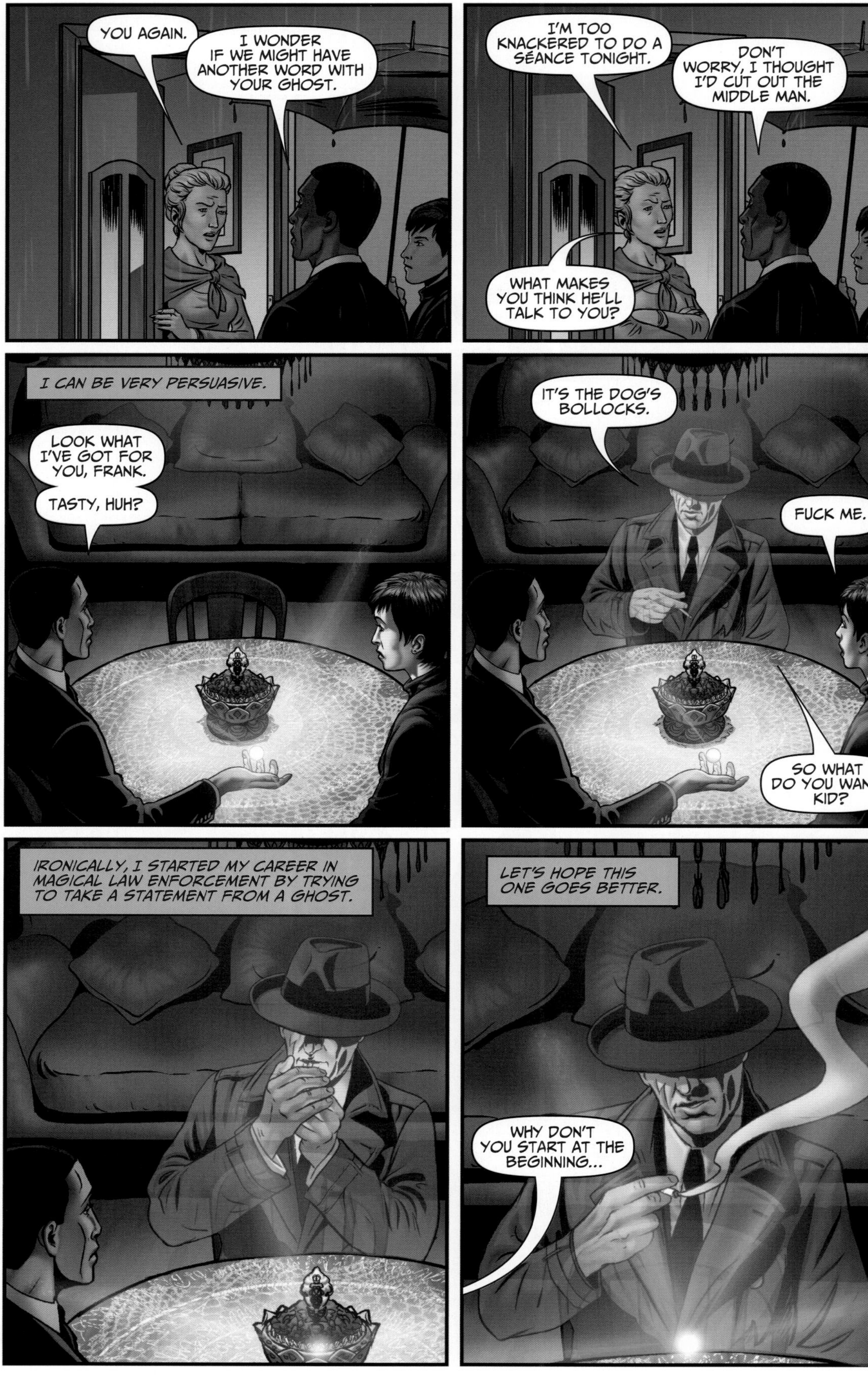
YOU AGAIN.
I WONDER IF WE MIGHT HAVE ANOTHER WORD WITH YOUR GHOST.
I'M TOO KNACKERED TO DO A SÉANCE TONIGHT.
DON'T WORRY, I THOUGHT I'D CUT OUT THE MIDDLE MAN.
WHAT MAKES YOU THINK HE'LL TALK TO YOU?
I CAN BE VERY PERSUASIVE.
LOOK WHAT I'VE GOT FOR YOU, FRANK.
TASTY, HUH?
IT'S THE DOG'S BOLLOCKS.
FUCK ME.
SO WHAT DO YOU WANT, KID?
IRONICALLY, I STARTED MY CAREER IN MAGICAL LAW ENFORCEMENT BY TRYING TO TAKE A STATEMENT FROM A GHOST.
LET'S HOPE THIS ONE GOES BETTER.
WHY DON'T YOU START AT THE BEGINNING...

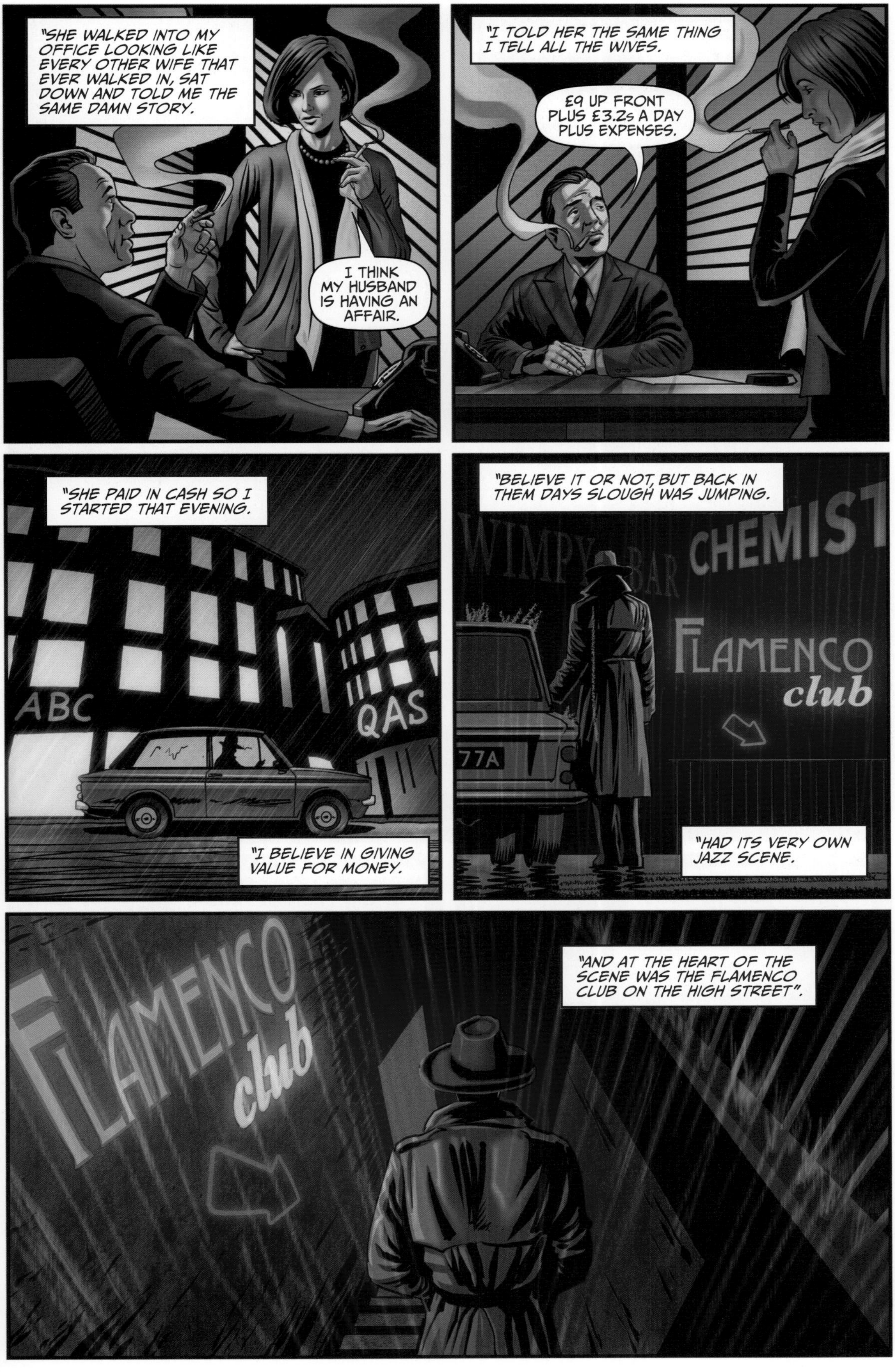
"SHE WALKED INTO MY OFFICE LOOKING LIKE EVERY OTHER WIFE THAT EVER WALKED IN, SAT DOWN AND TOLD ME THE SAME DAMN STORY.
I THINK MY HUSBAND IS HAVING AN AFFAIR.
"I TOLD HER THE SAME THING I TELL ALL THE WIVES.
£9 UP FRONT PLUS £3.2s A DAY PLUS EXPENSES.
"SHE PAID IN CASH SO I STARTED THAT EVENING.
ABC
QAS
"I BELIEVE IN GIVING VALUE FOR MONEY.
"BELIEVE IT OR NOT, BUT BACK IN THEM DAYS SLOUGH WAS JUMPING.
WIMPY BAR
CHEMIST
FLAMENCO club
77A
"HAD ITS VERY OWN JAZZ SCENE.
FLAMENCO club
"AND AT THE HEART OF THE SCENE WAS THE FLAMENCO CLUB ON THE HIGH STREET".

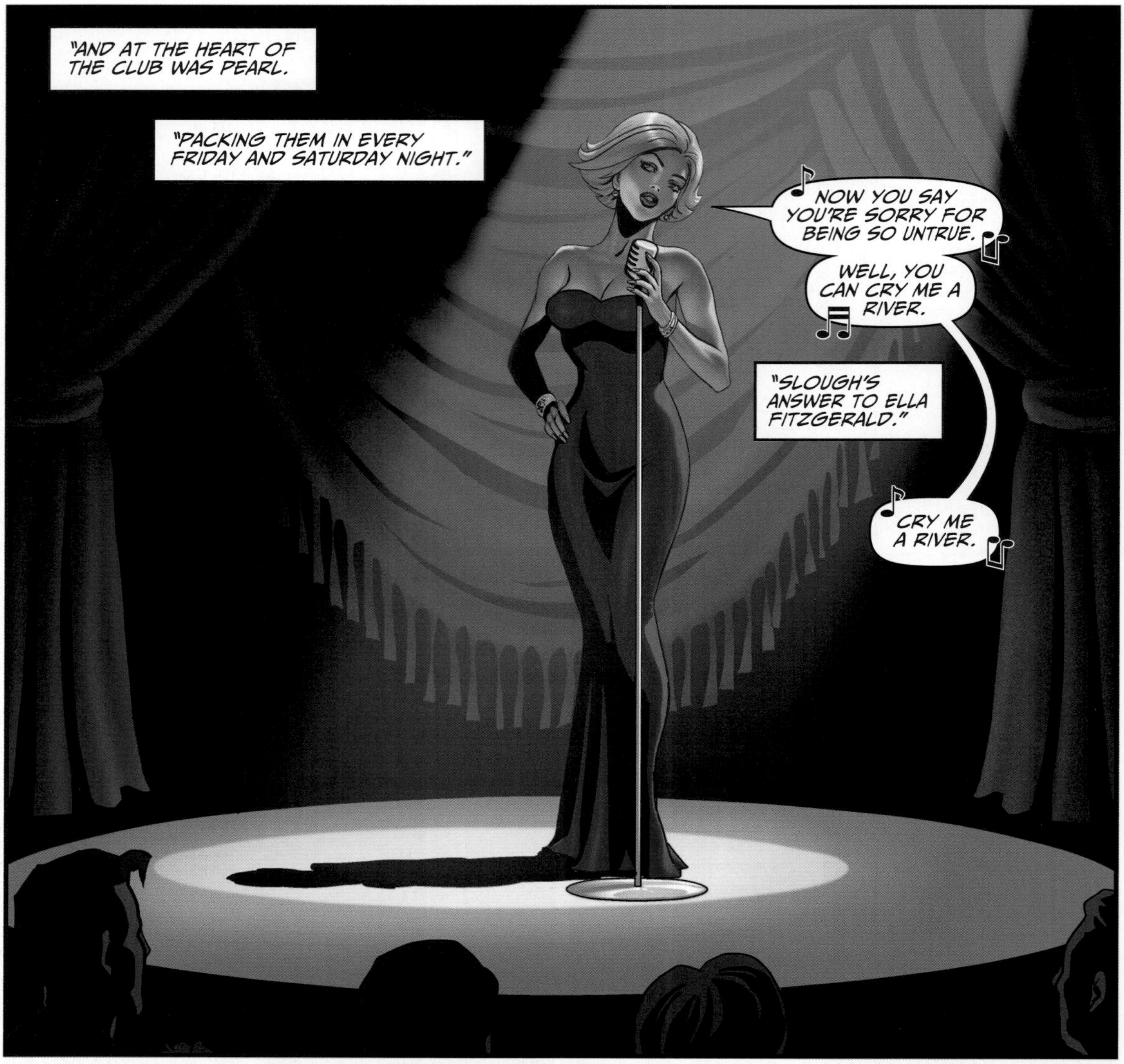
"AND AT THE HEART OF THE CLUB WAS PEARL.
"PACKING THEM IN EVERY FRIDAY AND SATURDAY NIGHT."
NOW YOU SAY YOU'RE SORRY FOR BEING SO UNTRUE.
WELL, YOU CAN CRY ME A RIVER.
"SLOUGH'S ANSWER TO ELLA FITZGERALD."
CRY ME A RIVER.

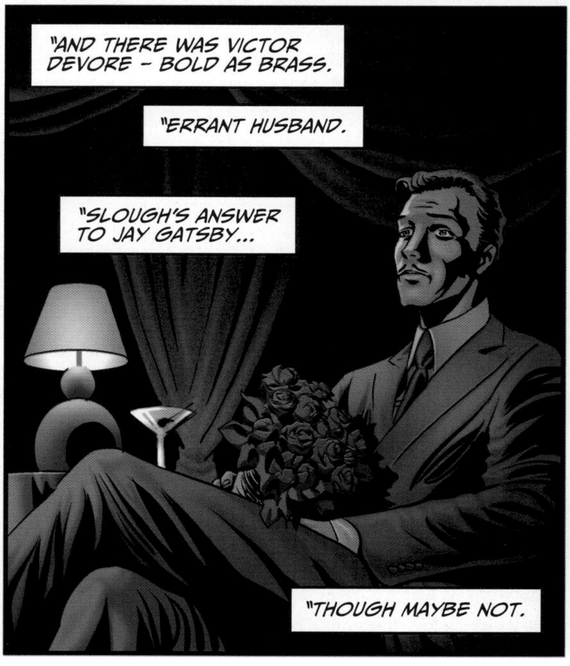
"AND THERE WAS VICTOR DEVORE - BOLD AS BRASS.
"ERRANT HUSBAND.
"SLOUGH'S ANSWER TO JAY GATSBY...
"THOUGH MAYBE NOT.

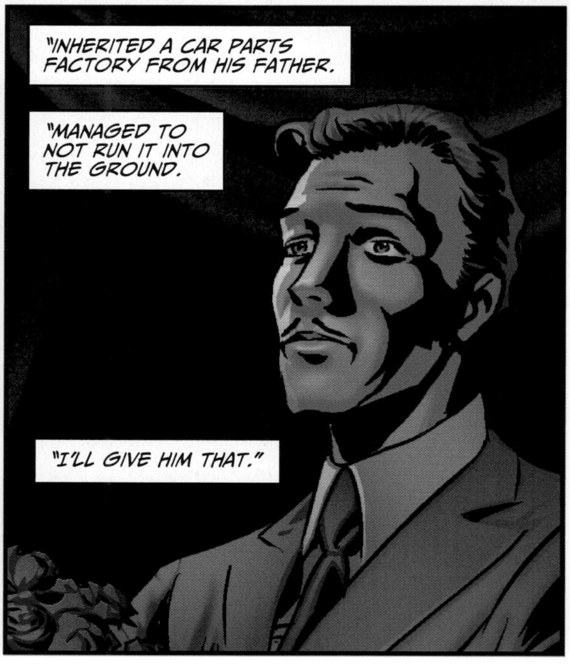
"INHERITED A CAR PARTS FACTORY FROM HIS FATHER.
"MANAGED TO NOT RUN IT INTO THE GROUND.
"I'LL GIVE HIM THAT."

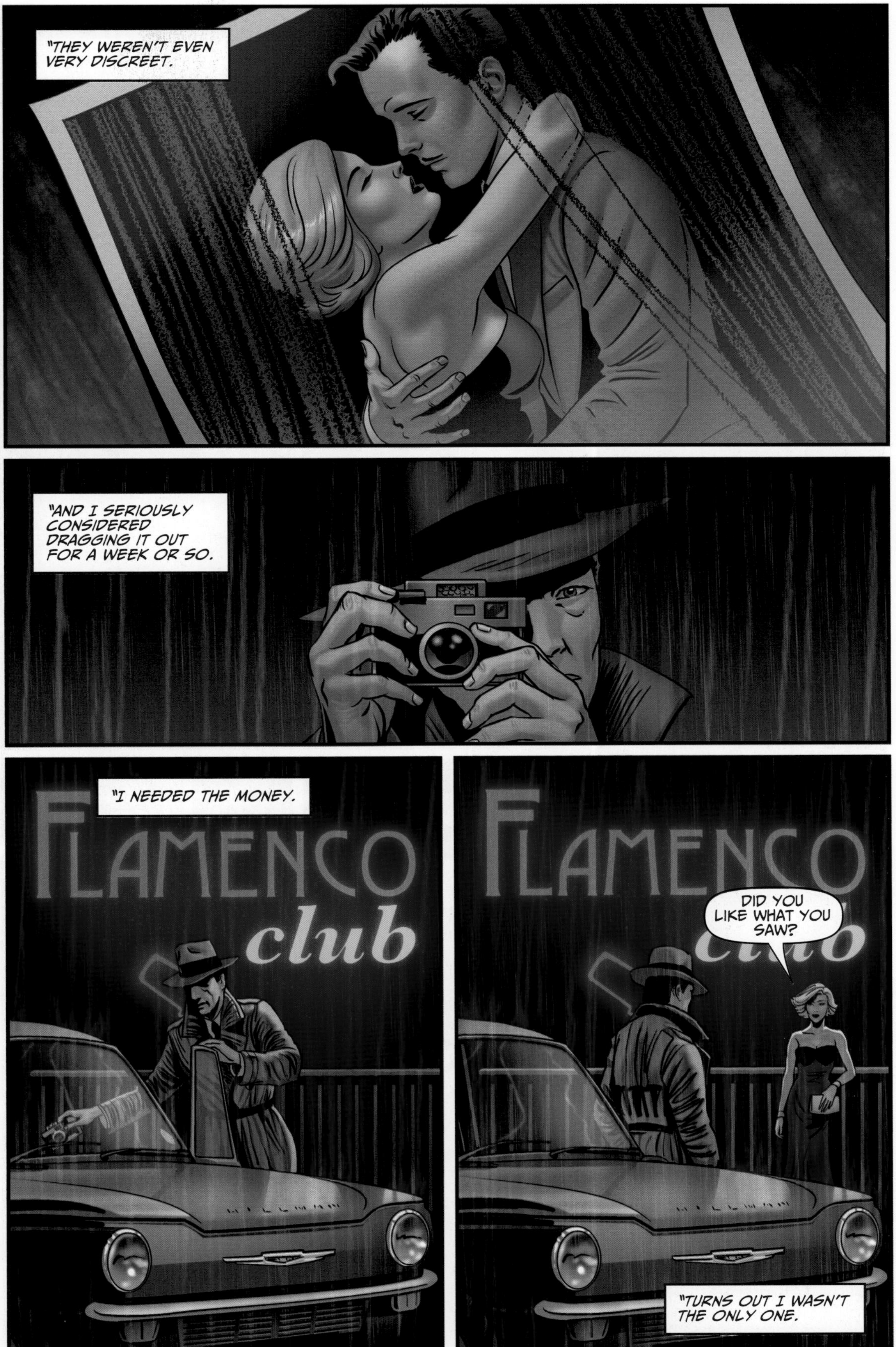
"THEY WEREN'T EVEN VERY DISCREET.
"AND I SERIOUSLY CONSIDERED DRAGGING IT OUT FOR A WEEK OR SO.
"I NEEDED THE MONEY.
FLAMENCO club
FLAMENCO
DID YOU LIKE WHAT YOU SAW?
"TURNS OUT I WASN'T THE ONLY ONE.

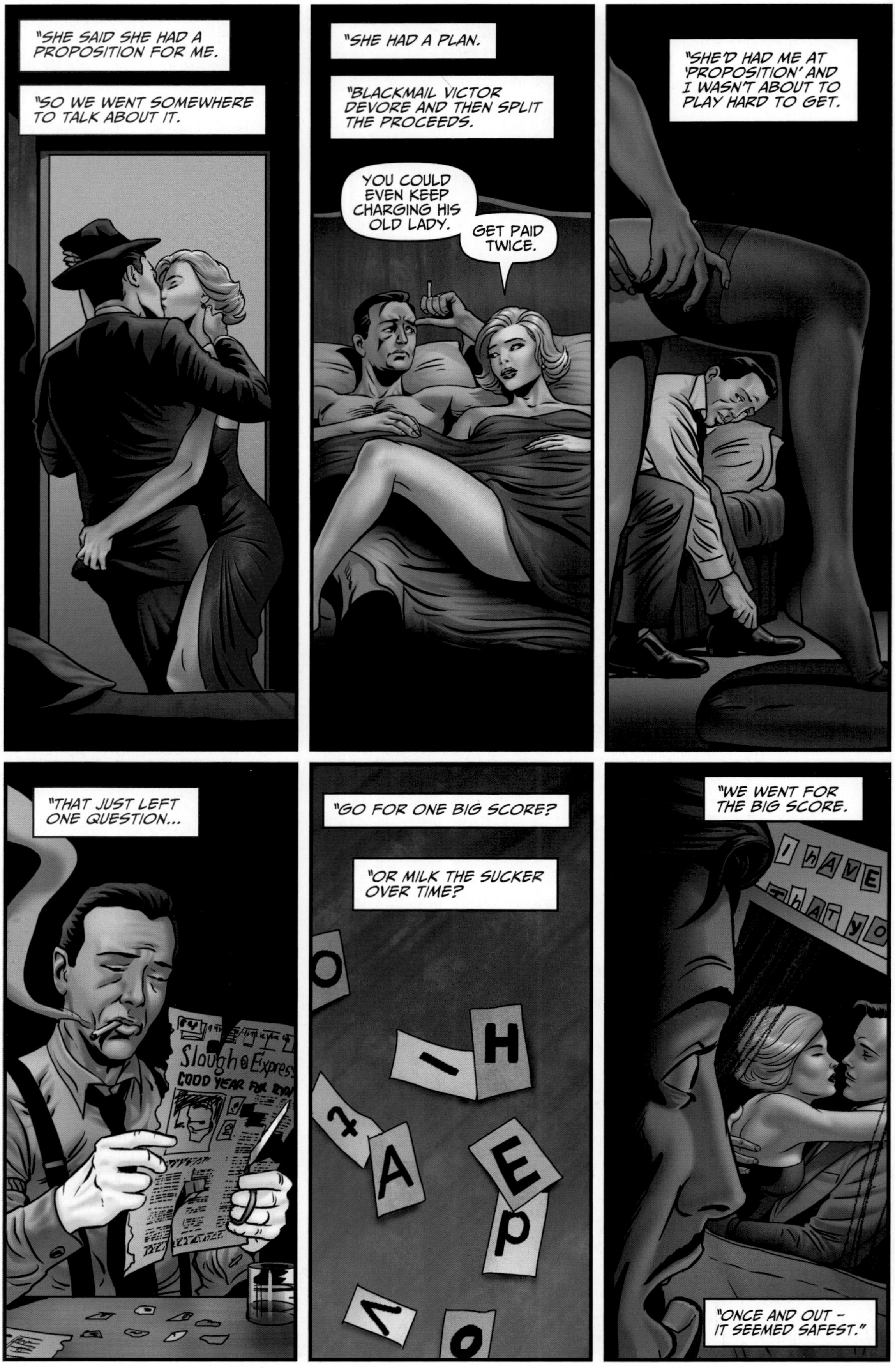
"SHE SAID SHE HAD A PROPOSITION FOR ME.
"SO WE WENT SOMEWHERE TO TALK ABOUT IT.
"SHE HAD A PLAN.
"BLACKMAIL VICTOR DEVORE AND THEN SPLIT THE PROCEEDS.
YOU COULD EVEN KEEP CHARGING HIS OLD LADY.
GET PAID TWICE.
"SHE'D HAD ME AT 'PROPOSITION' AND I WASN'T ABOUT TO PLAY HARD TO GET.
"THAT JUST LEFT ONE QUESTION...
Slough Express
"GO FOR ONE BIG SCORE?
"OR MILK THE SUCKER OVER TIME?
"WE WENT FOR THE BIG SCORE.
"ONCE AND OUT – IT SEEMED SAFEST."

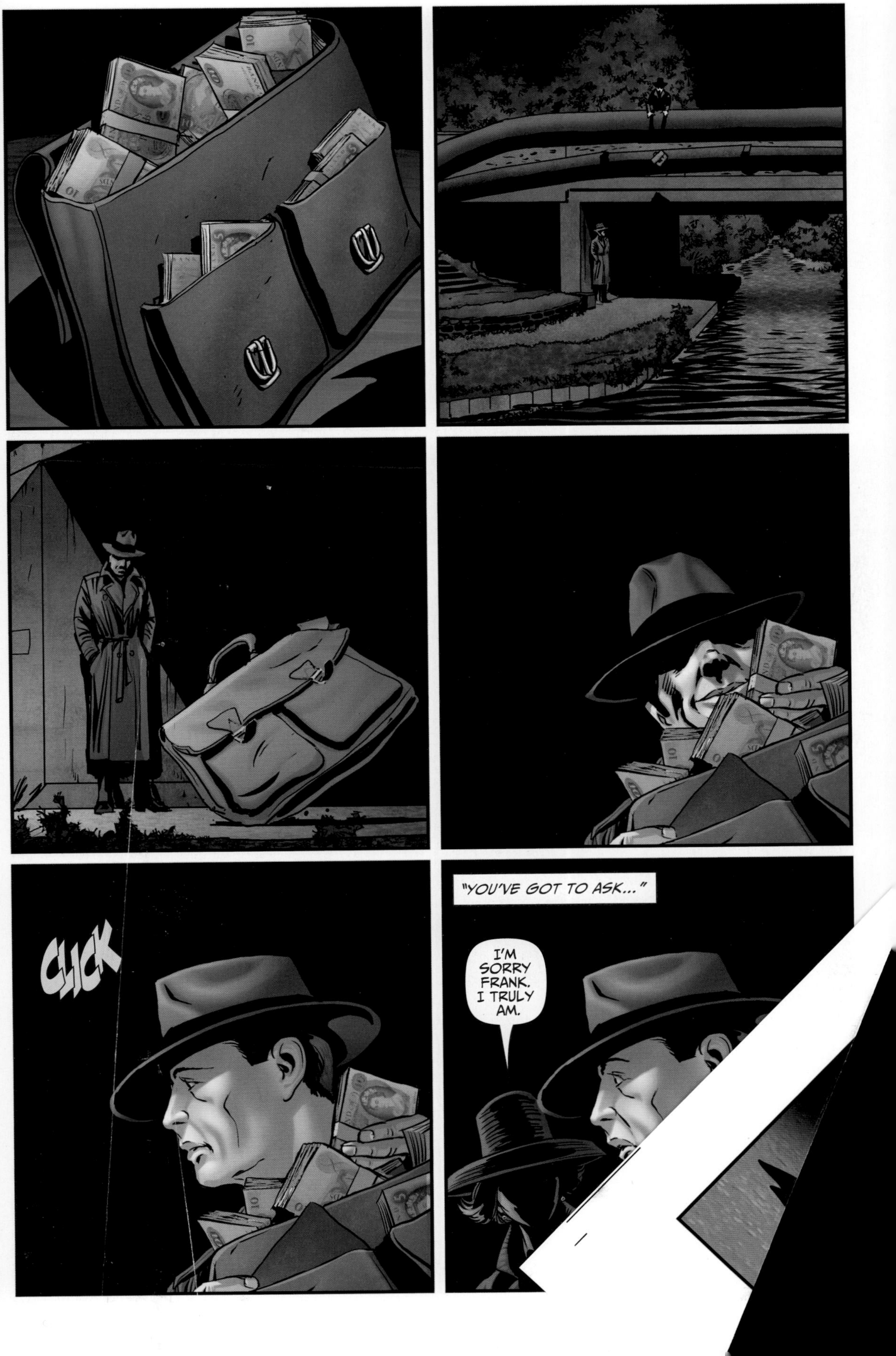
CLICK
"YOU'VE GOT TO ASK..."
I'M SORRY FRANK. I TRULY AM.

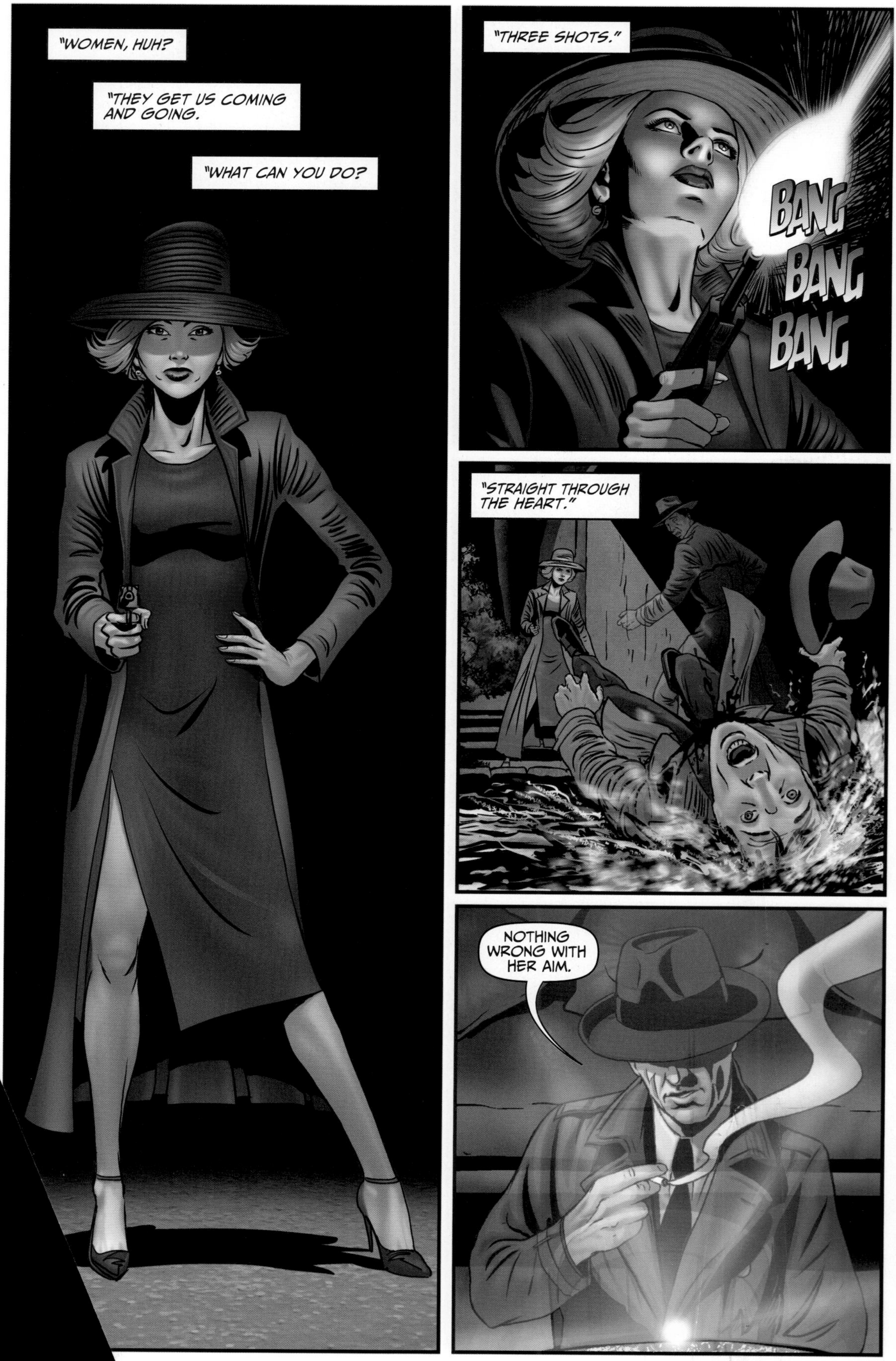
"WOMEN, HUH?
"THEY GET US COMING AND GOING.
"WHAT CAN YOU DO?
"THREE SHOTS."
BANG
BANG
BANG
"STRAIGHT THROUGH THE HEART."
NOTHING WRONG WITH HER AIM.

LEGALLY SPEAKING, WOULD YOU SAY THAT COUNTS AS A 'DYING DECLARATION?'

I WOULDN'T WANT TO GO INTO COURT WITH IT, SIR.

SO WHAT DID YOU DO ABOUT IT?

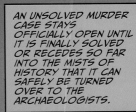

I WENT BACK TO MY ABCs.

BLACKSTONE'S
POLICE OPERATIONAL HANDBOOK: **PRACTICE & PROCEDURE**

Second Edition

PNLD

Editor: Dr Clive Harfield

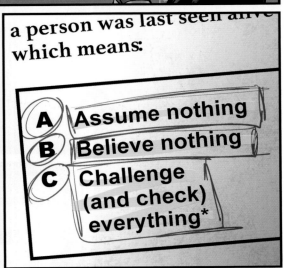

a person was last seen alive which means:

A Assume nothing

B Believe nothing

C Challenge (and check) everything*

AN UNSOLVED MURDER CASE STAYS OFFICIALLY OPEN UNTIL IT IS FINALLY SOLVED OR RECEDES SO FAR INTO THE MISTS OF HISTORY THAT IT CAN SAFELY BE TURNED OVER TO THE ARCHAEOLOGISTS.

FORTUNATELY THIS CASE WAS REVIEWED IN 1997, SO THE FILES AND THE STORED EVIDENCE HAD ALREADY BEEN CHECKED AND REPACKAGED TO MODERN STANDARDS.

THAMES VALLEY POLICE

COMPARATIVELY MODERN STANDARDS.

THAMES VALLEY POLICE

HAMES VALLEY POLICE

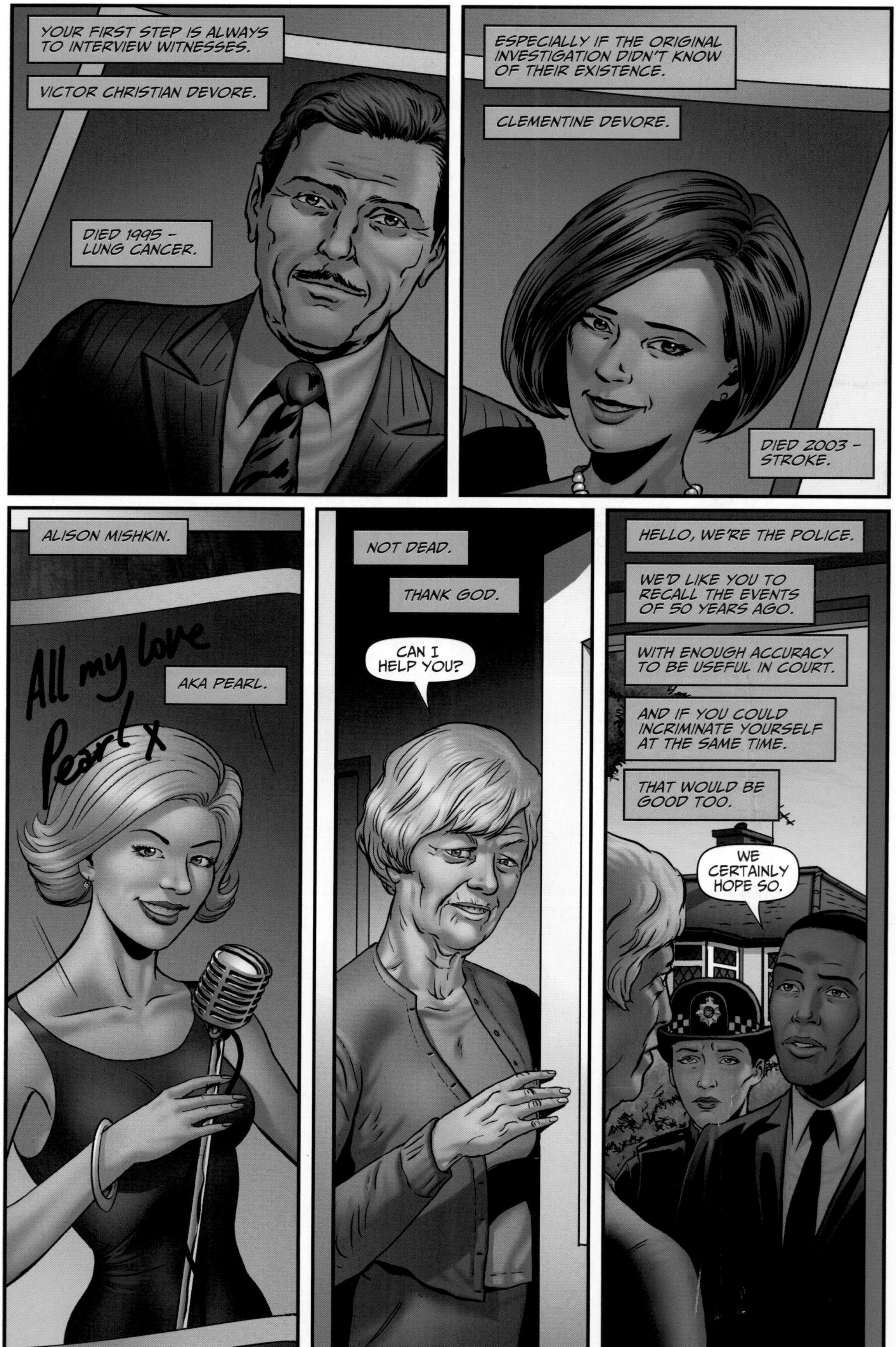
YOUR FIRST STEP IS ALWAYS TO INTERVIEW WITNESSES.
VICTOR CHRISTIAN DEVORE.
DIED 1995 - LUNG CANCER.
ESPECIALLY IF THE ORIGINAL INVESTIGATION DIDN'T KNOW OF THEIR EXISTENCE.
CLEMENTINE DEVORE.
DIED 2003 - STROKE.
ALISON MISHKIN.
AKA PEARL.
All my love Pearl x
NOT DEAD.
THANK GOD.
CAN I HELP YOU?
HELLO, WE'RE THE POLICE.
WE'D LIKE YOU TO RECALL THE EVENTS OF 50 YEARS AGO.
WITH ENOUGH ACCURACY TO BE USEFUL IN COURT.
AND IF YOU COULD INCRIMINATE YOURSELF AT THE SAME TIME.
THAT WOULD BE GOOD TOO.
WE CERTAINLY HOPE SO.

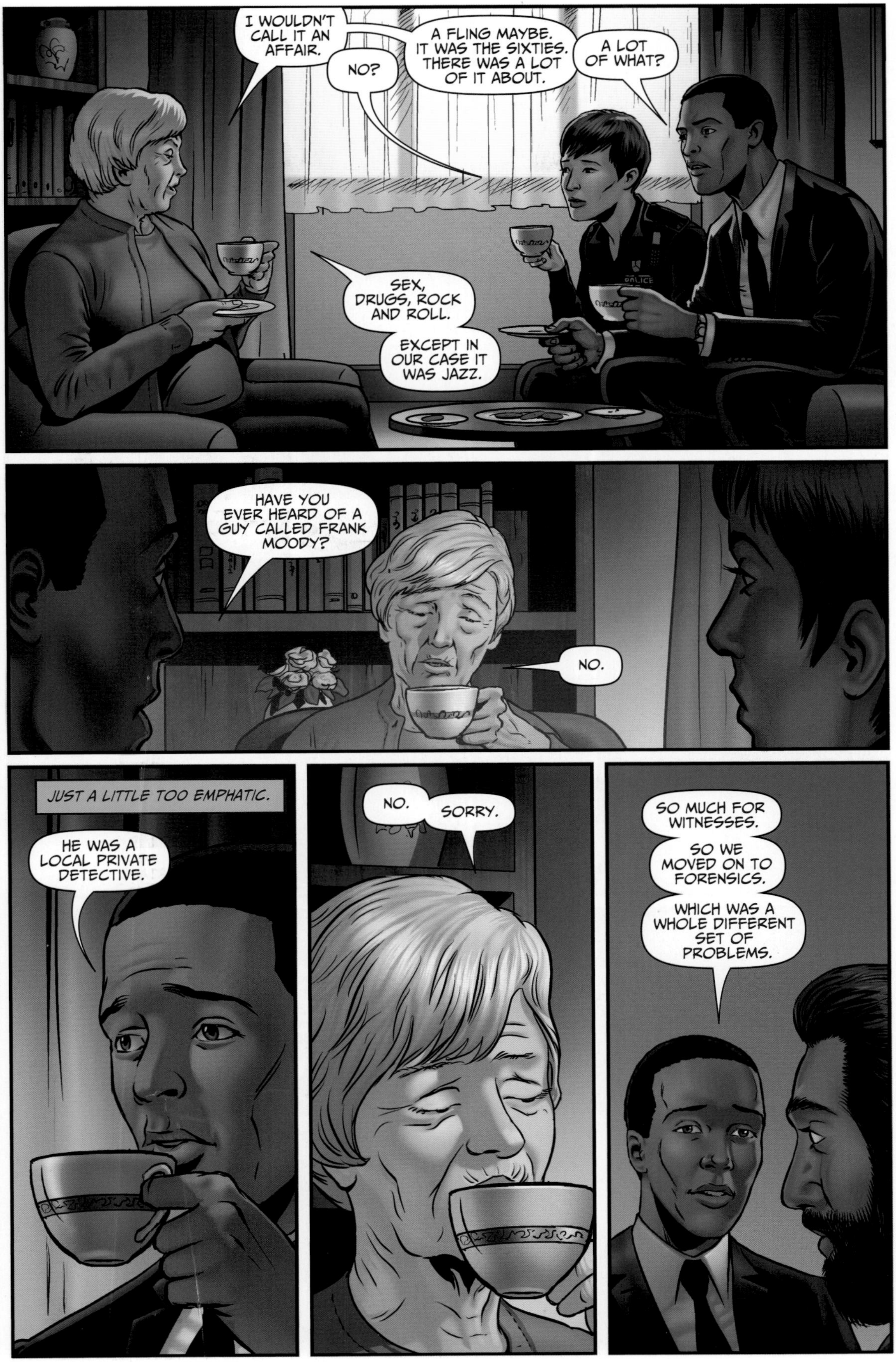
I WOULDN'T CALL IT AN AFFAIR.
NO?
A FLING MAYBE. IT WAS THE SIXTIES. THERE WAS A LOT OF IT ABOUT.
A LOT OF WHAT?
SEX, DRUGS, ROCK AND ROLL.
EXCEPT IN OUR CASE IT WAS JAZZ.
POLICE
HAVE YOU EVER HEARD OF A GUY CALLED FRANK MOODY?
NO.
JUST A LITTLE TOO EMPHATIC.
HE WAS A LOCAL PRIVATE DETECTIVE.
NO.
SORRY.
SO MUCH FOR WITNESSES.
SO WE MOVED ON TO FORENSICS.
WHICH WAS A WHOLE DIFFERENT SET OF PROBLEMS.

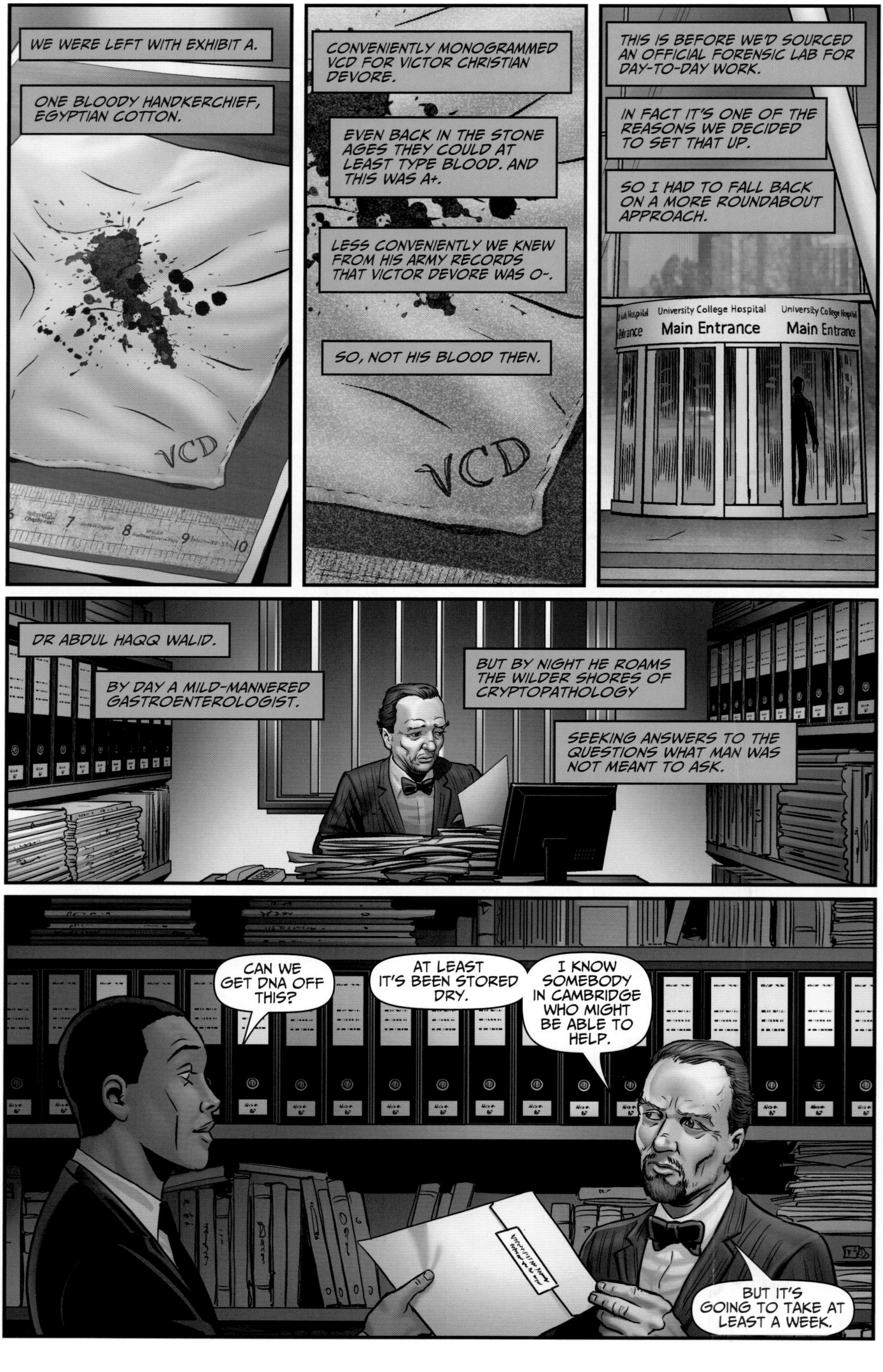
WE WERE LEFT WITH EXHIBIT A.
ONE BLOODY HANDKERCHIEF, EGYPTIAN COTTON.
VCD
CONVENIENTLY MONOGRAMMED VCD FOR VICTOR CHRISTIAN DEVORE.
EVEN BACK IN THE STONE AGES THEY COULD AT LEAST TYPE BLOOD. AND THIS WAS A+.
LESS CONVENIENTLY WE KNEW FROM HIS ARMY RECORDS THAT VICTOR DEVORE WAS O-.
SO, NOT HIS BLOOD THEN.
VCD
THIS IS BEFORE WE'D SOURCED AN OFFICIAL FORENSIC LAB FOR DAY-TO-DAY WORK.
IN FACT IT'S ONE OF THE REASONS WE DECIDED TO SET THAT UP.
SO I HAD TO FALL BACK ON A MORE ROUNDABOUT APPROACH.
University College Hospital
Main Entrance
University College Hospital
Main Entrance
DR ABDUL HAQQ WALID.
BY DAY A MILD-MANNERED GASTROENTEROLOGIST.
BUT BY NIGHT HE ROAMS THE WILDER SHORES OF CRYPTOPATHOLOGY
SEEKING ANSWERS TO THE QUESTIONS WHAT MAN WAS NOT MEANT TO ASK.
CAN WE GET DNA OFF THIS?
AT LEAST IT'S BEEN STORED DRY.
I KNOW SOMEBODY IN CAMBRIDGE WHO MIGHT BE ABLE TO HELP.
BUT IT'S GOING TO TAKE AT LEAST A WEEK.

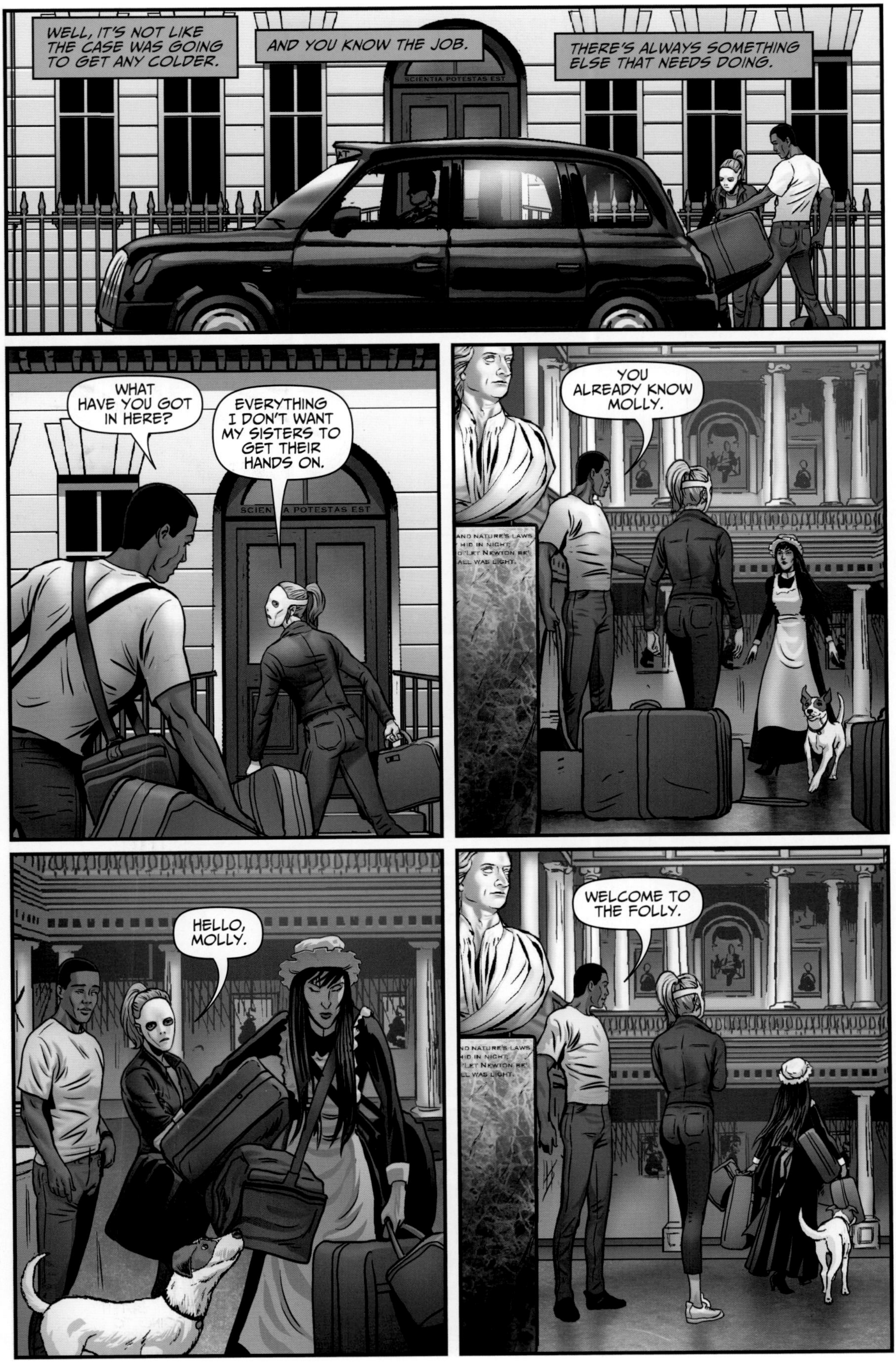
WELL, IT'S NOT LIKE THE CASE WAS GOING TO GET ANY COLDER.
AND YOU KNOW THE JOB.
THERE'S ALWAYS SOMETHING ELSE THAT NEEDS DOING.
SCIENTIA POTESTAS EST
WHAT HAVE YOU GOT IN HERE?
EVERYTHING I DON'T WANT MY SISTERS TO GET THEIR HANDS ON.
YOU ALREADY KNOW MOLLY.
HELLO, MOLLY.
WELCOME TO THE FOLLY.

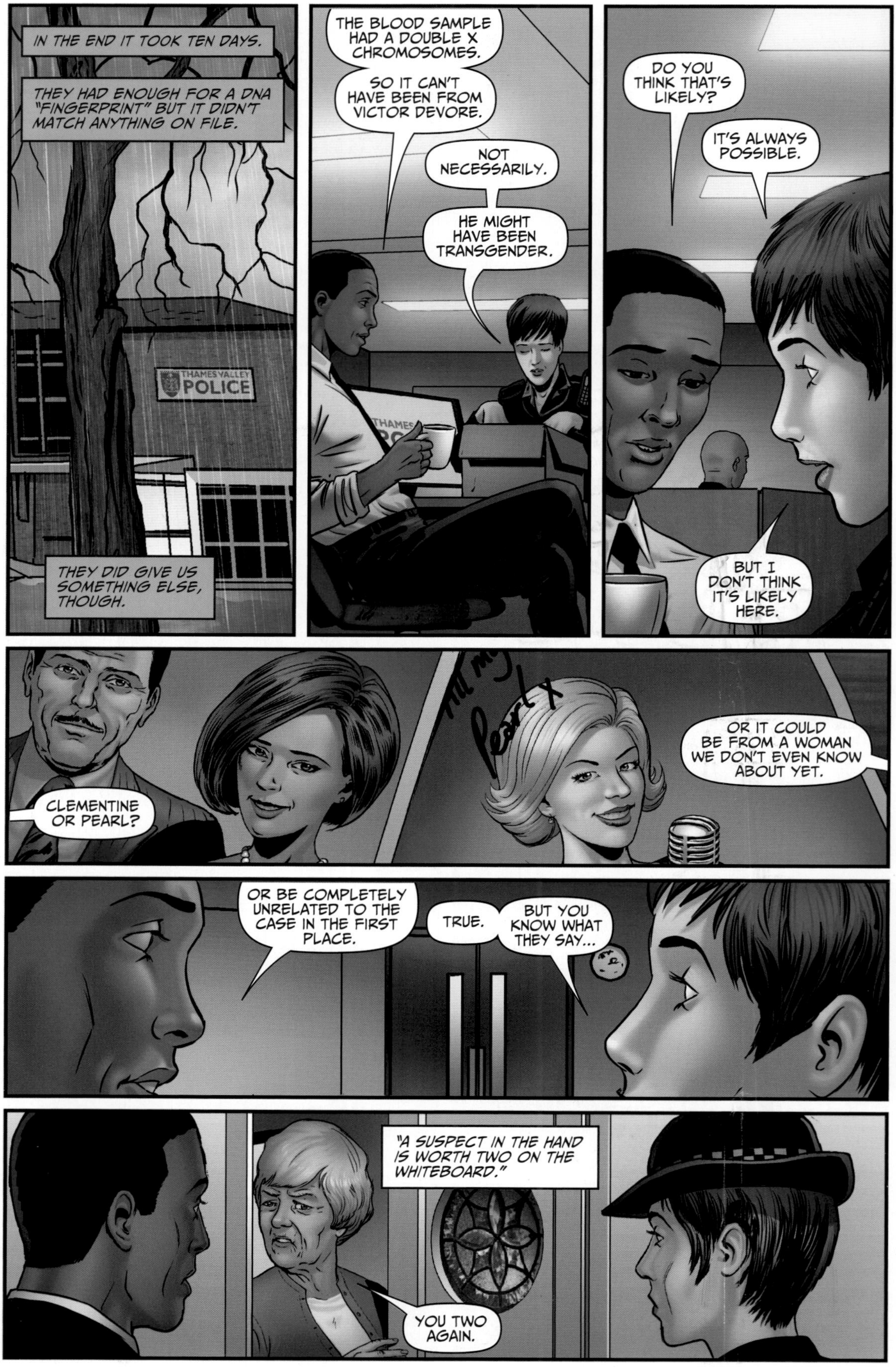
IN THE END IT TOOK TEN DAYS.
THEY HAD ENOUGH FOR A DNA "FINGERPRINT" BUT IT DIDN'T MATCH ANYTHING ON FILE.
THAMES VALLEY POLICE
THEY DID GIVE US SOMETHING ELSE, THOUGH.
THE BLOOD SAMPLE HAD A DOUBLE X CHROMOSOMES.
SO IT CAN'T HAVE BEEN FROM VICTOR DEVORE.
NOT NECESSARILY.
HE MIGHT HAVE BEEN TRANSGENDER.
DO YOU THINK THAT'S LIKELY?
IT'S ALWAYS POSSIBLE.
BUT I DON'T THINK IT'S LIKELY HERE.
CLEMENTINE OR PEARL?
Pearl x
OR IT COULD BE FROM A WOMAN WE DON'T EVEN KNOW ABOUT YET.
OR BE COMPLETELY UNRELATED TO THE CASE IN THE FIRST PLACE.
TRUE.
BUT YOU KNOW WHAT THEY SAY...
"A SUSPECT IN THE HAND IS WORTH TWO ON THE WHITEBOARD."
YOU TWO AGAIN.

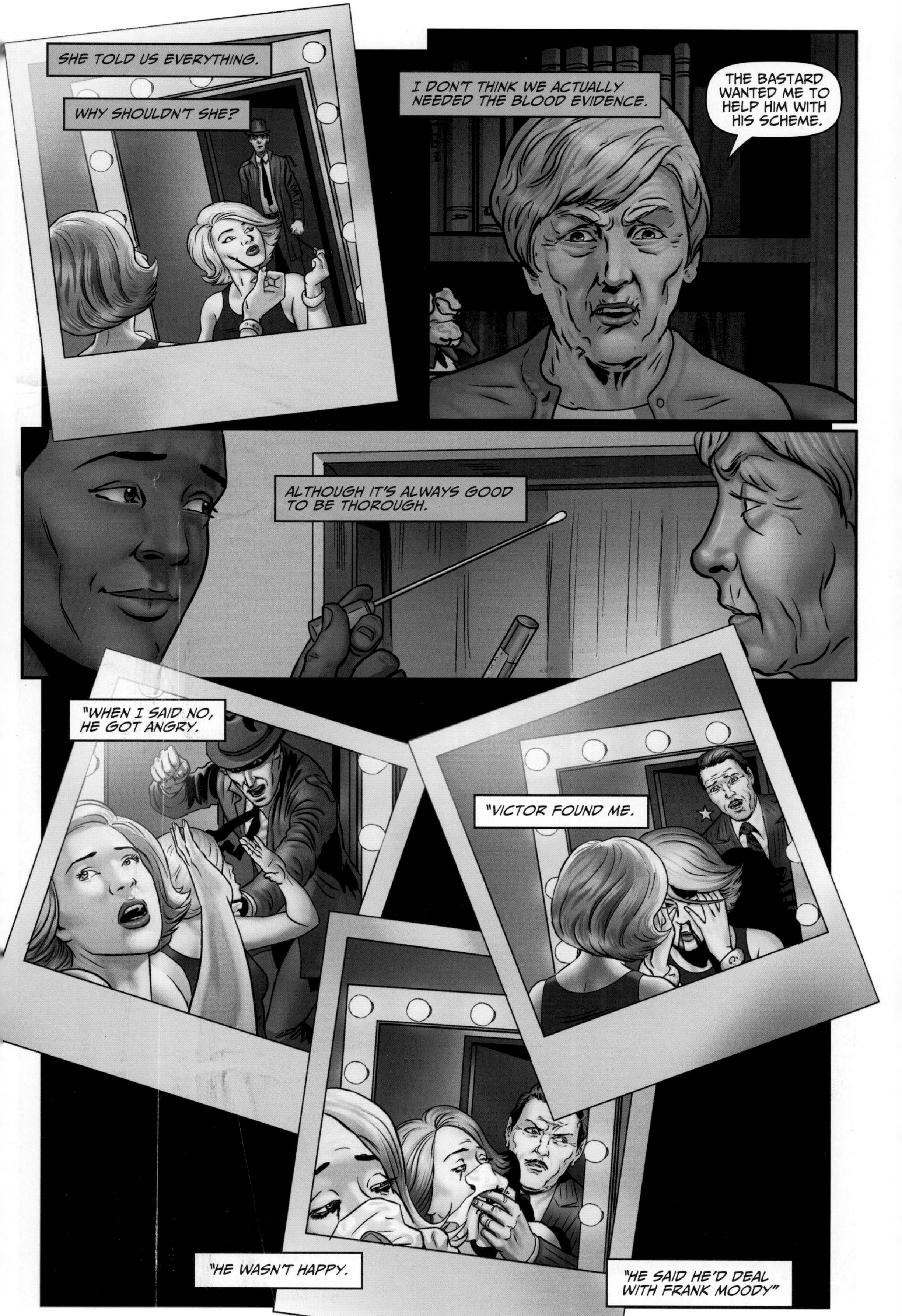
SHE TOLD US EVERYTHING.
WHY SHOULDN'T SHE?
I DON'T THINK WE ACTUALLY NEEDED THE BLOOD EVIDENCE.
THE BASTARD WANTED ME TO HELP HIM WITH HIS SCHEME.
ALTHOUGH IT'S ALWAYS GOOD TO BE THOROUGH.
"WHEN I SAID NO, HE GOT ANGRY.
"VICTOR FOUND ME.
"HE WASN'T HAPPY.
"HE SAID HE'D DEAL WITH FRANK MOODY"

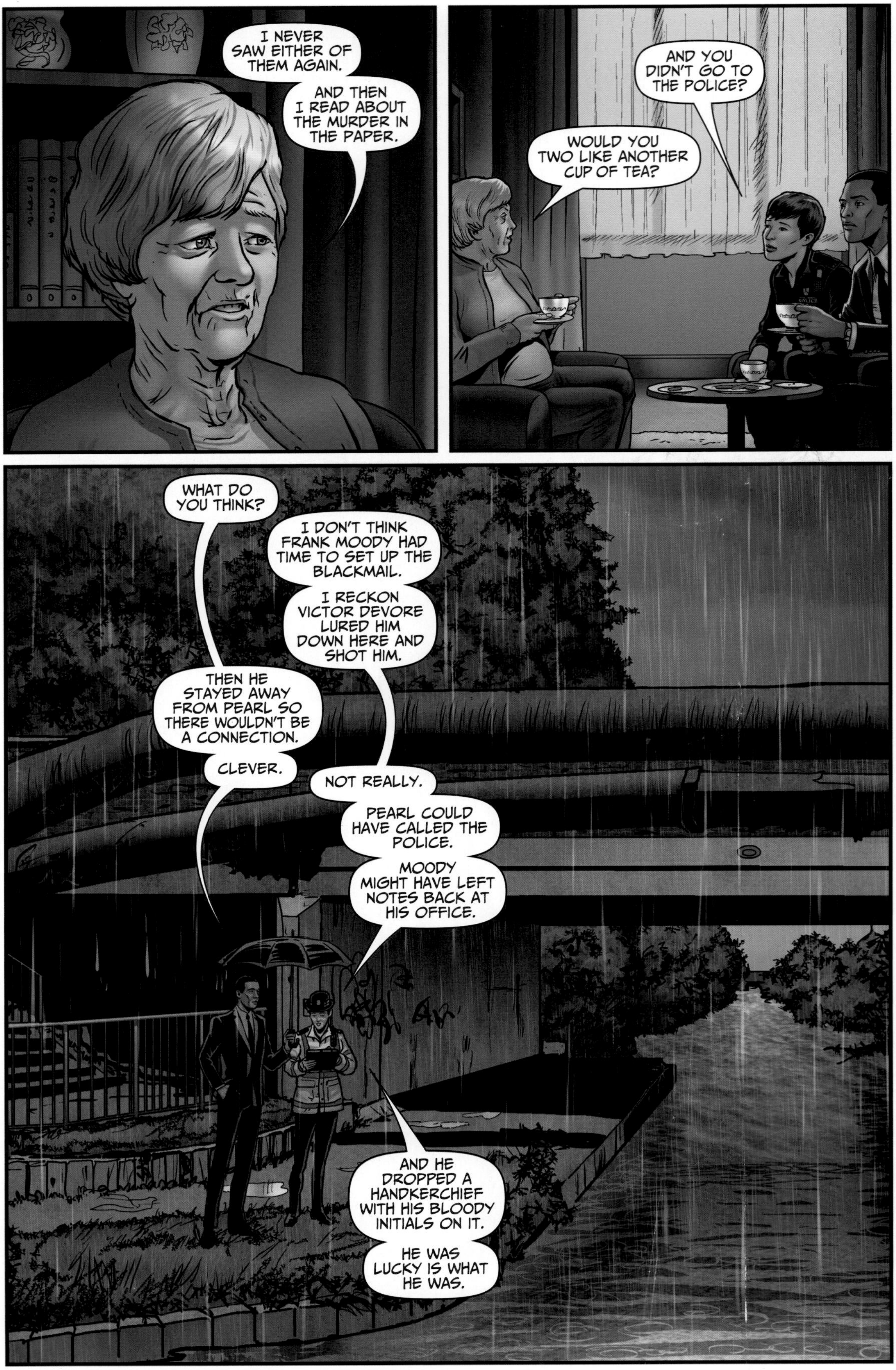
I NEVER SAW EITHER OF THEM AGAIN.
AND THEN I READ ABOUT THE MURDER IN THE PAPER.
AND YOU DIDN'T GO TO THE POLICE?
WOULD YOU TWO LIKE ANOTHER CUP OF TEA?
WHAT DO YOU THINK?
I DON'T THINK FRANK MOODY HAD TIME TO SET UP THE BLACKMAIL.
I RECKON VICTOR DEVORE LURED HIM DOWN HERE AND SHOT HIM.
THEN HE STAYED AWAY FROM PEARL SO THERE WOULDN'T BE A CONNECTION.
CLEVER.
NOT REALLY.
PEARL COULD HAVE CALLED THE POLICE.
MOODY MIGHT HAVE LEFT NOTES BACK AT HIS OFFICE.
AND HE DROPPED A HANDKERCHIEF WITH HIS BLOODY INITIALS ON IT.
HE WAS LUCKY IS WHAT HE WAS.

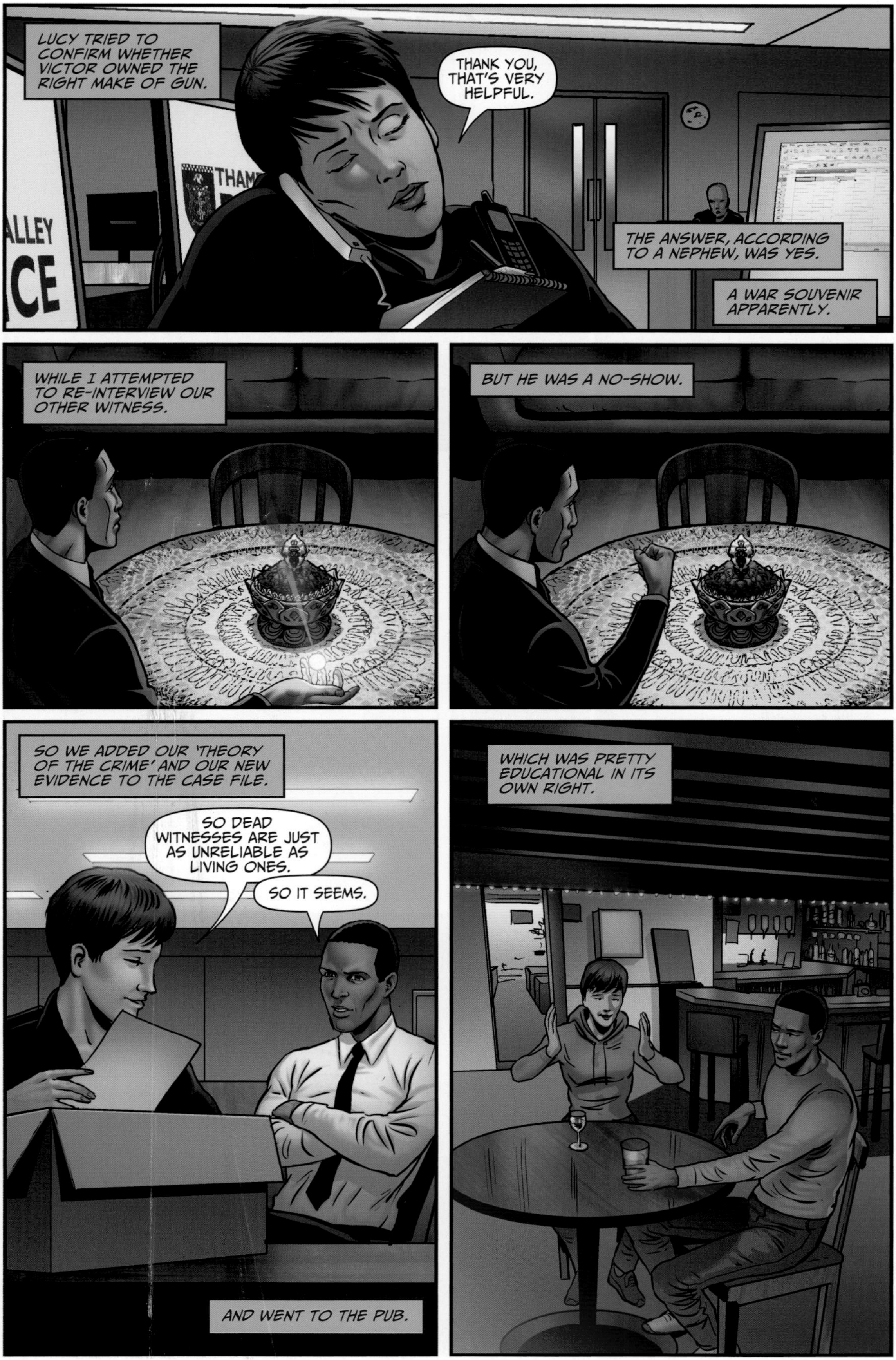
LUCY TRIED TO CONFIRM WHETHER VICTOR OWNED THE RIGHT MAKE OF GUN.
THANK YOU, THAT'S VERY HELPFUL.
THE ANSWER, ACCORDING TO A NEPHEW, WAS YES.
A WAR SOUVENIR APPARENTLY.
WHILE I ATTEMPTED TO RE-INTERVIEW OUR OTHER WITNESS.
BUT HE WAS A NO-SHOW.
SO WE ADDED OUR 'THEORY OF THE CRIME' AND OUR NEW EVIDENCE TO THE CASE FILE.
SO DEAD WITNESSES ARE JUST AS UNRELIABLE AS LIVING ONES.
SO IT SEEMS.
AND WENT TO THE PUB.
WHICH WAS PRETTY EDUCATIONAL IN ITS OWN RIGHT.

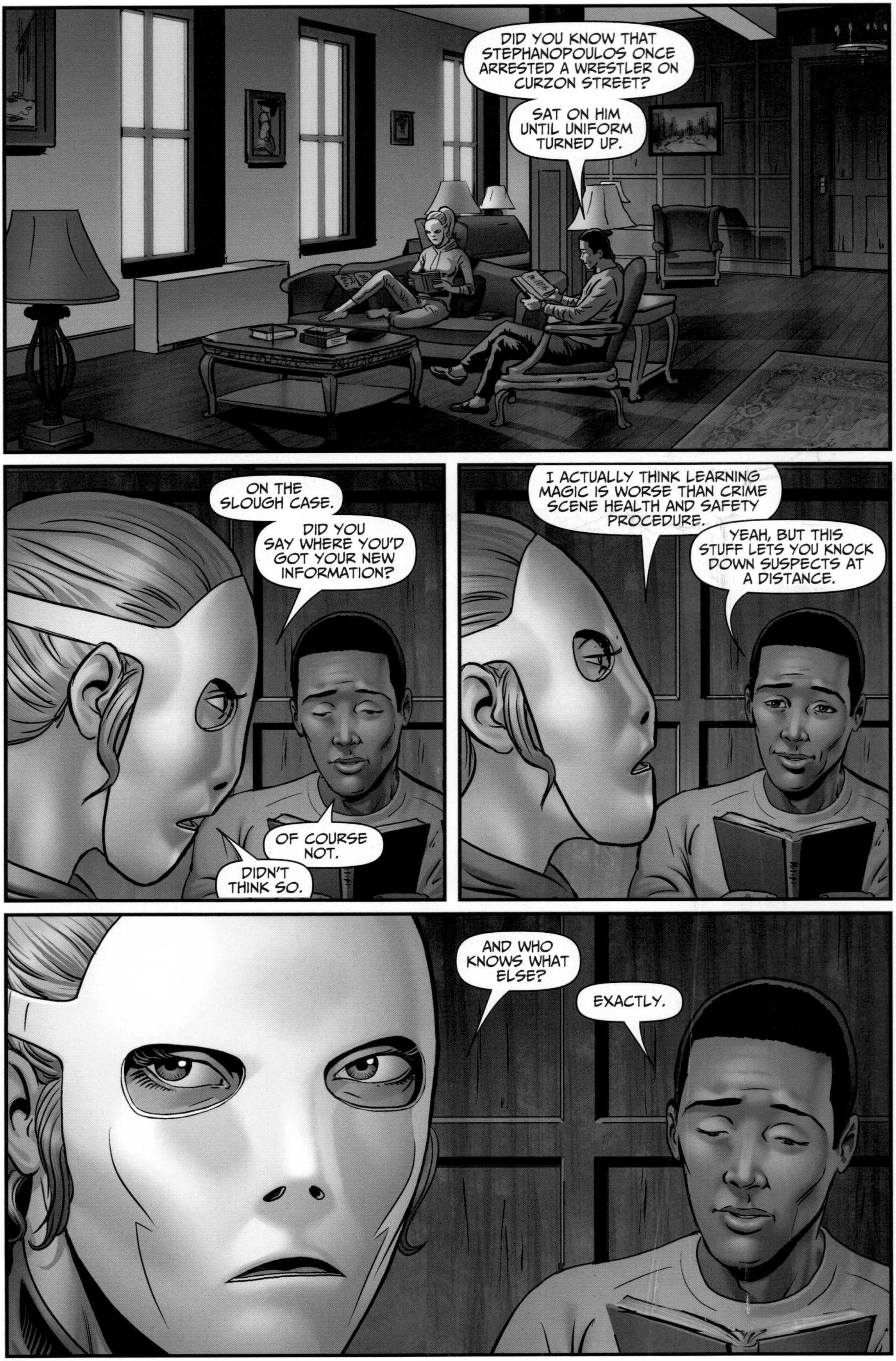
DID YOU KNOW THAT STEPHANOPOULOS ONCE ARRESTED A WRESTLER ON CURZON STREET?
SAT ON HIM UNTIL UNIFORM TURNED UP.
ON THE SLOUGH CASE.
DID YOU SAY WHERE YOU'D GOT YOUR NEW INFORMATION?
OF COURSE NOT.
DIDN'T THINK SO.
I ACTUALLY THINK LEARNING MAGIC IS WORSE THAN CRIME SCENE HEALTH AND SAFETY PROCEDURE.
YEAH, BUT THIS STUFF LETS YOU KNOCK DOWN SUSPECTS AT A DISTANCE.
AND WHO KNOWS WHAT ELSE?
EXACTLY.

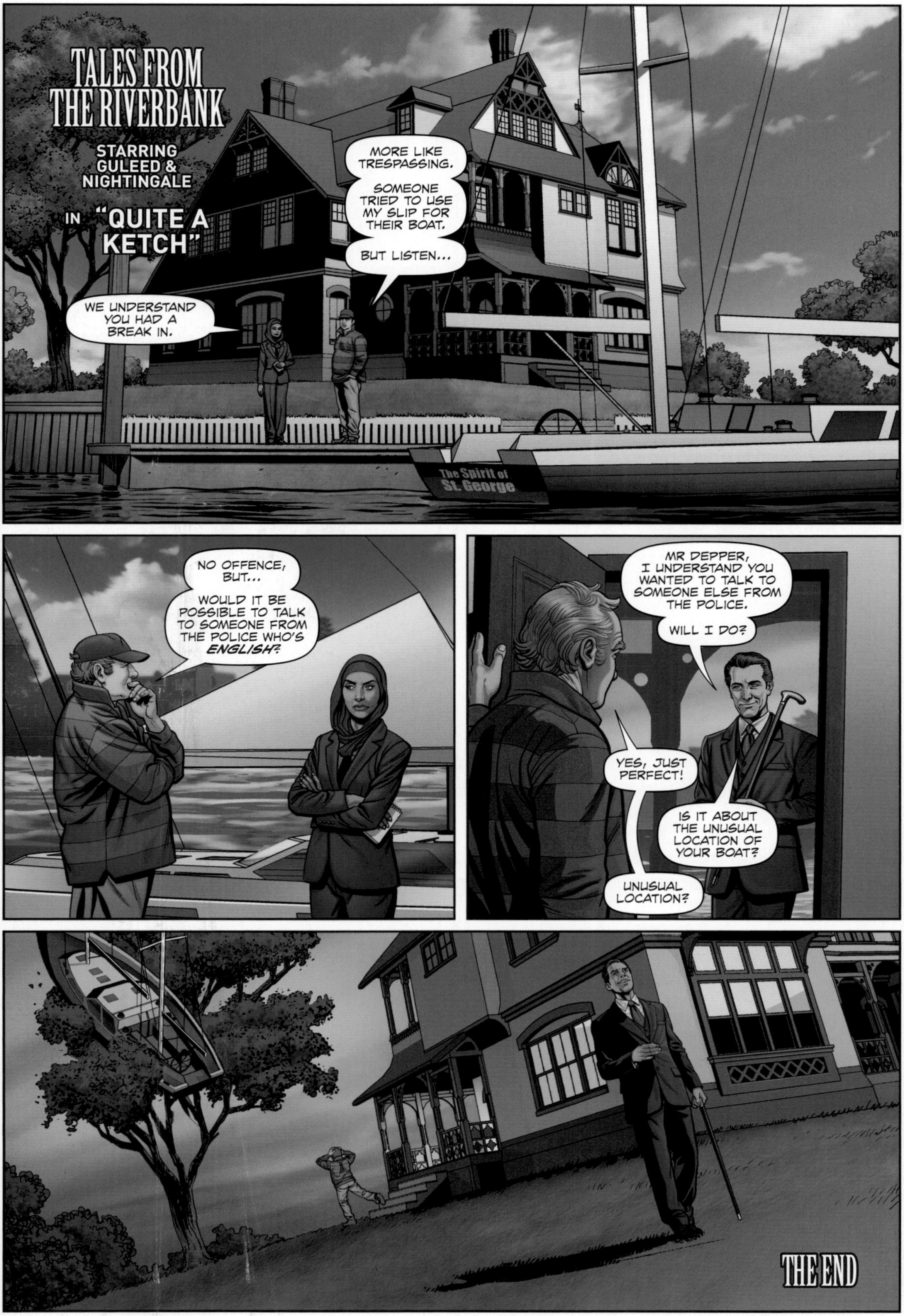
TALES FROM THE RIVERBANK
STARRING GULEED & NIGHTINGALE
IN "QUITE A KETCH"
WE UNDERSTAND YOU HAD A BREAK IN.
MORE LIKE TRESPASSING.
SOMEONE TRIED TO USE MY SLIP FOR THEIR BOAT.
BUT LISTEN...
The Spirit of St. George
NO OFFENCE, BUT...
WOULD IT BE POSSIBLE TO TALK TO SOMEONE FROM THE POLICE WHO'S ENGLISH?
MR DEPPER, I UNDERSTAND YOU WANTED TO TALK TO SOMEONE ELSE FROM THE POLICE.
WILL I DO?
YES, JUST PERFECT!
IS IT ABOUT THE UNUSUAL LOCATION OF YOUR BOAT?
UNUSUAL LOCATION?
THE END

TALES FROM THE FOLLY

STARRING DEBDEN, TOBY & NIGHTINGALE

IN "GRAB BAG"

THANK YOU FOR TAKING CHARGE OF TOBY THIS MORNING, TOM.

IT WAS A GREAT HELP.

AND IT LOOKS LIKE YOU ENJOYED YOURSELF.

I'M JUST IMAGINING THE LOOK ON SOMEONE'S FACE...

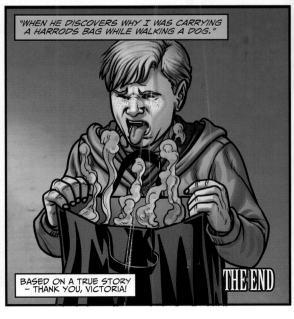

"WHEN HE DISCOVERS WHY I WAS CARRYING A HARRODS BAG WHILE WALKING A DOG."

BASED ON A TRUE STORY – THANK YOU, VICTORIA!

THE END

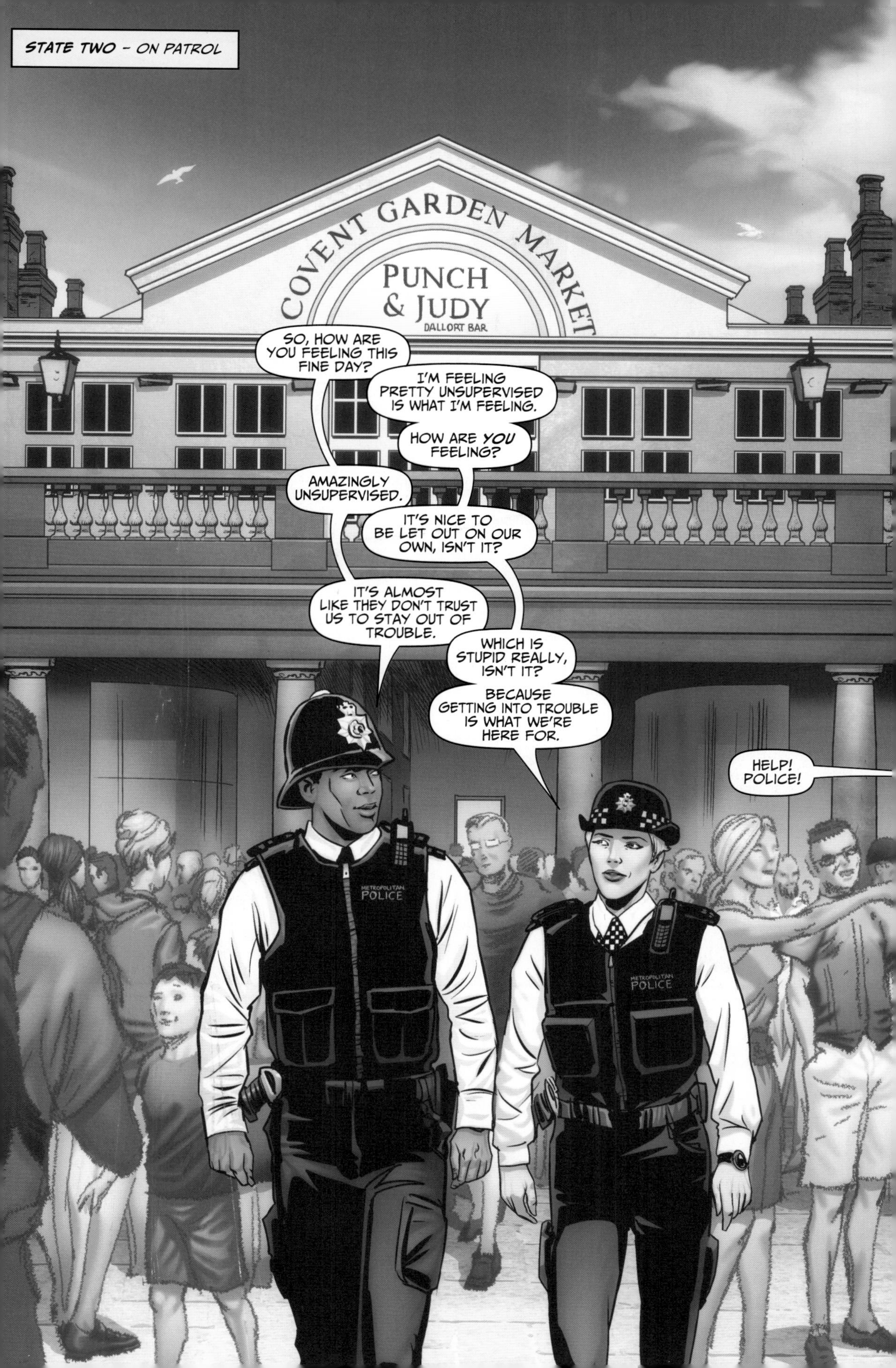
STATE TWO - ON PATROL
COVENT GARDEN MARKET
PUNCH & JUDY
DALLORT BAR
SO, HOW ARE YOU FEELING THIS FINE DAY?
I'M FEELING PRETTY UNSUPERVISED IS WHAT I'M FEELING.
HOW ARE *YOU* FEELING?
AMAZINGLY UNSUPERVISED.
IT'S NICE TO BE LET OUT ON OUR OWN, ISN'T IT?
IT'S ALMOST LIKE THEY DON'T TRUST US TO STAY OUT OF TROUBLE.
WHICH IS STUPID REALLY, ISN'T IT?
BECAUSE GETTING INTO TROUBLE IS WHAT WE'RE HERE FOR.
HELP! POLICE!
METROPOLITAN POLICE
METROPOLITAN POLICE

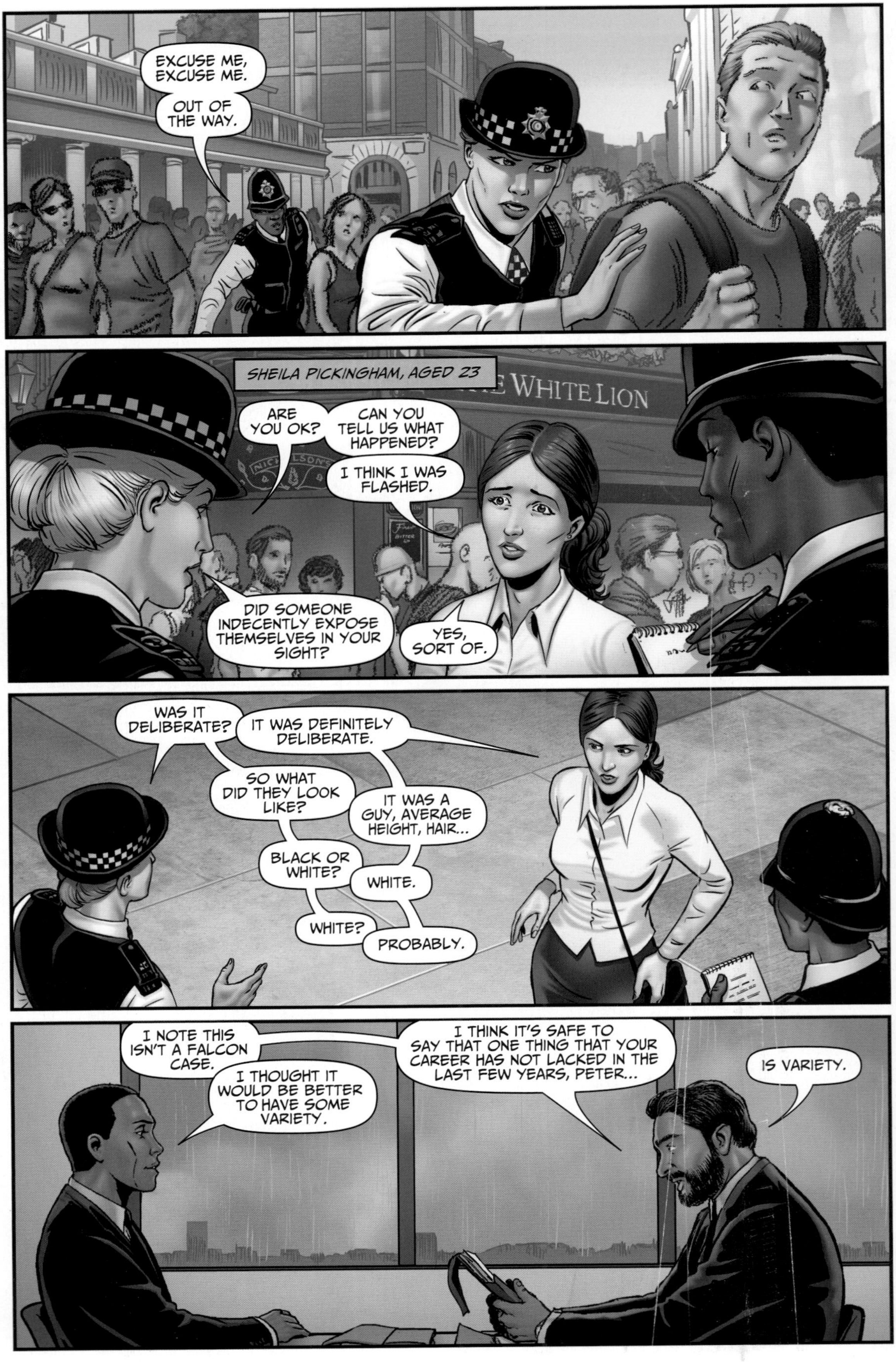

EXCUSE ME, EXCUSE ME.
OUT OF THE WAY.
SHEILA PICKINGHAM, AGED 23
THE WHITE LION
ARE YOU OK?
CAN YOU TELL US WHAT HAPPENED?
I THINK I WAS FLASHED.
DID SOMEONE INDECENTLY EXPOSE THEMSELVES IN YOUR SIGHT?
YES, SORT OF.
WAS IT DELIBERATE?
IT WAS DEFINITELY DELIBERATE.
SO WHAT DID THEY LOOK LIKE?
IT WAS A GUY, AVERAGE HEIGHT, HAIR...
BLACK OR WHITE?
WHITE.
WHITE?
PROBABLY.
I NOTE THIS ISN'T A FALCON CASE.
I THOUGHT IT WOULD BE BETTER TO HAVE SOME VARIETY.
I THINK IT'S SAFE TO SAY THAT ONE THING THAT YOUR CAREER HAS NOT LACKED IN THE LAST FEW YEARS, PETER...
IS VARIETY.

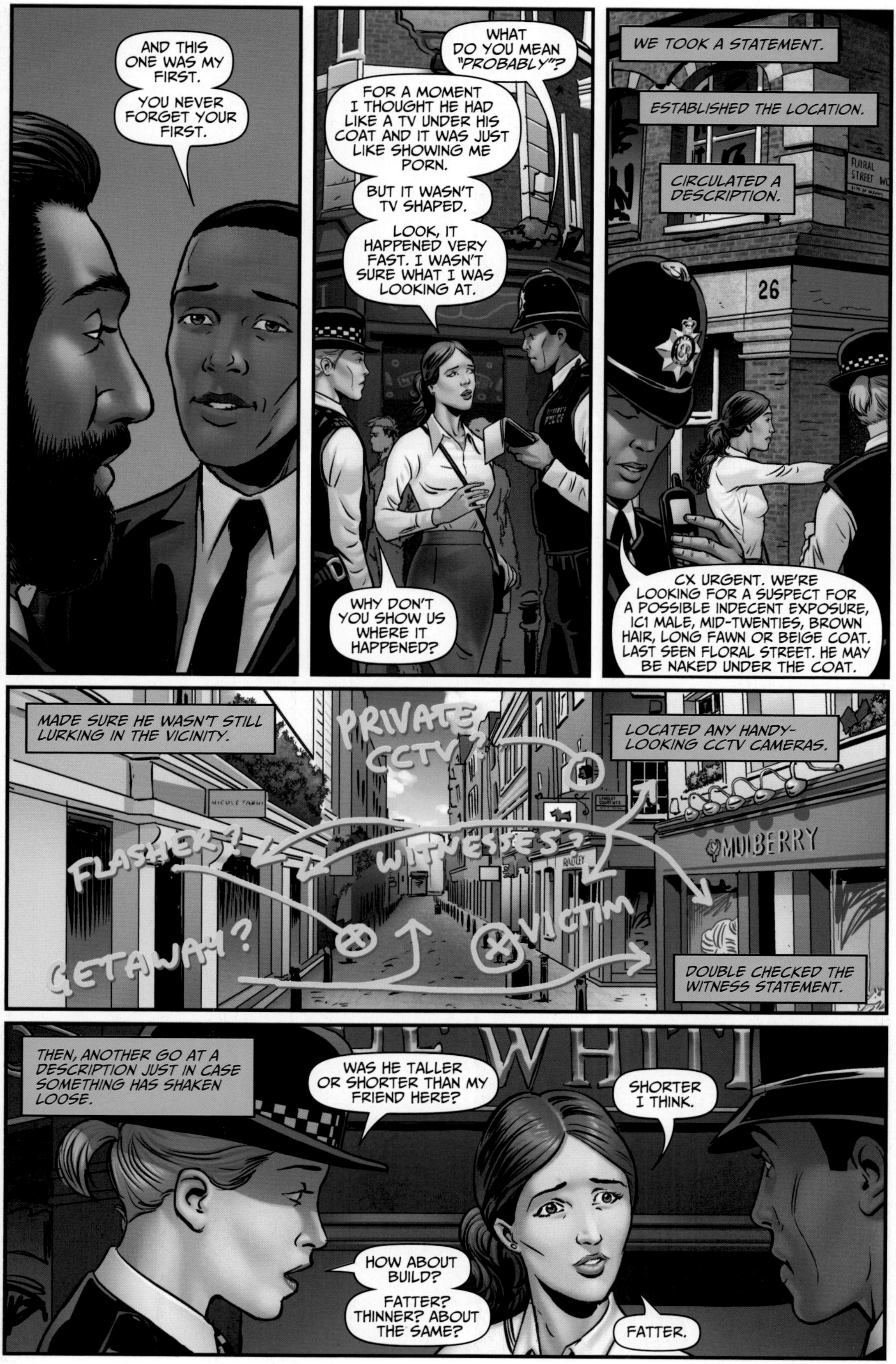
AND THIS ONE WAS MY FIRST.
YOU NEVER FORGET YOUR FIRST.
WHAT DO YOU MEAN "PROBABLY"?
FOR A MOMENT I THOUGHT HE HAD LIKE A TV UNDER HIS COAT AND IT WAS JUST LIKE SHOWING ME PORN.
BUT IT WASN'T TV SHAPED.
LOOK, IT HAPPENED VERY FAST. I WASN'T SURE WHAT I WAS LOOKING AT.
WHY DON'T YOU SHOW US WHERE IT HAPPENED?
WE TOOK A STATEMENT.
ESTABLISHED THE LOCATION.
CIRCULATED A DESCRIPTION.
FLORAL STREET
26
CX URGENT. WE'RE LOOKING FOR A SUSPECT FOR A POSSIBLE INDECENT EXPOSURE, IC1 MALE, MID-TWENTIES, BROWN HAIR, LONG FAWN OR BEIGE COAT. LAST SEEN FLORAL STREET. HE MAY BE NAKED UNDER THE COAT.
MADE SURE HE WASN'T STILL LURKING IN THE VICINITY.
PRIVATE CCTV?
LOCATED ANY HANDY-LOOKING CCTV CAMERAS.
NICOLE FARHI
FLASHER?
WITNESSES?
MULBERRY
RADLEY
VICTIM
GETAWAY?
DOUBLE CHECKED THE WITNESS STATEMENT.
THEN, ANOTHER GO AT A DESCRIPTION JUST IN CASE SOMETHING HAS SHAKEN LOOSE.
WAS HE TALLER OR SHORTER THAN MY FRIEND HERE?
SHORTER I THINK.
HOW ABOUT BUILD?
FATTER? THINNER? ABOUT THE SAME?
FATTER.

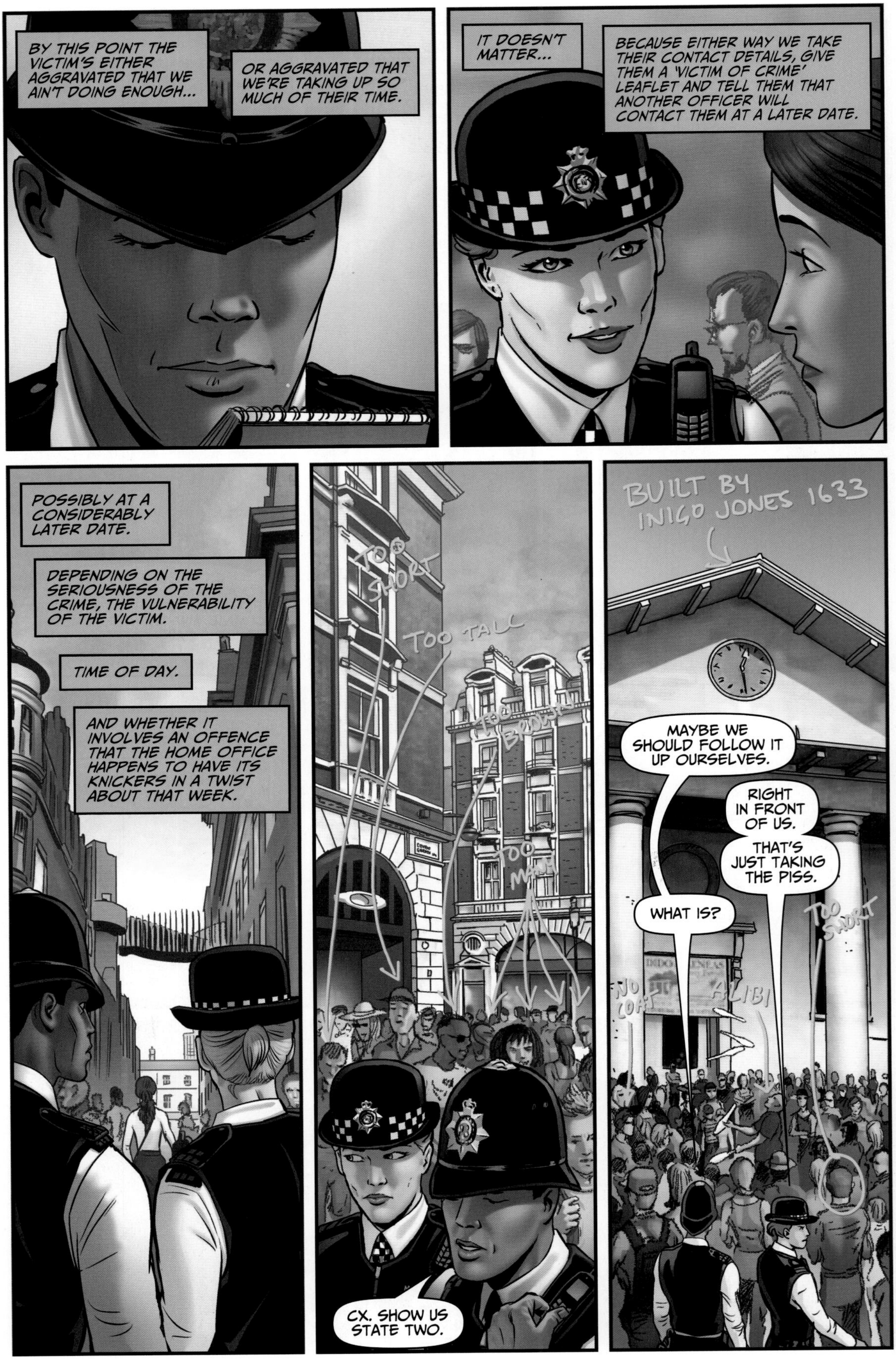
BY THIS POINT THE VICTIM'S EITHER AGGRAVATED THAT WE AIN'T DOING ENOUGH...
OR AGGRAVATED THAT WE'RE TAKING UP SO MUCH OF THEIR TIME.
IT DOESN'T MATTER...
BECAUSE EITHER WAY WE TAKE THEIR CONTACT DETAILS, GIVE THEM A 'VICTIM OF CRIME' LEAFLET AND TELL THEM THAT ANOTHER OFFICER WILL CONTACT THEM AT A LATER DATE.
POSSIBLY AT A CONSIDERABLY LATER DATE.
DEPENDING ON THE SERIOUSNESS OF THE CRIME, THE VULNERABILITY OF THE VICTIM.
TIME OF DAY.
AND WHETHER IT INVOLVES AN OFFENCE THAT THE HOME OFFICE HAPPENS TO HAVE ITS KNICKERS IN A TWIST ABOUT THAT WEEK.
TOO SHORT
TOO TALL
TOO BROWN
TOO MANY
CX. SHOW US STATE TWO.
BUILT BY INIGO JONES 1633
MAYBE WE SHOULD FOLLOW IT UP OURSELVES.
RIGHT IN FRONT OF US.
THAT'S JUST TAKING THE PISS.
WHAT IS?
TOO SHORT
NO COAT
ALIBI

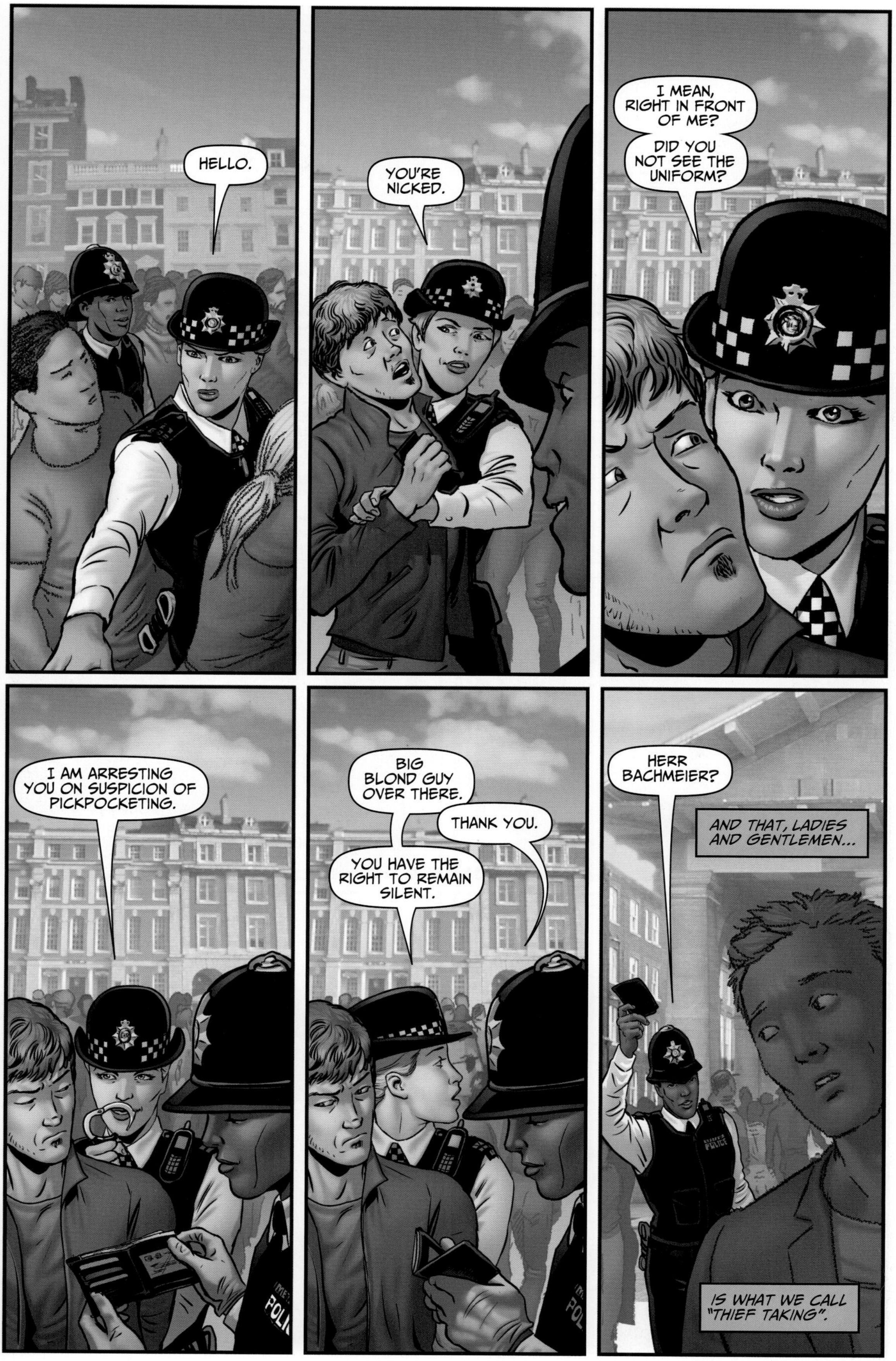
HELLO.
YOU'RE NICKED.
I MEAN, RIGHT IN FRONT OF ME?
DID YOU NOT SEE THE UNIFORM?
I AM ARRESTING YOU ON SUSPICION OF PICKPOCKETING.
BIG BLOND GUY OVER THERE.
THANK YOU.
YOU HAVE THE RIGHT TO REMAIN SILENT.
HERR BACHMEIER?
AND THAT, LADIES AND GENTLEMEN...
IS WHAT WE CALL "THIEF TAKING".

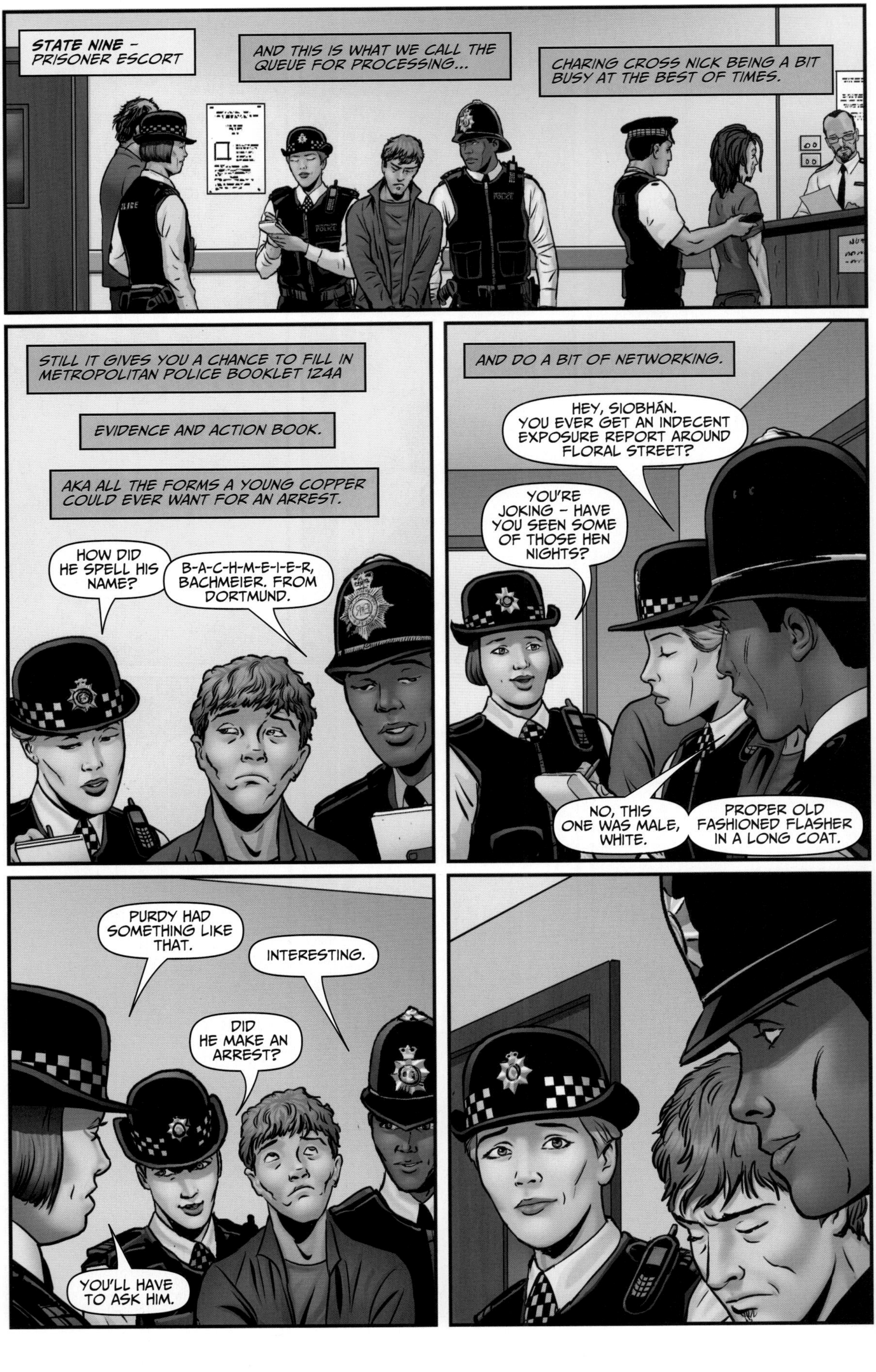
STATE NINE – PRISONER ESCORT
AND THIS IS WHAT WE CALL THE QUEUE FOR PROCESSING...
CHARING CROSS NICK BEING A BIT BUSY AT THE BEST OF TIMES.
STILL IT GIVES YOU A CHANCE TO FILL IN METROPOLITAN POLICE BOOKLET 124A
EVIDENCE AND ACTION BOOK.
AKA ALL THE FORMS A YOUNG COPPER COULD EVER WANT FOR AN ARREST.
HOW DID HE SPELL HIS NAME?
B-A-C-H-M-E-I-E-R, BACHMEIER. FROM DORTMUND.
AND DO A BIT OF NETWORKING.
HEY, SIOBHÁN. YOU EVER GET AN INDECENT EXPOSURE REPORT AROUND FLORAL STREET?
YOU'RE JOKING – HAVE YOU SEEN SOME OF THOSE HEN NIGHTS?
NO, THIS ONE WAS MALE, WHITE.
PROPER OLD FASHIONED FLASHER IN A LONG COAT.
PURDY HAD SOMETHING LIKE THAT.
INTERESTING.
DID HE MAKE AN ARREST?
YOU'LL HAVE TO ASK HIM.

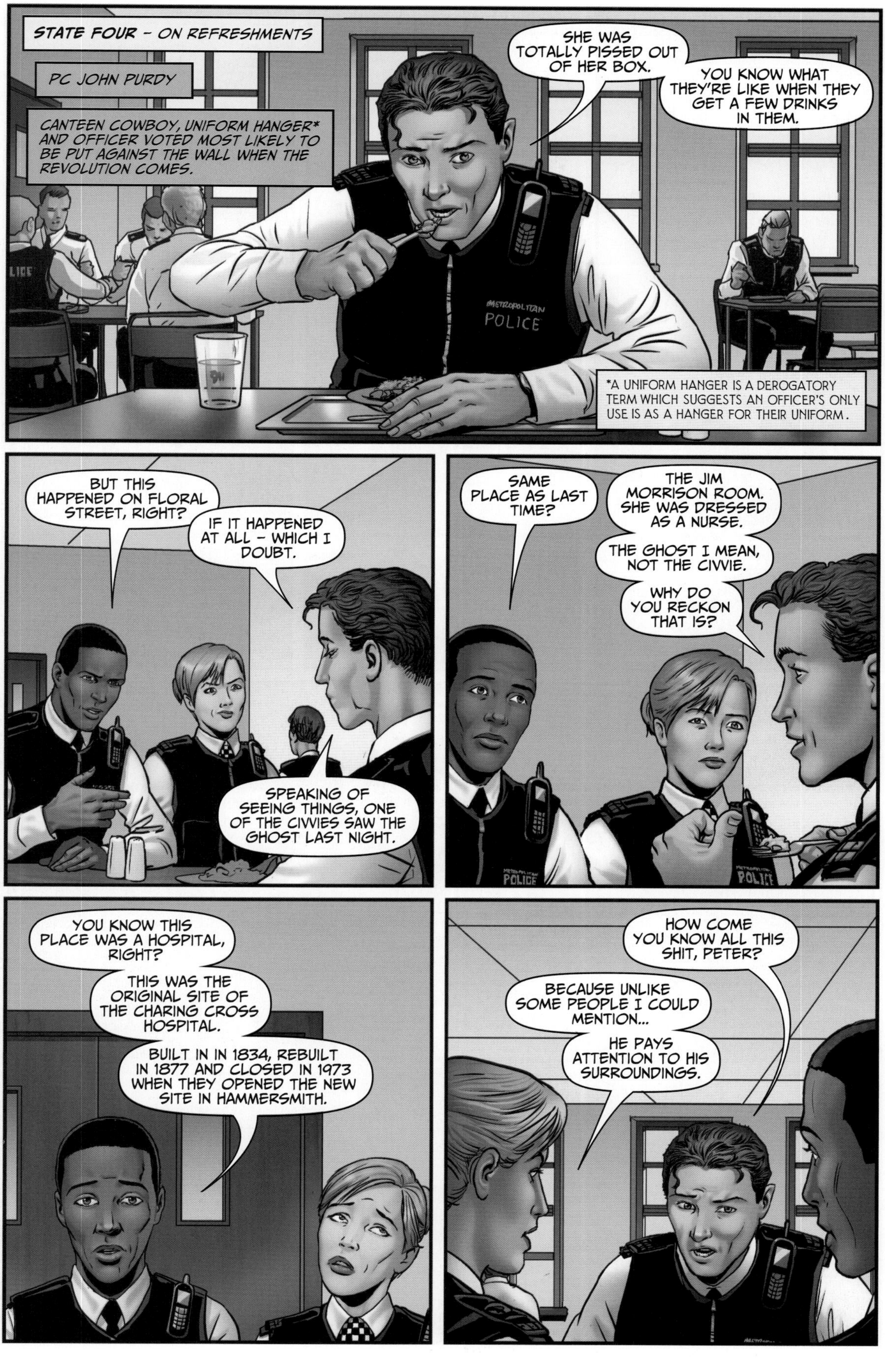
STATE FOUR - ON REFRESHMENTS
PC JOHN PURDY
CANTEEN COWBOY, UNIFORM HANGER* AND OFFICER VOTED MOST LIKELY TO BE PUT AGAINST THE WALL WHEN THE REVOLUTION COMES.
SHE WAS TOTALLY PISSED OUT OF HER BOX.
YOU KNOW WHAT THEY'RE LIKE WHEN THEY GET A FEW DRINKS IN THEM.
METROPOLITAN POLICE
*A UNIFORM HANGER IS A DEROGATORY TERM WHICH SUGGESTS AN OFFICER'S ONLY USE IS AS A HANGER FOR THEIR UNIFORM.
BUT THIS HAPPENED ON FLORAL STREET, RIGHT?
IF IT HAPPENED AT ALL - WHICH I DOUBT.
SPEAKING OF SEEING THINGS, ONE OF THE CIVVIES SAW THE GHOST LAST NIGHT.
SAME PLACE AS LAST TIME?
THE JIM MORRISON ROOM. SHE WAS DRESSED AS A NURSE.
THE GHOST I MEAN, NOT THE CIVVIE.
WHY DO YOU RECKON THAT IS?
YOU KNOW THIS PLACE WAS A HOSPITAL, RIGHT?
THIS WAS THE ORIGINAL SITE OF THE CHARING CROSS HOSPITAL.
BUILT IN IN 1834, REBUILT IN 1877 AND CLOSED IN 1973 WHEN THEY OPENED THE NEW SITE IN HAMMERSMITH.
HOW COME YOU KNOW ALL THIS SHIT, PETER?
BECAUSE UNLIKE SOME PEOPLE I COULD MENTION...
HE PAYS ATTENTION TO HIS SURROUNDINGS.

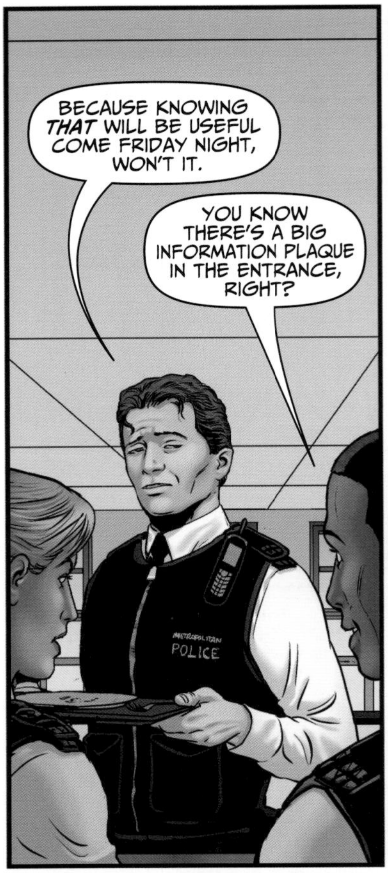
BECAUSE KNOWING THAT WILL BE USEFUL COME FRIDAY NIGHT, WON'T IT.
YOU KNOW THERE'S A BIG INFORMATION PLAQUE IN THE ENTRANCE, RIGHT?
METROPOLITAN POLICE

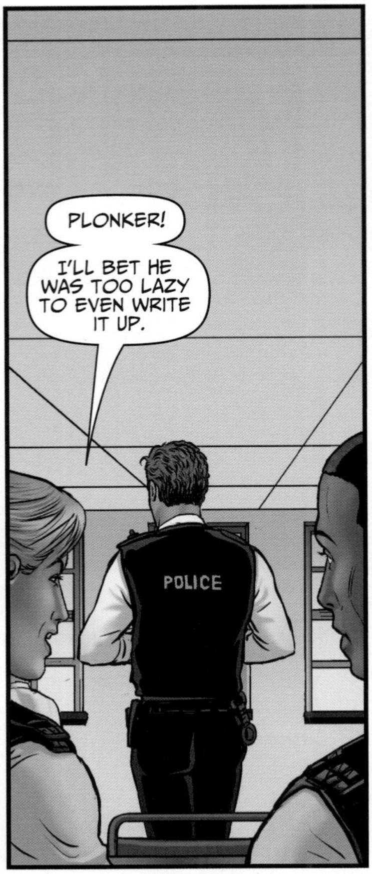
PLONKER!
I'LL BET HE WAS TOO LAZY TO EVEN WRITE IT UP.
POLICE

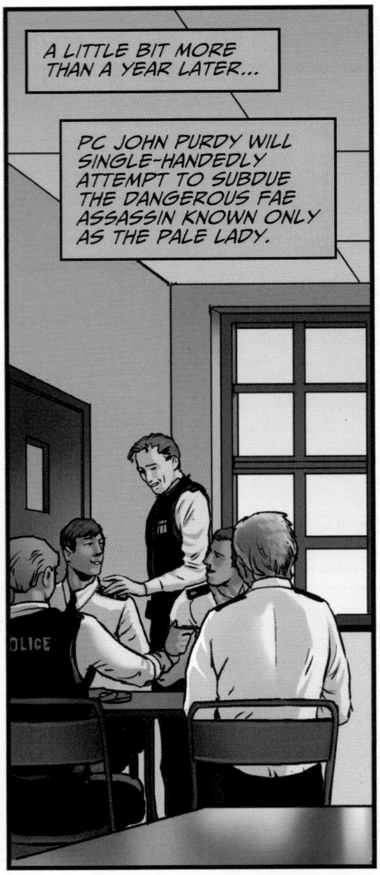
A LITTLE BIT MORE THAN A YEAR LATER...
PC JOHN PURDY WILL SINGLE-HANDEDLY ATTEMPT TO SUBDUE THE DANGEROUS FAE ASSASSIN KNOWN ONLY AS THE PALE LADY.
OLICE

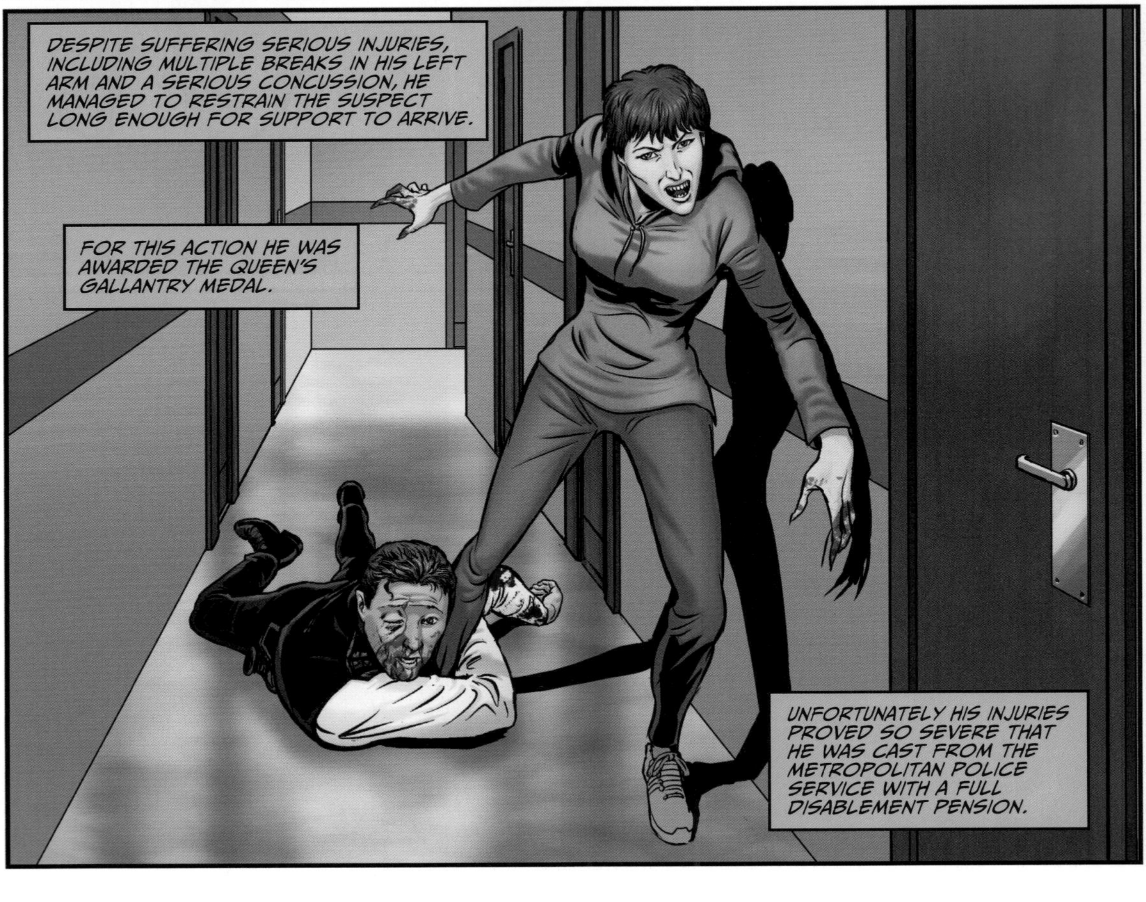
DESPITE SUFFERING SERIOUS INJURIES, INCLUDING MULTIPLE BREAKS IN HIS LEFT ARM AND A SERIOUS CONCUSSION, HE MANAGED TO RESTRAIN THE SUSPECT LONG ENOUGH FOR SUPPORT TO ARRIVE.
FOR THIS ACTION HE WAS AWARDED THE QUEEN'S GALLANTRY MEDAL.
UNFORTUNATELY HIS INJURIES PROVED SO SEVERE THAT HE WAS CAST FROM THE METROPOLITAN POLICE SERVICE WITH A FULL DISABLEMENT PENSION.

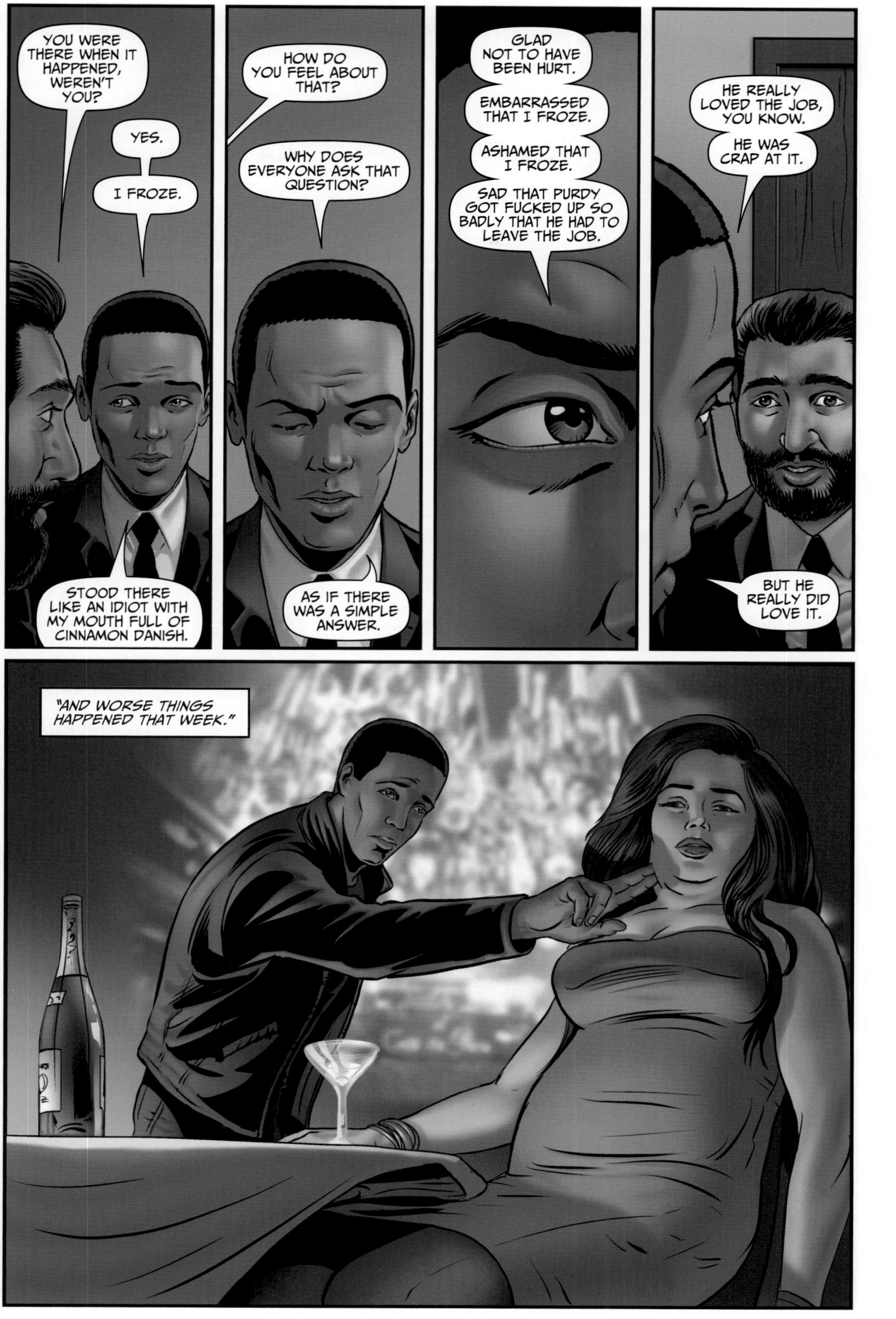
YOU WERE THERE WHEN IT HAPPENED, WEREN'T YOU?
YES.
I FROZE.
STOOD THERE LIKE AN IDIOT WITH MY MOUTH FULL OF CINNAMON DANISH.
HOW DO YOU FEEL ABOUT THAT?
WHY DOES EVERYONE ASK THAT QUESTION?
AS IF THERE WAS A SIMPLE ANSWER.
GLAD NOT TO HAVE BEEN HURT.
EMBARRASSED THAT I FROZE.
ASHAMED THAT I FROZE.
SAD THAT PURDY GOT FUCKED UP SO BADLY THAT HE HAD TO LEAVE THE JOB.
HE REALLY LOVED THE JOB, YOU KNOW.
HE WAS CRAP AT IT.
BUT HE REALLY DID LOVE IT.
"AND WORSE THINGS HAPPENED THAT WEEK."

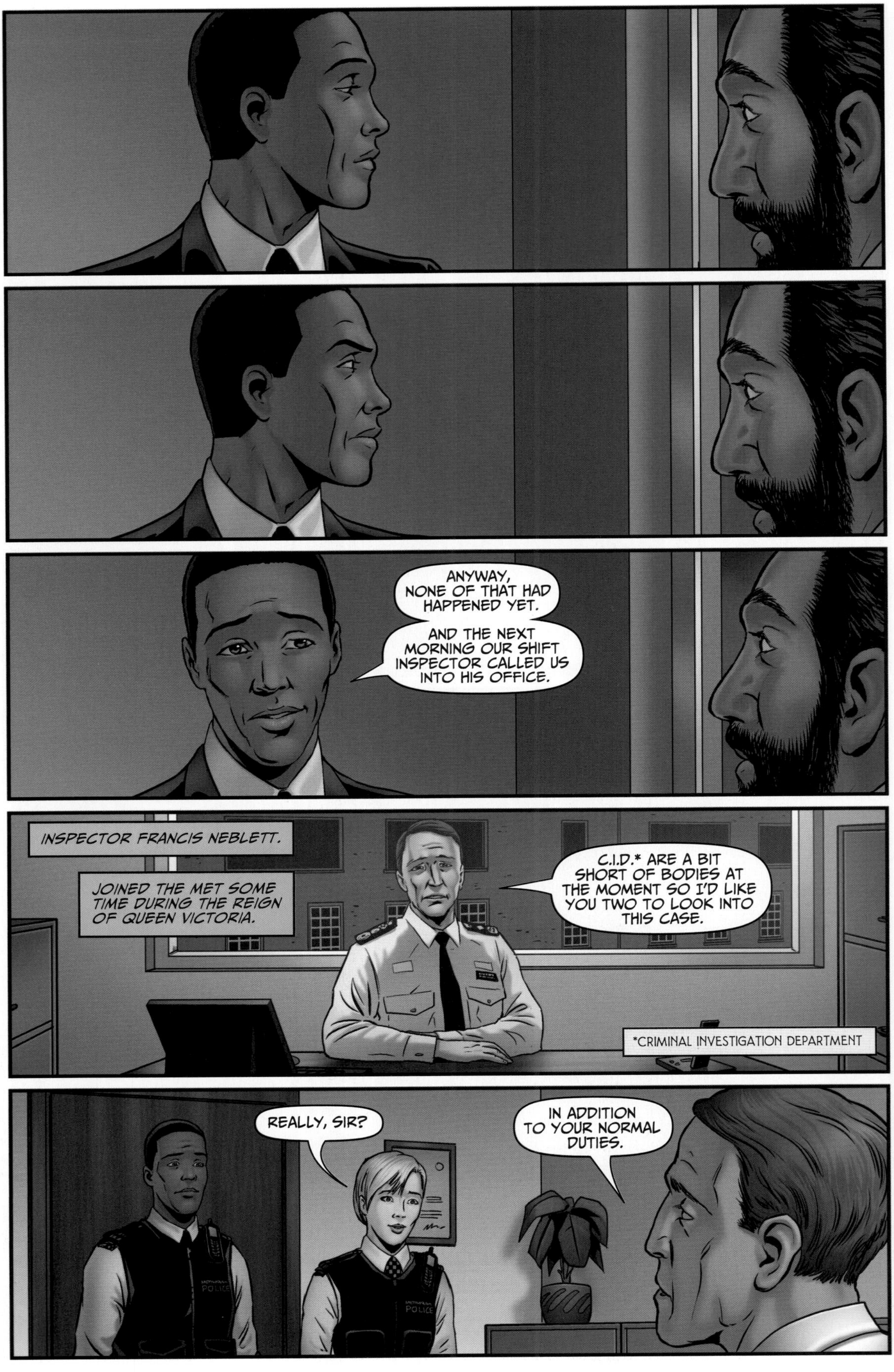
ANYWAY, NONE OF THAT HAD HAPPENED YET.
AND THE NEXT MORNING OUR SHIFT INSPECTOR CALLED US INTO HIS OFFICE.
INSPECTOR FRANCIS NEBLETT.
JOINED THE MET SOME TIME DURING THE REIGN OF QUEEN VICTORIA.
C.I.D.* ARE A BIT SHORT OF BODIES AT THE MOMENT SO I'D LIKE YOU TWO TO LOOK INTO THIS CASE.
*CRIMINAL INVESTIGATION DEPARTMENT
REALLY, SIR?
IN ADDITION TO YOUR NORMAL DUTIES.

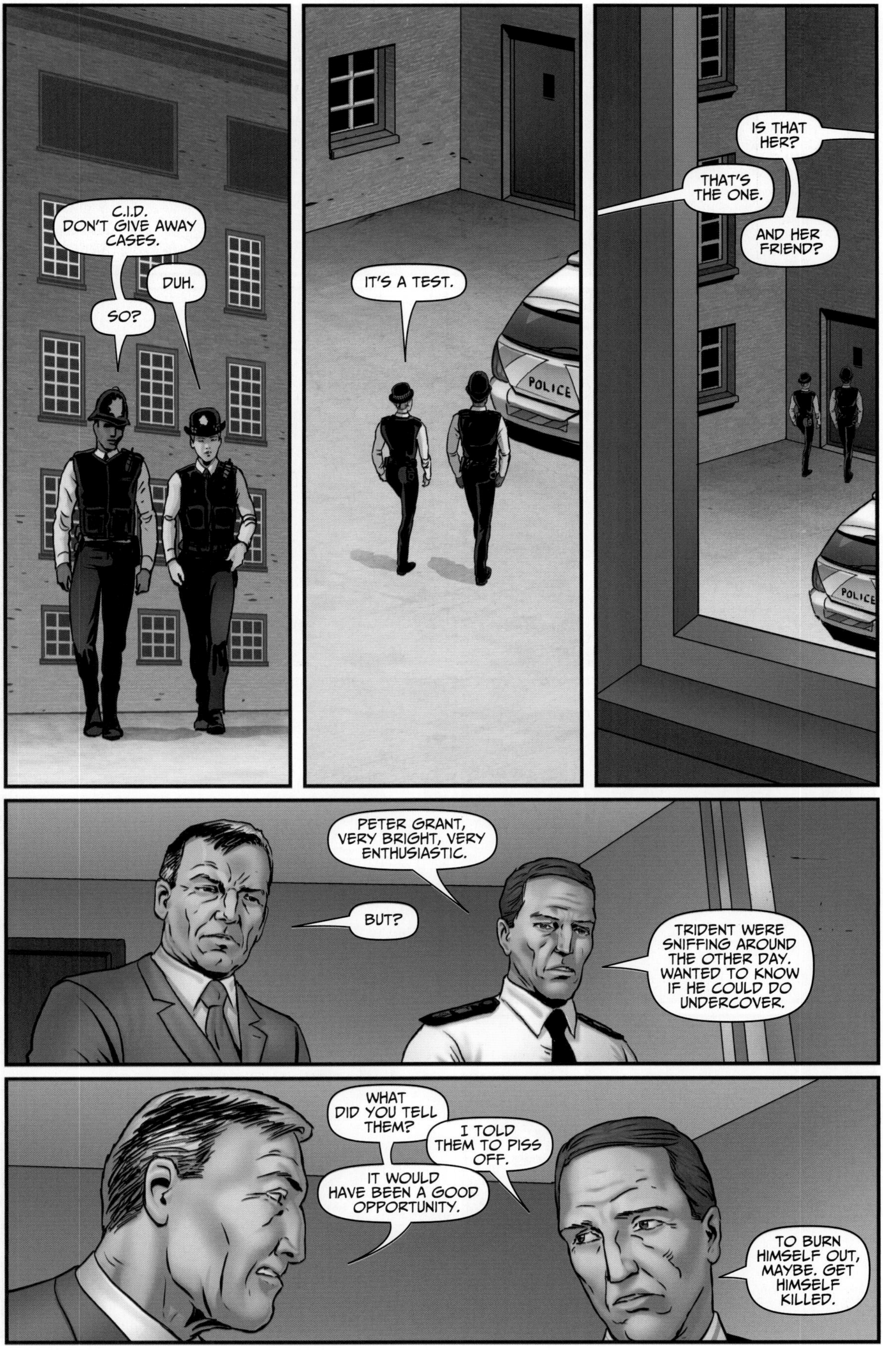
C.I.D. DON'T GIVE AWAY CASES.
SO?
DUH.
IT'S A TEST.
POLICE
IS THAT HER?
THAT'S THE ONE.
AND HER FRIEND?
POLICE
PETER GRANT, VERY BRIGHT, VERY ENTHUSIASTIC.
BUT?
TRIDENT WERE SNIFFING AROUND THE OTHER DAY. WANTED TO KNOW IF HE COULD DO UNDERCOVER.
WHAT DID YOU TELL THEM?
I TOLD THEM TO PISS OFF.
IT WOULD HAVE BEEN A GOOD OPPORTUNITY.
TO BURN HIMSELF OUT, MAYBE. GET HIMSELF KILLED.

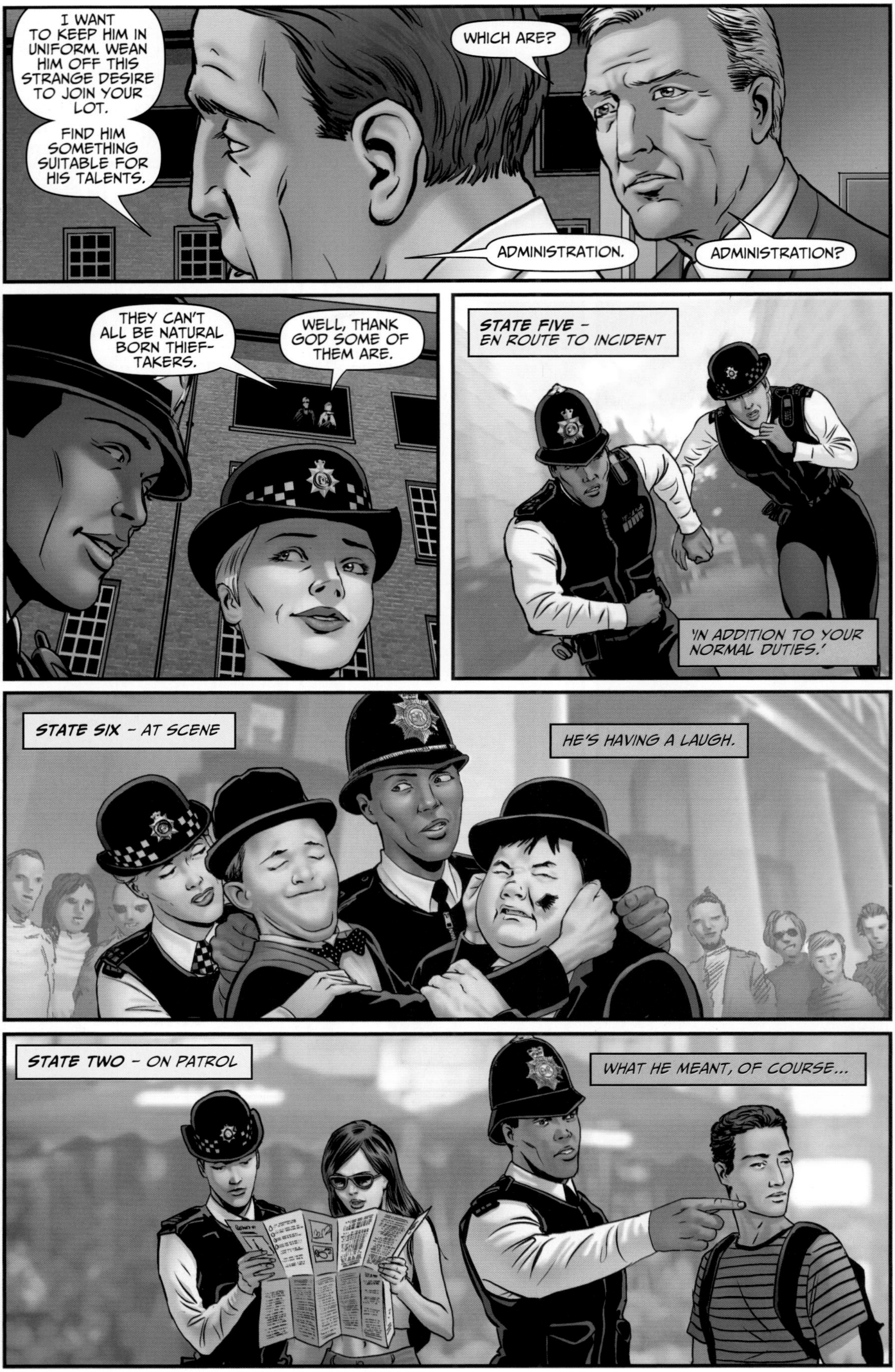
I WANT TO KEEP HIM IN UNIFORM. WEAN HIM OFF THIS STRANGE DESIRE TO JOIN YOUR LOT.
FIND HIM SOMETHING SUITABLE FOR HIS TALENTS.
WHICH ARE?
ADMINISTRATION.
ADMINISTRATION?
THEY CAN'T ALL BE NATURAL BORN THIEF-TAKERS.
WELL, THANK GOD SOME OF THEM ARE.
STATE FIVE – EN ROUTE TO INCIDENT
'IN ADDITION TO YOUR NORMAL DUTIES.'
STATE SIX – AT SCENE
HE'S HAVING A LAUGH.
STATE TWO – ON PATROL
WHAT HE MEANT, OF COURSE...

STATE FOUR – ON REFRESHMENTS

WAS DO IT IN YOUR FREE TIME.

WHICH IS A BIT OF A LIBERTY, BUT THEN AGAIN...

AWARE TERMINALS

WE WERE YOUNG.

WHAT ELSE WERE WE GOING TO DO WITH OUR FREE TIME?

LESLEY WAS RIGHT. PURDY HADN'T LOGGED A CRIME REPORT.

BUT THERE HAD BEEN OTHER COMPLAINTS AND THEY'D ALL ENDED UP ON CRIS.*

*CRIME REPORT INFORMATION SYSTEM

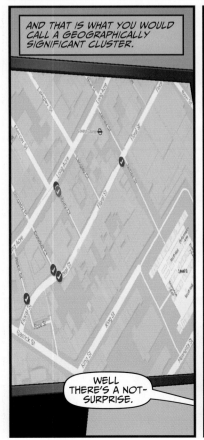

AND THAT IS WHAT YOU WOULD CALL A GEOGRAPHICALLY SIGNIFICANT CLUSTER.

WELL THERE'S A NOT-SURPRISE.

BUT CHECK THE INCIDENT TIMES.

THEY ALL TAKE PLACE BETWEEN 11:30 AND 2:00 PM...

WHICH SUGGESTS...

SOMEBODY'S BEING NAUGHTY DURING THEIR LUNCH HOUR.

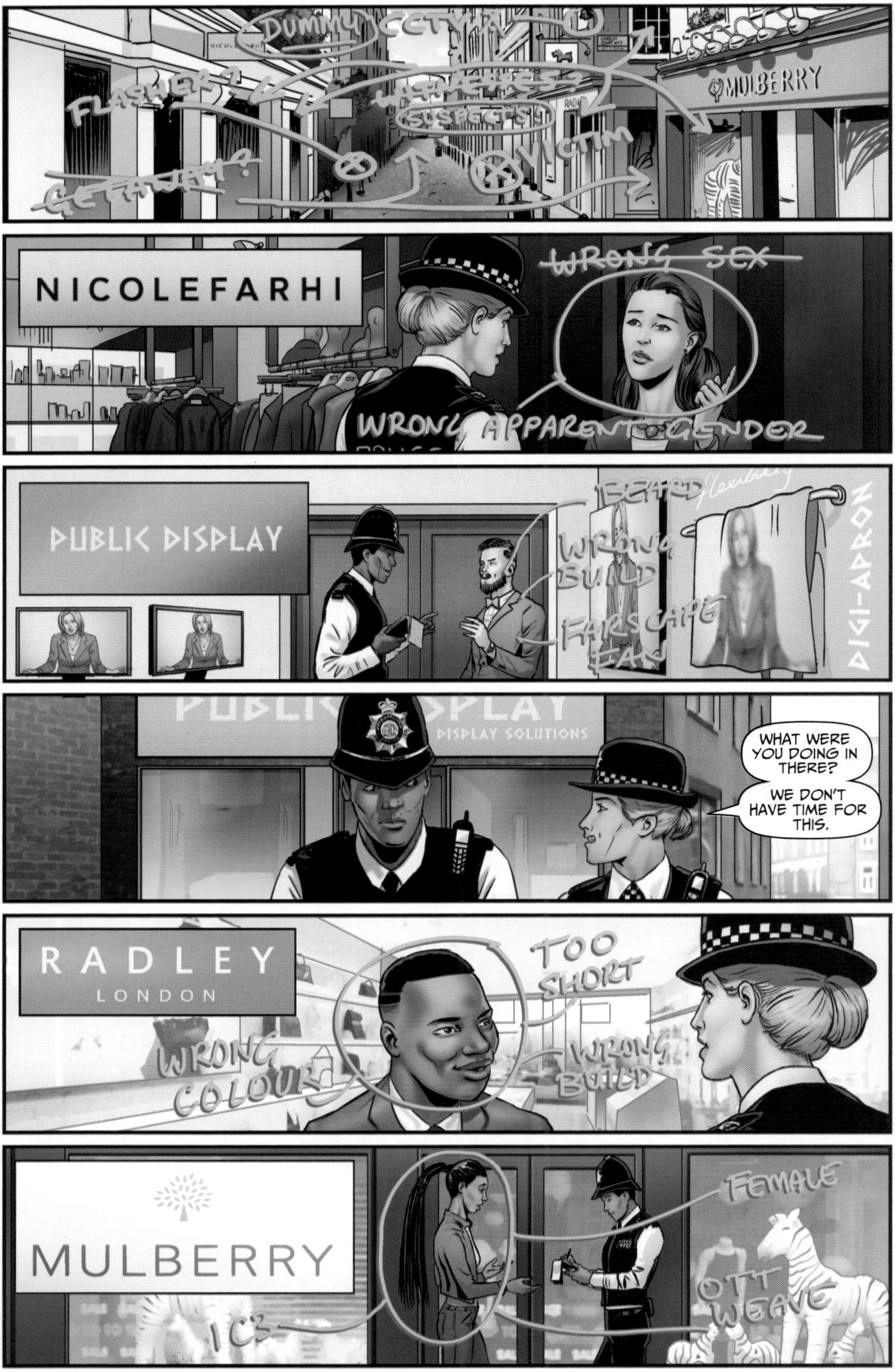
DUMMY CCTV
FLASHER?
WITNESSES?
SUSPECTS?
VICTIM
GETAWAY?
MULBERRY
NICOLEFARHI
WRONG SEX
WRONG APPARENT GENDER
PUBLIC DISPLAY
BEARD
Flexibility
WRONG BUILD
FARSCAPE FAN
DIGI-APRON
PUBLIC DISPLAY
DISPLAY SOLUTIONS
WHAT WERE YOU DOING IN THERE?
WE DON'T HAVE TIME FOR THIS.
RADLEY
LONDON
TOO SHORT
WRONG COLOUR
WRONG BUILD
MULBERRY
FEMALE
OTT WEAVE
IC3

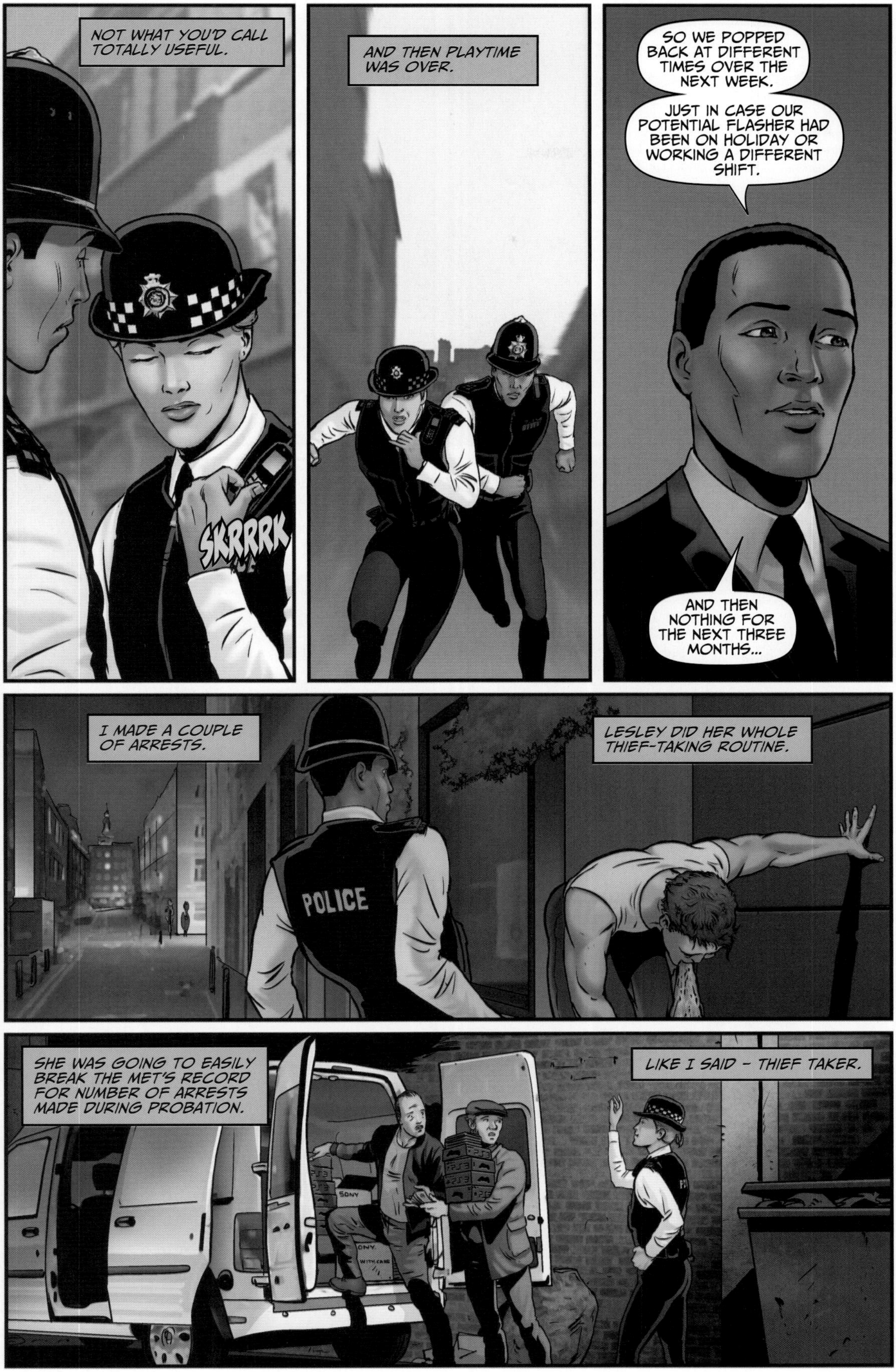
NOT WHAT YOU'D CALL TOTALLY USEFUL.
SKRRRK
AND THEN PLAYTIME WAS OVER.
SO WE POPPED BACK AT DIFFERENT TIMES OVER THE NEXT WEEK.
JUST IN CASE OUR POTENTIAL FLASHER HAD BEEN ON HOLIDAY OR WORKING A DIFFERENT SHIFT.
AND THEN NOTHING FOR THE NEXT THREE MONTHS...
I MADE A COUPLE OF ARRESTS.
POLICE
LESLEY DID HER WHOLE THIEF-TAKING ROUTINE.
SHE WAS GOING TO EASILY BREAK THE MET'S RECORD FOR NUMBER OF ARRESTS MADE DURING PROBATION.
LIKE I SAID - THIEF TAKER.

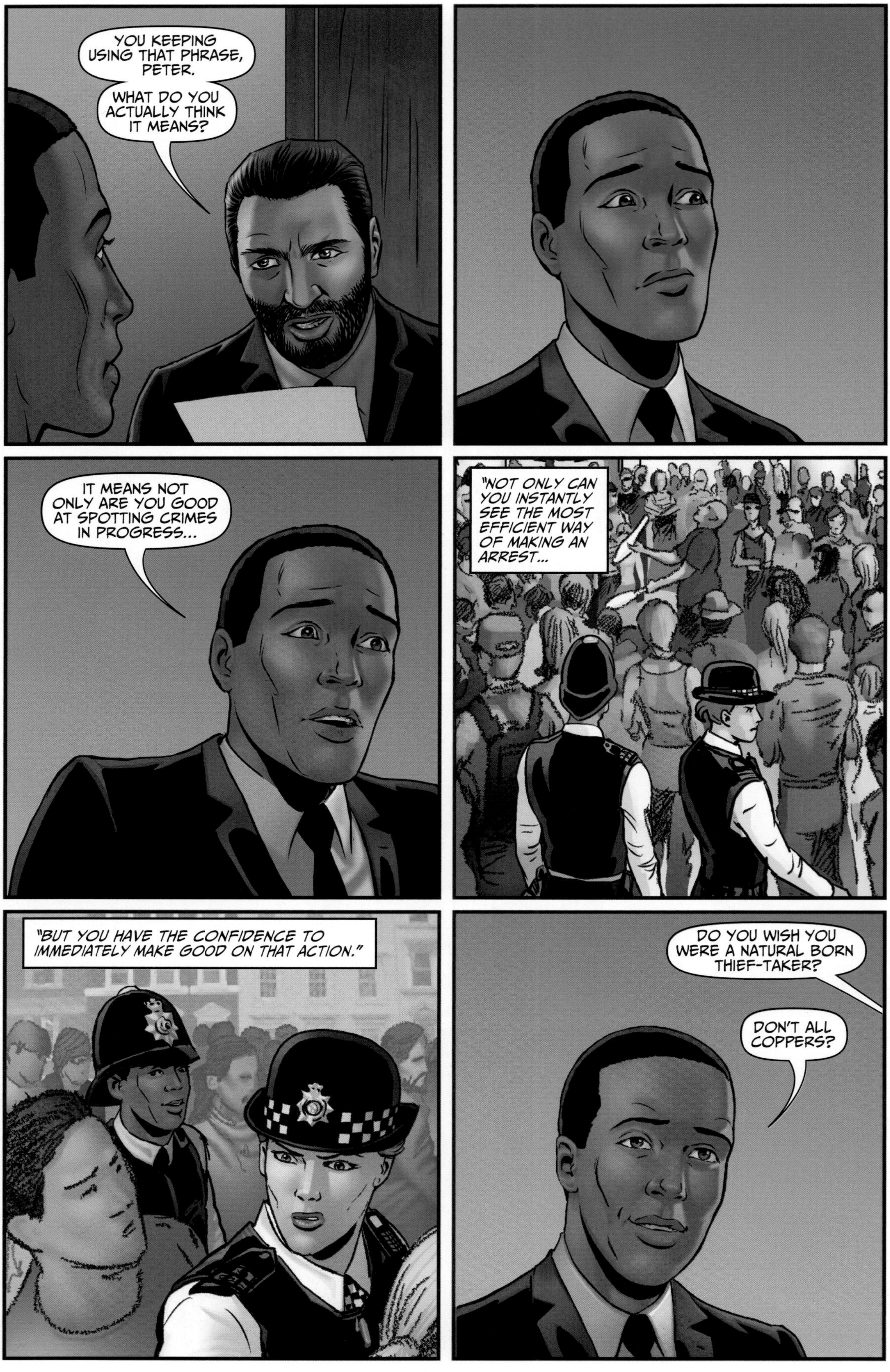
YOU KEEPING USING THAT PHRASE, PETER.
WHAT DO YOU ACTUALLY THINK IT MEANS?
IT MEANS NOT ONLY ARE YOU GOOD AT SPOTTING CRIMES IN PROGRESS...
"NOT ONLY CAN YOU INSTANTLY SEE THE MOST EFFICIENT WAY OF MAKING AN ARREST...
"BUT YOU HAVE THE CONFIDENCE TO IMMEDIATELY MAKE GOOD ON THAT ACTION."
DO YOU WISH YOU WERE A NATURAL BORN THIEF-TAKER?
DON'T ALL COPPERS?

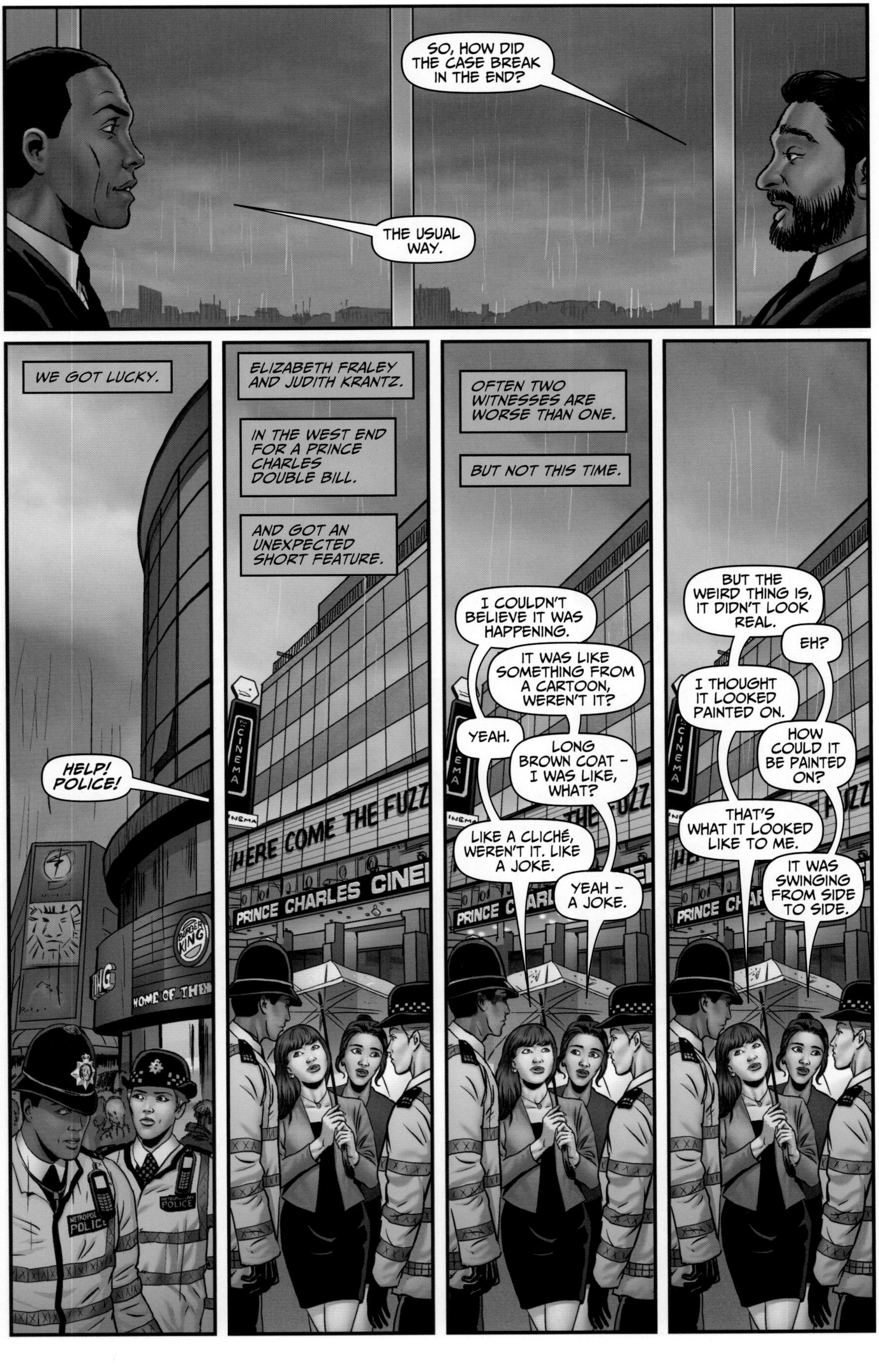

SO, HOW DID THE CASE BREAK IN THE END?
THE USUAL WAY.
WE GOT LUCKY.
HELP! POLICE!
HOME OF THE
ELIZABETH FRALEY AND JUDITH KRANTZ.
IN THE WEST END FOR A PRINCE CHARLES DOUBLE BILL.
AND GOT AN UNEXPECTED SHORT FEATURE.
HERE COME THE FUZZ
PRINCE CHARLES CINE
OFTEN TWO WITNESSES ARE WORSE THAN ONE.
BUT NOT THIS TIME.
I COULDN'T BELIEVE IT WAS HAPPENING.
IT WAS LIKE SOMETHING FROM A CARTOON, WEREN'T IT?
YEAH.
LONG BROWN COAT – I WAS LIKE, WHAT?
LIKE A CLICHÉ, WEREN'T IT. LIKE A JOKE.
YEAH – A JOKE.
BUT THE WEIRD THING IS, IT DIDN'T LOOK REAL.
EH?
I THOUGHT IT LOOKED PAINTED ON.
HOW COULD IT BE PAINTED ON?
THAT'S WHAT IT LOOKED LIKE TO ME.
IT WAS SWINGING FROM SIDE TO SIDE.

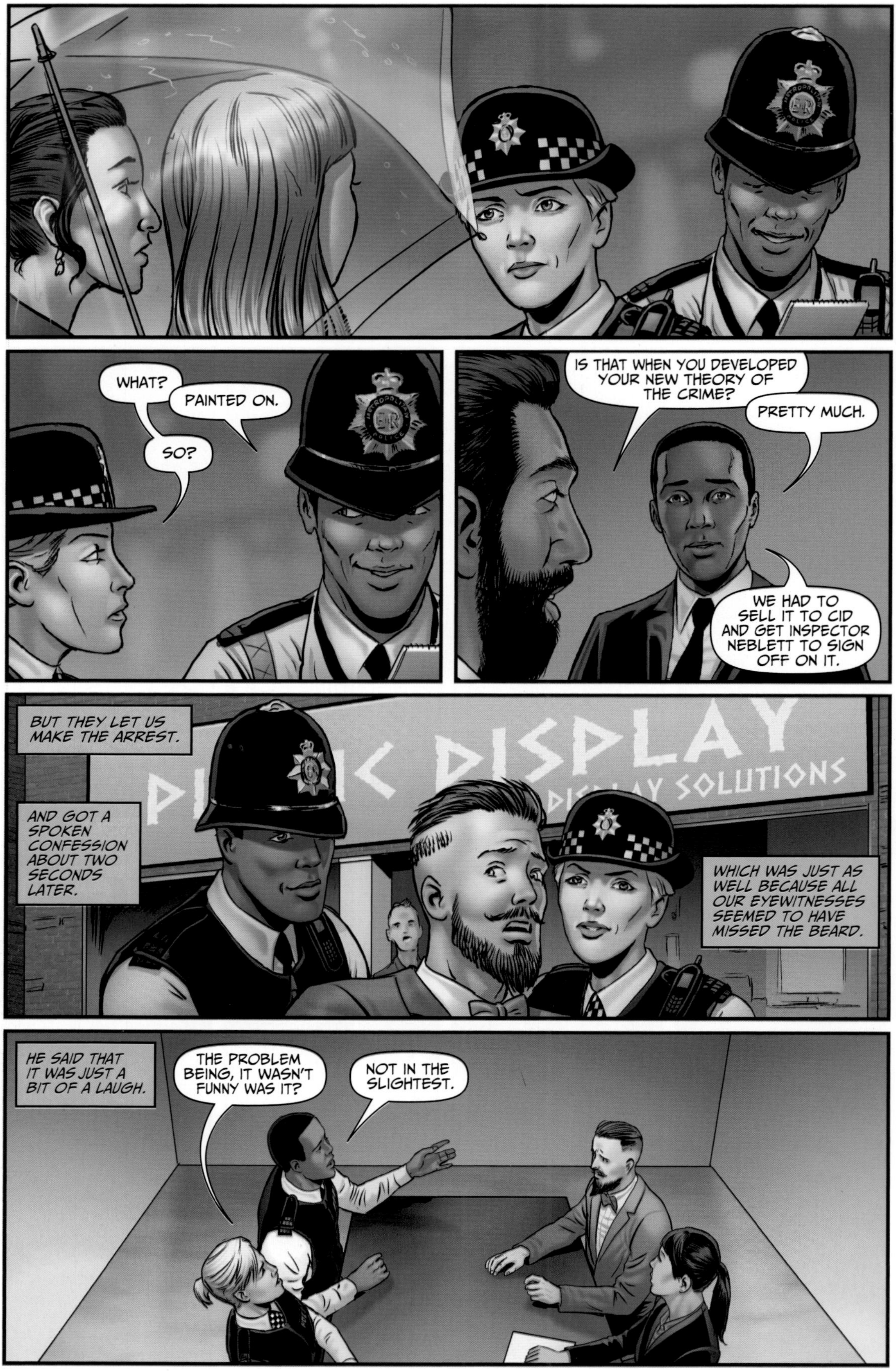

WHAT?
PAINTED ON.
SO?
IS THAT WHEN YOU DEVELOPED YOUR NEW THEORY OF THE CRIME?
PRETTY MUCH.
WE HAD TO SELL IT TO CID AND GET INSPECTOR NEBLETT TO SIGN OFF ON IT.
BUT THEY LET US MAKE THE ARREST.
DISPLAY
DISPLAY SOLUTIONS
AND GOT A SPOKEN CONFESSION ABOUT TWO SECONDS LATER.
WHICH WAS JUST AS WELL BECAUSE ALL OUR EYEWITNESSES SEEMED TO HAVE MISSED THE BEARD.
HE SAID THAT IT WAS JUST A BIT OF A LAUGH.
THE PROBLEM BEING, IT WASN'T FUNNY WAS IT?
NOT IN THE SLIGHTEST.

WHICH WAS A LIE.

IT **WAS** A BIT FUNNY.

A DIGITAL APRON. CYBERFLASHING. WHAT A MARVELLOUS MODERN AGE WE LIVE IN.

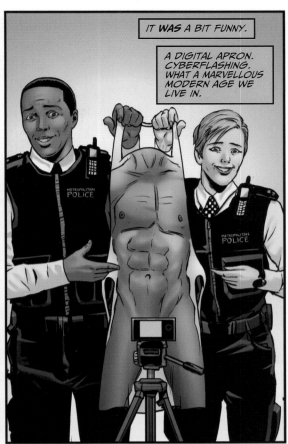

WHAT NOBODY COULD FIGURE OUT WAS WHETHER, TECHNICALLY, IT WAS AN OFFENCE.

BUT FORTUNATELY THAT WAS A PROBLEM FOR THE CPS*, NOT US.

AND WE GOT TO CALL SHEILA PICKINGHAM AND TELL HER WE'D CAUGHT THE GUY WHO SCARED HER.

*CROWN PROSECUTION SERVICE

BECAUSE WHAT PEOPLE REALLY WANT TO KNOW...

IS THAT SOMEBODY GIVES A SHIT.

PARDON MY FRENCH.

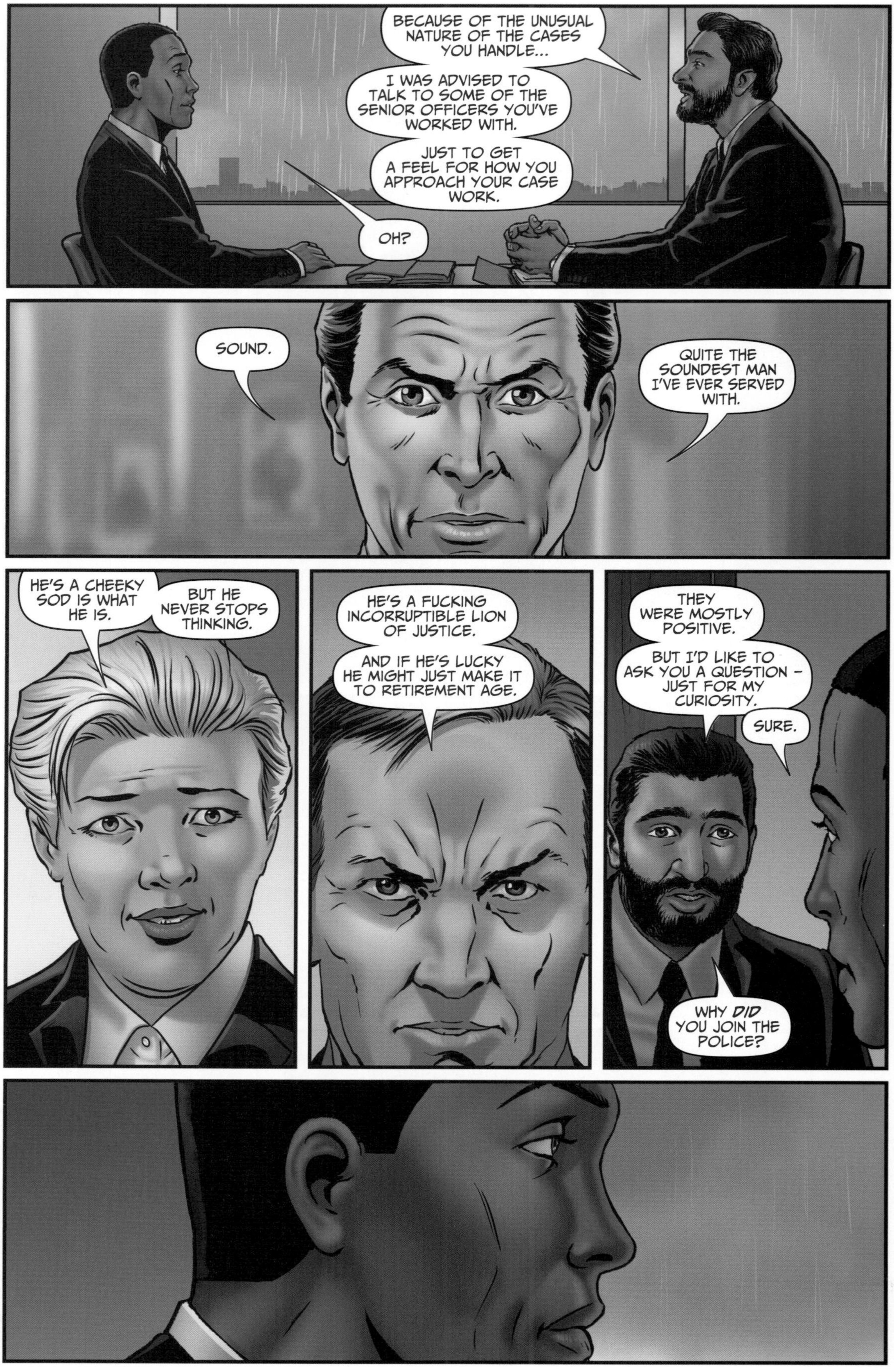
BECAUSE OF THE UNUSUAL NATURE OF THE CASES YOU HANDLE...
I WAS ADVISED TO TALK TO SOME OF THE SENIOR OFFICERS YOU'VE WORKED WITH.
JUST TO GET A FEEL FOR HOW YOU APPROACH YOUR CASE WORK.
OH?
SOUND.
QUITE THE SOUNDEST MAN I'VE EVER SERVED WITH.
HE'S A CHEEKY SOD IS WHAT HE IS.
BUT HE NEVER STOPS THINKING.
HE'S A FUCKING INCORRUPTIBLE LION OF JUSTICE.
AND IF HE'S LUCKY HE MIGHT JUST MAKE IT TO RETIREMENT AGE.
THEY WERE MOSTLY POSITIVE.
BUT I'D LIKE TO ASK YOU A QUESTION – JUST FOR MY CURIOSITY.
SURE.
WHY *DID* YOU JOIN THE POLICE?

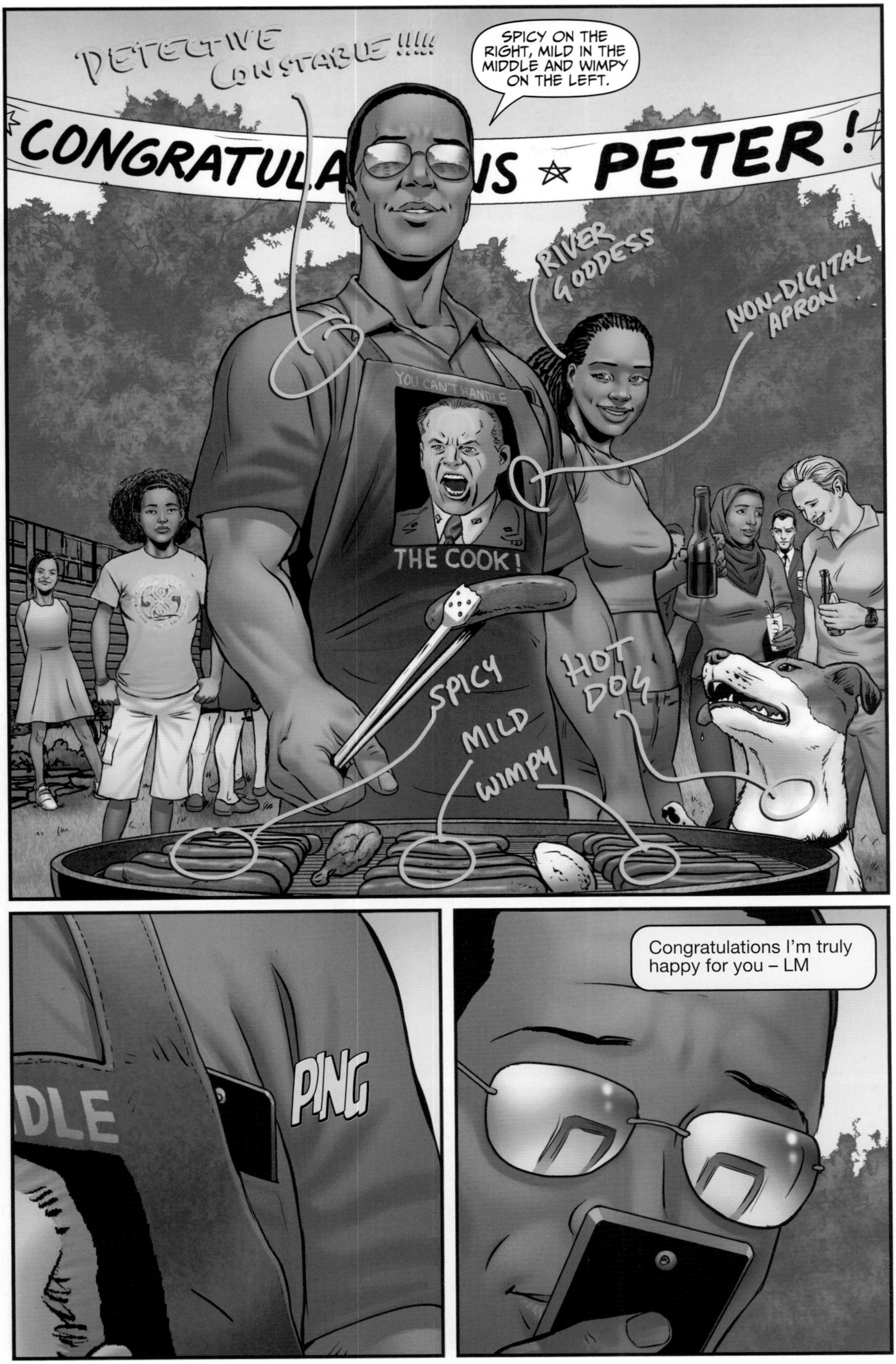
SPICY ON THE RIGHT, MILD IN THE MIDDLE AND WIMPY ON THE LEFT.
DETECTIVE CONSTABLE!!!!!
CONGRATULA NS ★ PETER!
RIVER GODDESS
NON-DIGITAL APRON
YOU CAN'T HANDLE
THE COOK!
SPICY
MILD
WIMPY
HOT DOG
DLE
PING
Congratulations I'm truly happy for you – LM

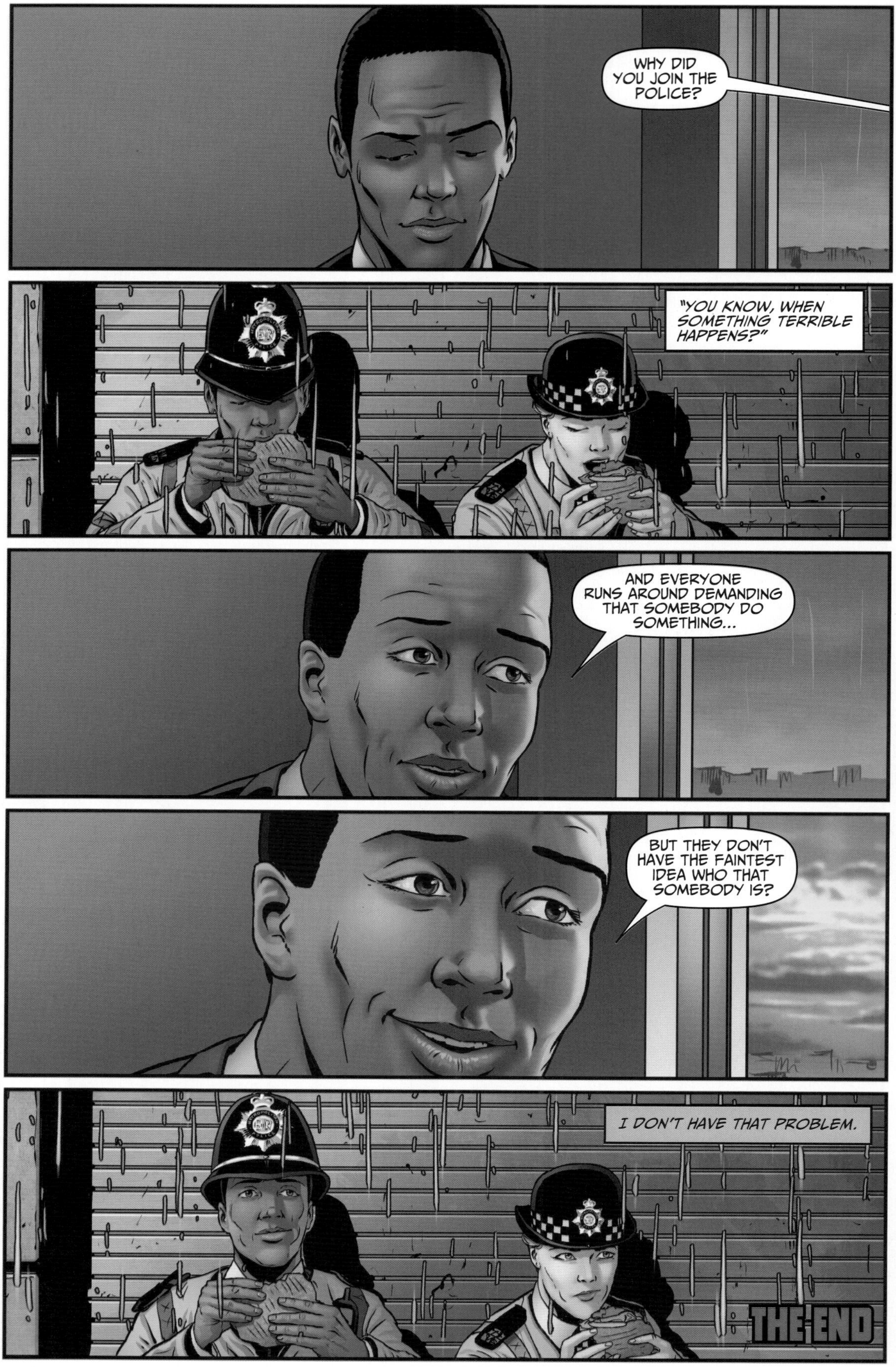
WHY DID YOU JOIN THE POLICE?
"YOU KNOW, WHEN SOMETHING TERRIBLE HAPPENS?"
AND EVERYONE RUNS AROUND DEMANDING THAT SOMEBODY DO SOMETHING...
BUT THEY DON'T HAVE THE FAINTEST IDEA WHO THAT SOMEBODY IS?
I DON'T HAVE THAT PROBLEM.
THE END

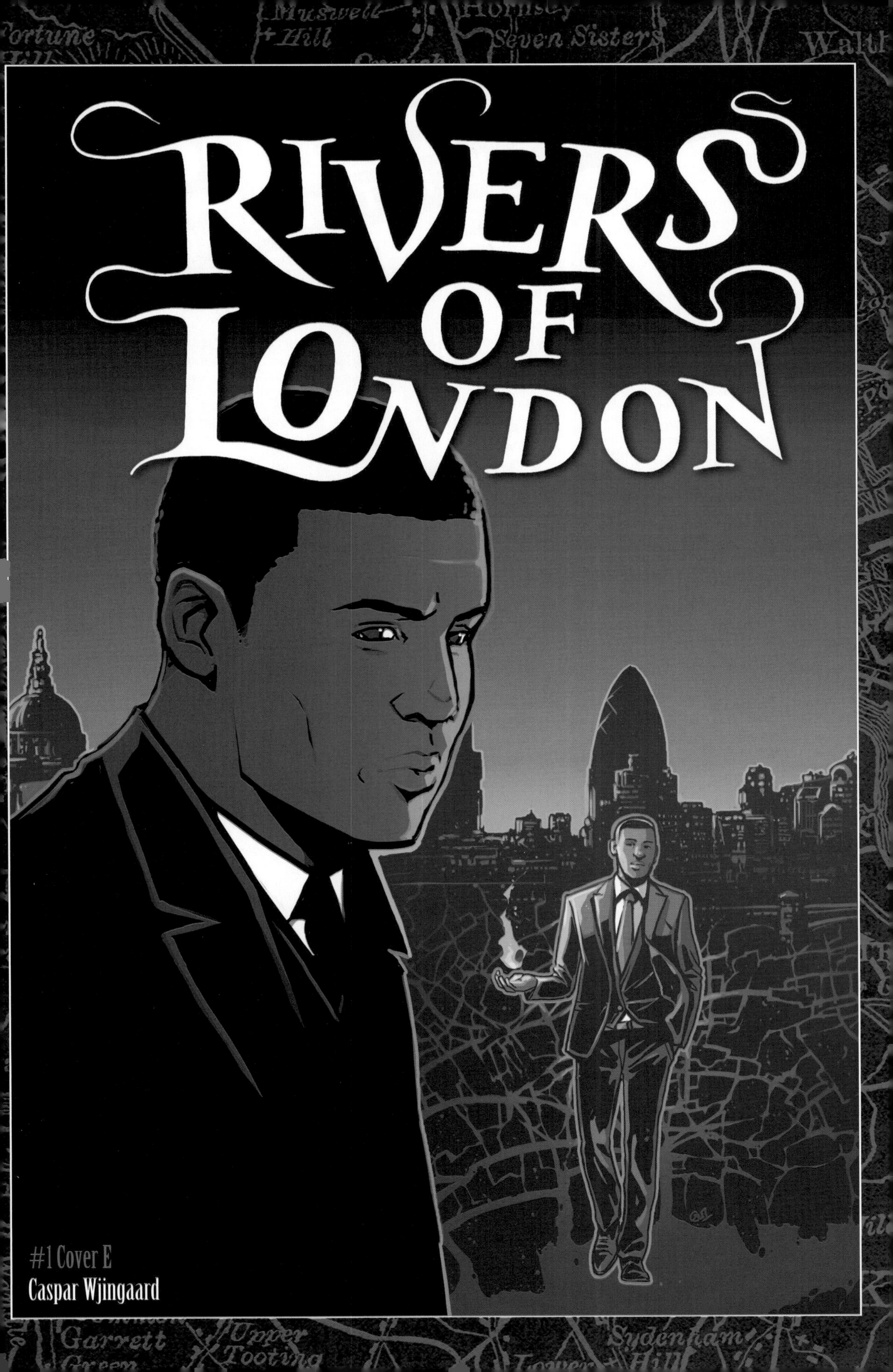
Muswell Hill
Seven Sisters
RIVERS OF LONDON
#1 Cover E
Caspar Wjingaard
Garrett
Upper Tooting
Sydenham Hill

PEELERS
A VERY BRIEF HISTORY OF THE MET

"If my profession – that's thief catcher, not wizard – could be said to have started anywhere in London, then it started in Bow Street with Henry Fielding, magistrate, satirical author, and founder of what came to be known as the Bow Street Runners." – **Peter Grant**

Known by many as the rozzers or the peelers (for reasons that will become apparent), the Met, or by the Metropolitan Police Service, was established by the Metropolitan Police act in 1829, but who were the proto-rozzers?

The definition of policing is to ensure that people keep the peace and obey the law. The definition of a policeman is such persons given power/authority by the state to enforce the law, protect property, and prevent civil disorder. The actual concept of policing originates with the Saxons, with appointed representatives given the responsibility of maintaining order and ensuring tribal customs were followed.

This developed into a 'tything' system, with one man in every ten becoming a group representative or 'tything-man'; ten tythings were grouped into ten with their joint representative a 'hundred-man', who reported to the 'Shire-reeve' – or county Sheriff.

When the Normans came in and introduced feudalism to the mix, the tything-man gradually evolved into the parish constable, and his boss, the sheriff, became the local Justice of the Peace. Parish constables were elected or appointed men of the parish who served for a year, undertaking their law enforcement role on a voluntary basis as a public service.

Bow Street

Bow Street Court

In larger towns, supplementary enforcement fell to the guilds or other citizen groups, and town Watches were raised for the purposes of guarding the entrance to the settlement and patrolling the streets at night.

There were massive socio-economic changes in the 18th Century that led to considerable population growth and movement into towns and cities. The system of parish constables and Watches was never particularly well-organised, and was failing to cope with the increased demand that the social changes brought. Plus, criminal investigation – as we would recognise it today – varied from ad-hoc to non-existent.

Generally, private individuals who'd been the victim of a crime – and who could afford to – would hire a 'thief-taker' (a bit like a bounty hunter) to track down the perpetrator and bring him to an official representative of the law such as a parish constable or Watchman. But there was no official regulation of this, and corruption and incompetence led to

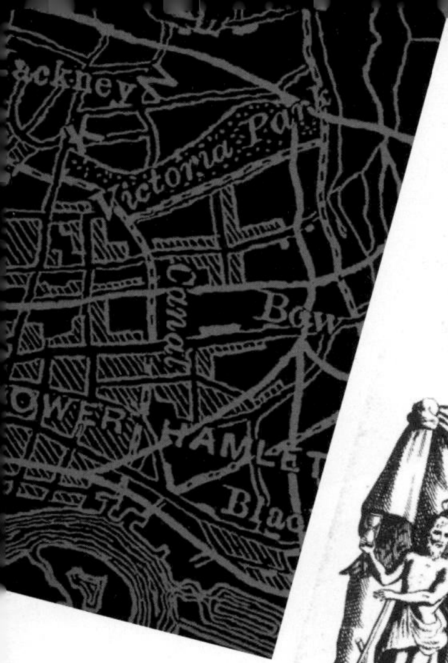
Victoria Park
Bow

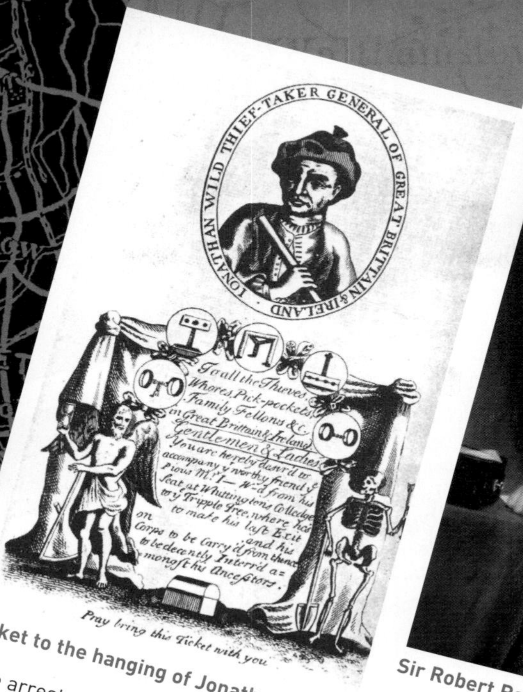
JONATHAN WILD THIEF-TAKER GENERAL OF GREAT BRITTAIN & IRELAND
To all the Thieves, Whores, Pick-pockets, Family Fellons &c. in Great Brittain & Ireland.
Gentlemen & Ladies
You are hereby desir'd to accompany y^r worthy friend ye Pious M^r J— W—d from his Seat at Whittingtons Colledge to y^e Tripple Tree, where he'l to make his last Exit on ... and his Corps to be Carry'd from thence to be decently Interr'd amongst his Ancestors.
Pray bring this Ticket with you

Ticket to the hanging of Jonathan Wild

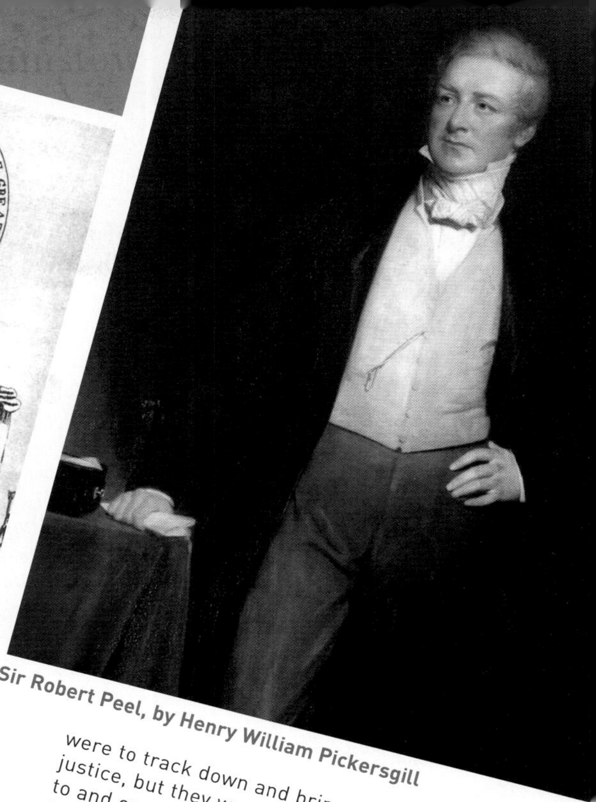

Sir Robert Peel, by Henry William Pickersgill

false arrests – and worse. The infamous Jonathan Wild took advantage of the power that his role as self-titled 'Thief-Taker General' enabled him to play both sides of the law, a sort of Harvey Dent/Two-Face of his time. He was hanged from the Tyburn tree in front of a huge crowd.

By the middle of the 18th Century, the novelist and magistrate Henry Fielding had fielded (haha!) a solution to the law enforcement needs of the growing metropolis. Operating from the magistrate's court at 4 Bow Street, London, he employed a group of men who would come to be nicknamed the 'Bow Street Runners' by the public. Like the thief-takers, these men were to track down and bring offenders to justice, but they were answerable directly to and operating with the authority of Bow Street magistrates court, and they were paid by public funds. In addition to the officers, Fielding employed clerks whose job it was to keep a record of the officers' activities – a sort of Case Progression Unit of its time. In this way, the role was formalised and

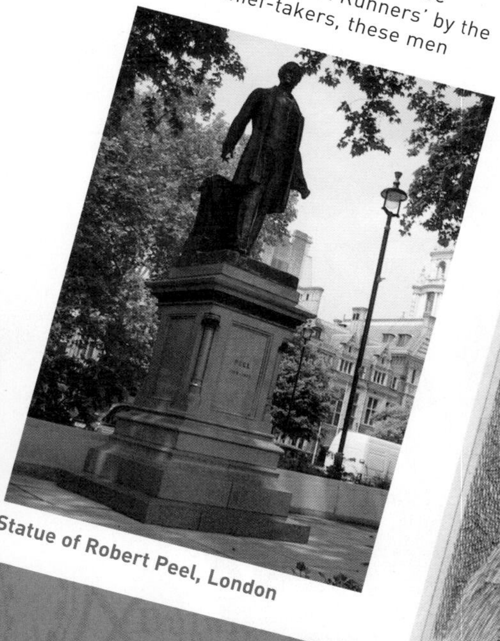

Statue of Robert Peel, London

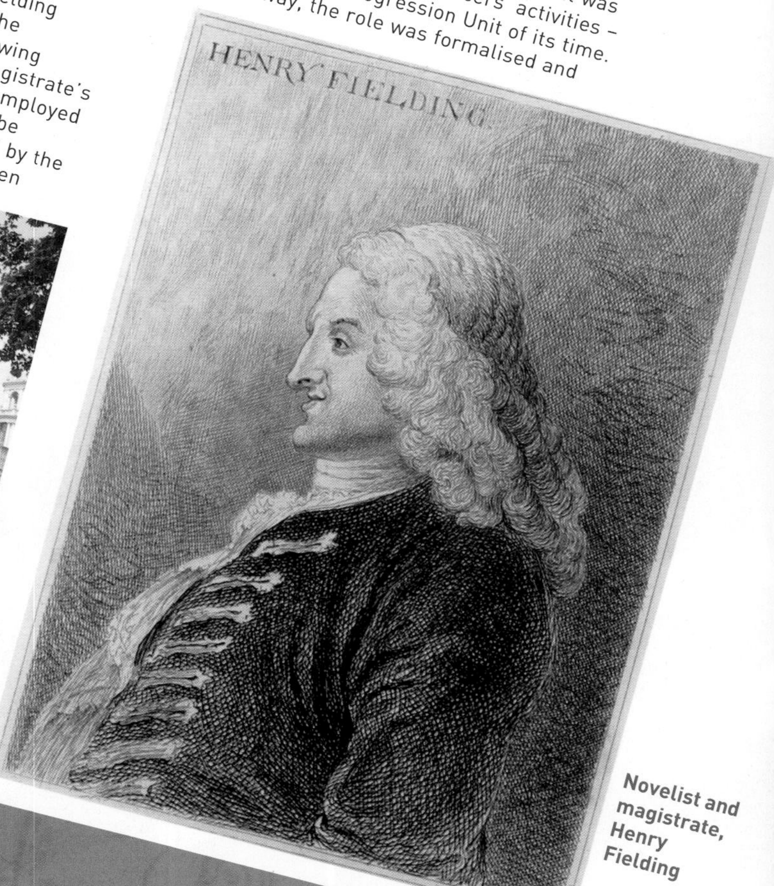
HENRY FIELDING

Novelist and magistrate, Henry Fielding

professionalised; the Runners carried proper identification and could travel the length and breadth of the country to exercise their duties. What they didn't do was patrol the streets – at this point this was still left to the Watch.

In the 1820s, Home Secretary Sir Robert Peel established a parliamentary committee to look at fully standardising and modernising the policing system. He favoured a civilian, rather than military, force; paid, professionalised and answerable to the public – policing by consent. These "Peelian principles" and the Bow Street Runners' operational model formed the basis of the Metropolitan Police, which was established by an Act of Parliament in 1829. The new police force incorporated some of the pre-existing professional institutions – including the Bow Street Runners, their uniformed cousins the Bow Street Horse Patrol (who dealt with highway robbery) and the Marine Police. These remained nominally independent until they were finally rolled into the Met in 1839.

The City maintained their own, independent policing system, which it retains to this day, now better known as the Metropolitan Police Service.

"A police whistle on Bow Street. For a moment I felt a connection, like a vestigium, with the night, the streets, the whistle and the smell of blood and my own fear, with all the other uniforms of London down the ages who wondered what the hell they were doing out so late."
Peter Grant

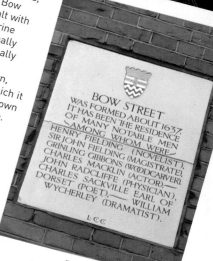

BOW STREET
WAS FORMED ABOUT 1637.
IT HAS BEEN THE RESIDENCE
OF MANY NOTABLE MEN
AMONG WHOM WERE –
HENRY FIELDING (NOVELIST).
SIR JOHN FIELDING (MAGISTRATE).
GRINLING GIBBONS (WOODCARVER).
CHARLES MACKLIN (ACTOR).
JOHN RADCLIFFE (PHYSICIAN).
CHARLES SACKVILLE EARL OF
DORSET (POET). — WILLIAM
WYCHERLEY (DRAMATIST).

L.C.C.

Plaque on Bow Street

Sir Thomas de Veil

De Veil was Bow Street's first magistrate, setting up the court and contributing to the development of Britain's policing and justice system. Sir Thomas was known to be pretty hands-on, taking part in many investigations himself and solving some of the most notorious crimes of the time. He was also known to be rather 'hands-on' with the fairer sex.

Sir Thomas de Veil, by Thomas Ryley

Sir Thomas de Veil, as depicted by William Hogarth in Night

COVERS GALLERY

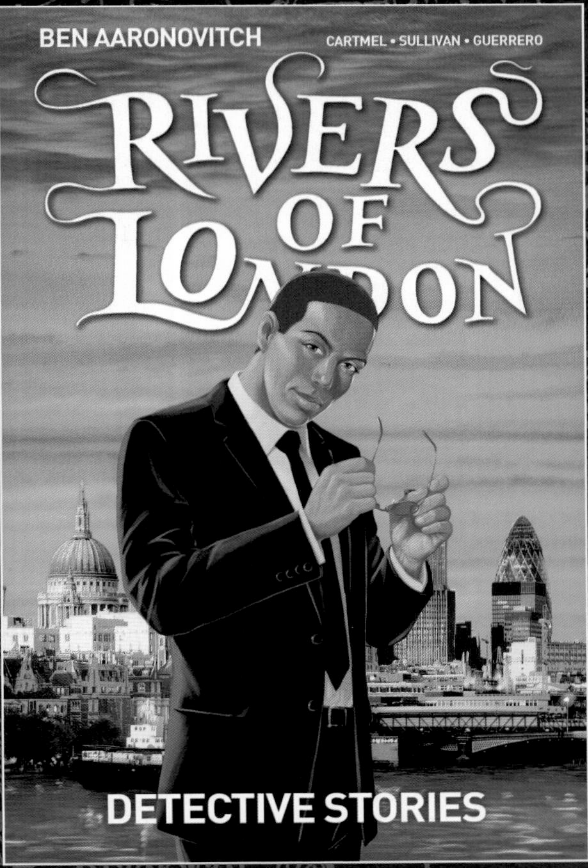
BEN AARONOVITCH
CARTMEL • SULLIVAN • GUERRERO
RIVERS OF LONDON
DETECTIVE STORIES

ISSUE 1 - Cover B
Lee Sullivan

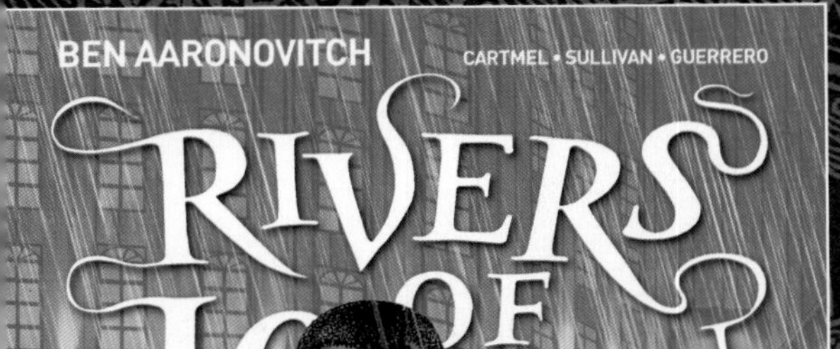
BEN AARONOVITCH
CARTMEL • SULLIVAN • GUERRERO
RIVERS OF LONDON
DETECTIVE STORIES

ISSUE 2 - Cover A
Gary Erskine & Yel Zamor

COVERS GALLERY

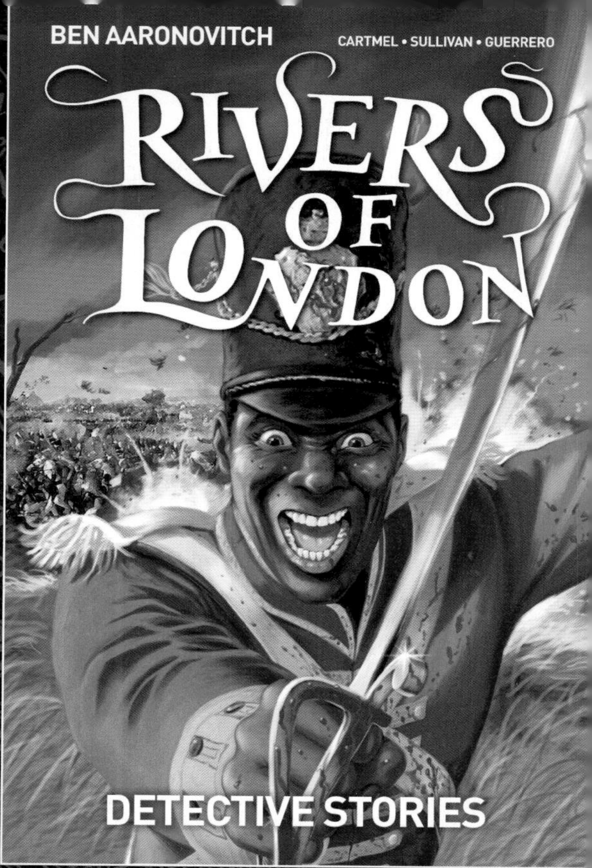
BEN AARONOVITCH
CARTMEL • SULLIVAN • GUERRERO
RIVERS OF LONDON
DETECTIVE STORIES

ISSUE 2 - Cover B
Lee Sullivan

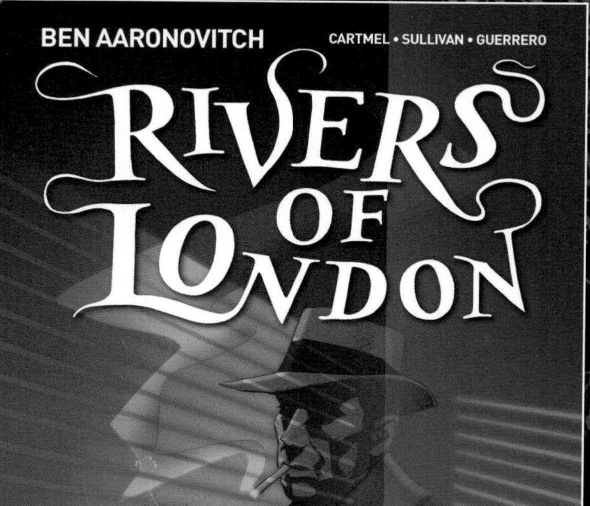
BEN AARONOVITCH
CARTMEL • SULLIVAN • GUERRERO
RIVERS OF LONDON
DETECTIVE STORIES

ISSUE 3 - Cover A
Lee Sullivan & Luis Guerrero

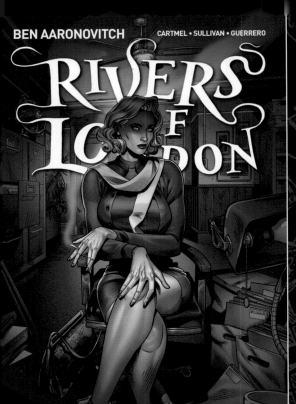

COVERS GALLERY

RIVERS OF LONDON

BEN AARONOVITCH

CARTMEL • SULLIVAN • GUERRERO

DETECTIVE STORIES

ISSUE 3 - Cover B
Rachael Stott & Luis Guerrero

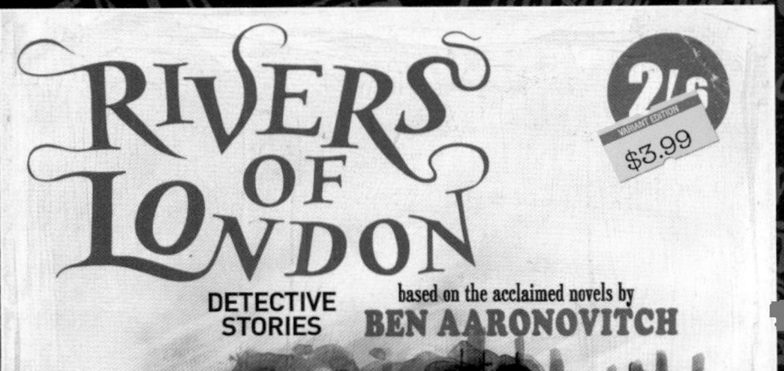

RIVERS OF LONDON

DETECTIVE STORIES

based on the acclaimed novels by
BEN AARONOVITCH

by **BEN AARONOVITCH,
ANDREW CARTMEL,
LEE SULLIVAN, &
LUIS GUERRERO**

$3.99

ISSUE 4 - Cover A
Robert Hack

RIVERS OF LONDON READER'S GUIDE

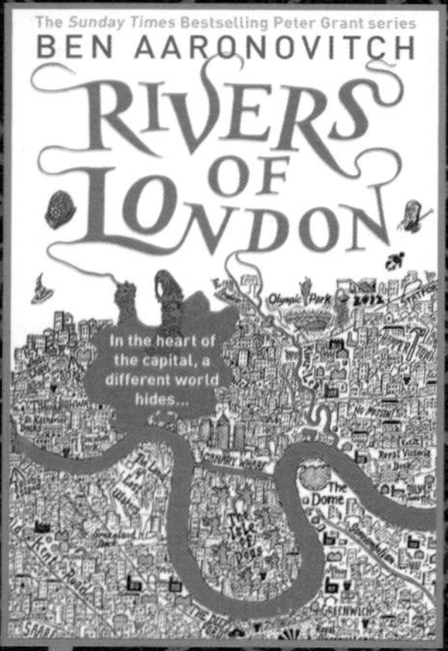
The Sunday Times Bestselling Peter Grant series
BEN AARONOVITCH
RIVERS OF LONDON
In the heart of the capital, a different world hides...

RIVERS OF LONDON / MIDNIGHT RIOT
Novel 1

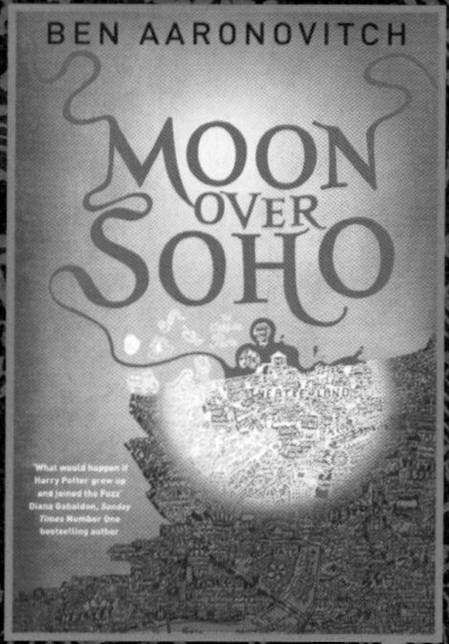
BEN AARONOVITCH
MOON OVER SOHO
'What would happen if Harry Potter grew up and joined the Fuzz' Diana Gabaldon, Sunday Times Number One bestselling author

MOON OVER SOHO
Novel 2

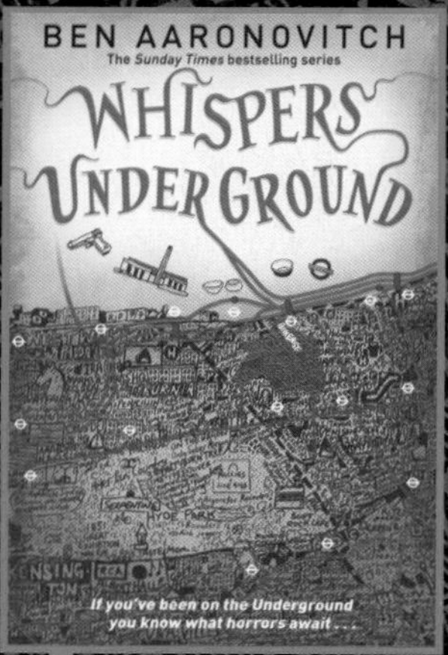
BEN AARONOVITCH
The Sunday Times bestselling series
WHISPERS UNDER GROUND
If you've been on the Underground you know what horrors await . . .

WHISPERS UNDER GROUND
Novel 3

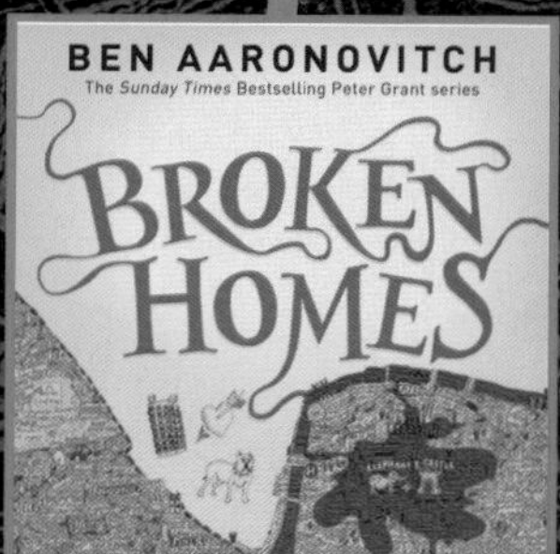
BEN AARONOVITCH
The Sunday Times Bestselling Peter Grant series
BROKEN HOMES
Stuff gets serious South of the River . . .

BROKEN HOMES
Novel 4

The *Rivers of London* comics and graphics novels are an essential part of the saga. Though they each stand alone, together they add compelling depth to the wider world of Peter and the Folly!

This helpful guide shows where each book fits in the ever-growing timeline of the *Rivers of London* universe!

Fit for Rugby

WITHDRAWN

LIVERPOOL POLYTECHNIC LIBRARY

3 1111 00409 6663